Put Me Back On My Bike

William Fotheringham writes for the *Guardian* and *Observer* on cycling and rugby. A racing cyclist and launch editor of *Procycling* and *Cycle Sport* magazines, he has reported on over twenty Tours de France. He is the critically lauded author of *Fallen Angel, Roule Britannia*, and *Put Me Back on My Bike*, which *Vélo* magazine called 'the best cycling biography ever written', and the bestselling biography of Eddy Merckx.

Also by William Fotheringham

Roule Britannia: Great Britain and the Tour de France

Fallen Angel: The Passion of Fausto Coppi

Cyclopedia: It's All About the Bike

A Century of Cycling

Fotheringham's Sporting Trivia

Fotheringham's Sporting Trivia: The Greatest Sporting Trivia Book Ever II

Merckx: Half Man, Half Bike

Racing Hard: 20 Tumultuous Years in Cycling

Tom Simpson was an Olympic medallist, world champion and the first Briton to wear the fabled yellow jersey of the Tour de France. He died a tragic early death on the barren moonscape of the Mont Ventoux during the 1967 Tour. A man of contradictions, Simpson was one of the first cyclists to admit to using banned drugs, and was accused of fixing races, yet the dapper 'Major Tom' inspired awe and affection for the obsessive will to win which was ultimately to cost him his life.

Put Me Back on My Bike revisits the places and people associated with Simpson to produce the definitive story of Britain's greatest ever cyclist.

William Fotheringham

Put Me Back On My Bike

IN SEARCH OF TOM SIMPSON

YELLOW JERSEY PRESS
LONDON

Published by Yellow Jersey Press 2014

2 4 6 8 10 9 7 5 3 1

First published in Great Britain in 2002 by
Yellow Jersey Press
Random House, 20 Vauxhall Bridge Road,
London SW1V 2SA

www.vintage-books.co.uk

Addresses for companies within The Random House Group Limited can be
found at: www.randomhouse.co.uk/offices.htm

The Random House Group Limited Reg. No. 954009

A CIP catalogue record for this book
is available from the British Library

ISBN 9780224092395

The Random House Group Limited supports The Forest Stewardship
Council® (FSC®), the leading international forest-certification organisation.
Our books carrying the FSC label are printed on FSC®-certified paper.
FSC is the only forest-certification scheme supported by the leading
environmental organisations, including Greenpeace. Our
paper procurement policy can be found at
www.randomhouse.co.uk/environment

Printed and bound in Great Britain by Clays Ltd, St Ives plc

CYCLING GLOSSARY

Attack
A cyclist making an attempt to break free of the bunch –
often for the stage win or to take time out of the leaders,
either alone or as part of a small group. Popular places to
attack include on climbs or down daring descents.

Autobus
A group of riders, usually on a mountainous stage, banding
together to finish the stage within the cut-off time.

Bidon
A cyclist's bottle for liquids, attached to the bike.

Bonk
The much-feared physical condition when a cyclist's body
has run out of fuel. Symptoms include light-headedness,
hallucinations, fatigue.

Break/breakaway
A group of riders splitting from the main bunch to attack.
Will often be chased down by the **peloton**.

Bunch sprint
A chaotic end to a stage where teams engineer their sprinters to the front to contest the stage win. Only certain stages (usually flat ones) will be suitable for a sprint finish.

Cadence
The rate at which a cyclist turns the pedals.

Category one climb
A system of categorising climbs: the lower the number, the steeper the route. *Hors categorie* (literally, without category) is the toughest.

Chamois (chammy) cream
A cream liberally applied to avoid saddle sores.

Classic
A one-day professional bike race in Europe. Many have been running for decades. Famous classics include: Paris–Roubaix, Tour of Flanders, Milan–San Remo.

Cleats
Bits of plastic attached to your shoe that clip on to the bike's pedals. Can refer to the entire shoe.

Cofidis affair
An infamous drug raid in 2004 that was exposed after cyclists' phones were tapped by French police. Multiple riders were arrested and charged with possessing illegal drugs and the scandal rocked professional cycling.

Criterium
A race organised in a city centre that involves multiple laps of a closed-off route. Usually a short race, as opposed to a standard road race.

Directeur sportif
The person in charge of a cycling team, with a similar role to that of a football team's manager.

Domestique
A support rider in a team, whose responsibilities include fetching food and drink from the team car for their leader, pacing the leader up climbs, chasing down breakaway groups.

Echelon
A horizontal formation of riders often deployed in crosswinds. Riders across different teams take it in turns to be in the most exposed position, with other riders being able to shelter and conserve energy.

EPO
A synthetic hormone that allows blood to carry more oxygen around the body and therefore improves performance in endurance sports. Using EPO is a type of blood doping.

Etape
A stage in a multi-day bike race.

Festina affair
A drugs bust in 1998 during the Tour de France where a significant haul of drugs was found in a team car. Nine riders were arrested and many teams were investigated during the race.

Green Jersey
The jersey awarded in the Tour de France to the rider with the most points. Points are awarded to the first riders to reach the end of a stage, or who win an intermediate sprint during a stage.

Gruppetto
The Italian term for the *autobus*.

Lead out
The formation used by a team to get their sprinter to the front before a sprint finish.

Musette
A cyclist's bag of food to be eaten during the race. Often collected by a *domestique* or handed out at a feed station by a *soigneur*.

Peloton
The main group of riders during a bike race, often numbering over 100.

Polka Dot Jersey
Awarded to the 'King of the Mountains' during the Tour de France – the rider who picks up the most points during mountain stages, awarded for arriving first at the peaks.

Rainbow Jersey
Worn by the world champion in their discipline – time trial, team time trial, road race. The jersey is white with a band of five stripes (green, yellow, black, red, blue).

Ramp
The slope where a rider waits immediately before they are cleared to begin their time trial.

Sitting on someone's wheel
The practice of conserving energy by riding just behind another rider in their slipstream, which can reduce effort by roughly 20 per cent.

Skinsuit
The skin-tight outfit riders wear in time trials to be as aerodynamic as possible.

Skis
The special handlebars on a time trial bike which force the rider to adopt an aerodynamic position.

Soigneur
The member of a team's support crew responsible for distributing *musettes, bidons* and administering massages to the riders after a day's racing.

Sportive
A short mass ride open to amateurs, often to raise money for charity.

Sprocket
The toothed wheel that a bike's chain rolls over.

Time trial
A race or stage in a multi-day race where riders compete individually against the clock.

Torque
A measure of power output.

Turbo trainer
A stationary bike used for training or for warming up.

VAM
A measure of elevation gain (usually metres per hour), which is used as an indicator of fitness and speed.

White Jersey
The jersey awarded to the best young rider in the Tour de France.

Yellow Jersey / *Maillot Jaune*
The jersey awarded to the leader of the Tour de France.

This book is dedicated to the late Geoffrey Nicholson, whose vision of the Tour de France inspired me as a teenager and guided me as a journalist.

Contents

Acknowledgements

This book could not have been written without the cooperation of the following in giving up their time to be interviewed: Bob Addy, Lucien Aimar, Jacques Augendre, Albert Beurick, Chris Brasher, Peter Bryan, Vin Denson, Harry Hall, Helen and Barry Hoban, Jean-Marie Leblanc, Colin Lewis, the late Arthur Metcalfe, Dr Jean-Pierre de Mondenard, George Morris, Peter Parkin, Raymond Poulidor, Alan Ramsbottom, Brian Robinson, Pete Ryalls, Norman Sheil, Harry Simpson, Jean Stablinski, Michael Wright.

George Shaw's collection of letters from Tom were invaluable, particularly in writing chapter three: I owe him my sincere thanks. Vital material for chapter eight, the interview with Dr Pierre Dumas, was kindly provided by Philippe Brunel, who also gave considerable help and encouragement. Ray Pascoe's willingness to share Simpson material was much appreciated. Dr Chris Jarvis's advice and information on physiology were crucial for chapter nine, while Peter Keen's advice on body core temperatures was also helpful.

In the *Equipe* archive, Serge Laget provided time, advice and encouragement in equal measure. My brother, Alasdair, hunted down Spanish cyclists on my behalf. My father, Alex, provided valuable 1950s background information. Willy Voet assisted with background on Gus Naessens. In the Avignon archive, Mme Hollard dug out documents on my behalf. Martin Ayres and Dave Marsh provided names and addresses.

For the photos, thanks go to Michael Loasby, Presse Sports/Offside, Photosport International and Pete Ryalls.

I should also like to thank my sports editor at the *Guardian*, Ben Clissitt, for his support, and my colleagues Tim Clifford and Ian Austen for their advice and encouragement. To Rachel Cugnoni at Random House, many thanks for cutting the dead wood and the occasional boot in the backside.

This book owes most, however, to Caroline Arthur, whose constant patience, keen eye, and brutally honest comments at the manuscript stage made the whole thing happen.

Foreword

Put Me Back on My Bike closes with a brief look into a bag of letters. The bag belongs to Helen Hoban, Helen Simpson as was, and contains the hundreds of messages she received after her first husband's death. As a whole, there could be no better expression of how Tom Simpson's public felt about him 40 years ago.

Another batch of letters, those prompted by the publication of this biography, underlines how the emotions Simpson engendered among cycling fans have endured for four decades: amusement, admiration, love, frustration, annoyance, grief.

Such is the power of the Simpson story that it has its own momentum. In the five years since this book originally appeared, the story has moved on, with new revelations from fresh sources, and new investigations into his life and death.

Inevitably, in exploring subject matter so controversial, the book led to a few arguments on its own account. Equally inevitably, the Simpson story was not one that I could leave behind once I had finished typing. For all that he has been dead for 40 years, Simpson gets under your skin, and interviews for a later book, *Roule Britannia*, often led back to Tom. For the sake of completeness, all this is worth looking at, and the new material appears in a fresh final chapter.

When writing this book, I occasionally pondered the value of looking into the death and life and character of a man who had died so long ago, under such controversial circumstances. The poems, press cuttings, tall tales, rants and recollections that have arrived on my doorstep since June 2002 leave me in no doubt that it was worth the effort.

Simpson clearly still matters, immensely, to a huge number of people, and not solely to cycling fans. That vindicates my original decision to portray him as a three-dimensional character, the less likeable qualities as well as the good. Anything else would have been a disservice; as with the film that inspired this book, it is a choice between seeing the man in colour, or leaving him in black and white.

CHAPTER ONE

'Something to Aim At'

It is not the average Sunday afternoon at the movies. For one thing, there is something unusual about the audience at the Riverside Theatre in Hammersmith on a dark day in January 2001. I'm perhaps the youngest of the two hundred of us. We're nearly all men, mostly aged over 50, thin and with a healthy glow, the same men you will see in the lanes of the Home Counties on Saturday mornings pedalling immaculate bikes to garden centre cafés to drink tea and gossip. Veteran cyclists.

What we have come to see is not the normal Sunday afternoon matinée either. *Something to Aim At* has never gone on general release, and its name would mean nothing to normal members of the public or to cinema critics. It is unpolished, amateurish in places. That reflects both its budget, and the fact that it is as much a 75-minute labour of love as a piece of cinema. It is part enthusiast's film, part work of art. It tells the story of Tom Simpson, Britain's greatest ever cyclist, and was made by a lifelong fan of Simpson's named Ray Pascoe. In 1967, when his hero died on Mont Ventoux in the 13th stage of the Tour de France, Pascoe set out with his camera and tape recorder, seeking out old newsreel footage, interviewing Simpson's associates and family.

The film's name comes from an anecdote told by Simpson's mechanic. Simpson was out to win that Tour de France and before it started, he went into the Mercedes showroom in Ghent, where he lived. He put down a deposit on the best car they had, the one on the turntable going round in the window. He knew the thought of the car and the cash he needed for it would stay in the back of his mind and motivate him. As he said: 'It gives you something to aim at.'

Pascoe is a balding, earnest-looking man, a former racing cyclist who saw Simpson race, loved his style, his aggression, his charisma. He can remember first meeting Simpson in 1961 when he was an awestruck young cyclist racing in Ghent, staying where all the British cyclists stayed, in Simpson's friend Albert Beurick's guest house. They met a few times over the next few years, exchanged a few words now and then. That was enough to feed Pascoe's passion.

A film enthusiast and technician, Pascoe has gone through 30 years of emotional effort, a bank loan, five-figures' worth of his own money, and countless unpaid hours in making his two films about Simpson: *Tribute to Tom Simpson*, in 1972, and *Something to Aim At*, completed in 1995. He has tracked down Simpson's mentors, Simpson's widow, Helen, his clubmates and his teammates. In the film, they talk of the man's drive, ambition, and talent. And Pascoe has unearthed archive footage which takes most of the audience back to their adolescence, and which can cause a shiver down the spine.

The great cycling stars of the past exist as two-dimensional figures, seen in black and white photographs, known for a string of racing results and little else. Pascoe's film changes that. We can see Simpson in colour. We can see the fluidity of his pedalling style. We can listen to Simpson's voice as he tells a joke about the Duke of Norfolk and a racehorse to the BBC interviewer Eamonn Andrews. We can admire his polite response as Andrews asks questions which display a wince-making ignorance of cycling.

Simpson's voice, his accent a mix of Nottinghamshire and lilting Durham, bridges the 33 years since he died and connects directly with my experience of cycling. His voice has been turned slightly flat and nasal by the tone of

Flanders: the same has happened to all the English cyclists I have ever known who have been based in Belgium.

Pascoe found both the home where Simpson was brought up in the Nottinghamshire mining village of Harworth and the house which he built in his adopted city of Ghent yet barely lived in. Early in his research, Pascoe interviewed Simpson's parents, who have long since died, and most touching of all, he was loaned some home movies of Simpson and his two daughters. Here is Tom skiing, with one child falling over in the snow as they all build a snowman; here he is on the beach in Corsica, lifting his daughters one by one over a stream so that they don't get their feet wet. The cycling idol as Mr Everyman. After Pascoe sent a copy of the film *Something to Aim At* to Simpson's daughter Jane, who was four when her father died, she wrote to him: 'I had never heard my daddy's voice before.'

Most of us have never heard Simpson's voice either, or seen the way he pedalled and how his expressive face worked, and this only makes his death all the crueller as it is played out for us in the grainy black and white television footage of the fatal day in the 1967 Tour. As he zigzags painfully up the mountain, the camera pans ahead to the leaders he is chasing: they are only a few hundred metres away from him. It might as well be 100 miles. Like a ship foundering in a storm, his torso rolls slowly from side to side with each turn of the pedals as he struggles up the mountain. The gasping mouth never closes: he has the look of a man drowning. The end is sudden, a brutal transformation from struggling man to inert body on a bike, held up, lowered gently down, his chest pumped vigorously by the desperate doctor.

After the showing, two of the men interviewed by Pascoe for the film take to the stage for a question and answer session. One is Simpson's friend and supporter Beurick, an unhealthy-looking mountain of a man who has trouble walking; the other is Vin Denson, Simpson's close friend and his teammate on the race when he died. They are joined by another professional cyclist of the time, Keith Butler. The emotions are still raw; the film has rubbed salt into the long-open wound. The tears come easily to Beurick, who can barely speak coherently when he is asked about Simpson. It's hard for Denson as well: on top of reliving Simpson's death, Denson has just had to watch images of his late wife Vi, who is interviewed alongside him in the film. Both men speak as if Simpson had died only yesterday. Clearly, the tragedy was a life-changing event with which Denson and Beurick have still to come to terms. Butler, who was more distant from it all, remains more dispassionate.

The vividness of Denson's and Beurick's grief is striking, more than 30 years on, but is understandable. What intrigues me more are the undercurrents which are still steering the two men. They cannot help but bring hidden issues to the surface, unwittingly or not. There are few questions from the audience – Denson and Beurick need little prompting, they clearly have a need to talk – and there are no clear answers. There is no confusion about the character of the man, his athletic class and mesmerising charisma, but both men seem as confused now as they were way back in 1967 about the reasons for Simpson's death and the issue it raises: the use of banned drugs.

No one in the audience actually mentions drugs. Pascoe's film had dodged gently around the issue in a 'lift your skirt to step over the puddle' kind of way, just as much of the material written about Simpson has done. But amphetamine pills were found in his pockets; the drug was in his urine and stomach contents. And amphetamines are the first thing in Beurick's mind once he has dried his eyes and collected his thoughts.

He does not need to be asked. All he needs is a public

platform where he can be allowed to speak for his friend. He is adamant that drugs did not cause Simpson's death. Simpson rarely used drugs, he says. On the occasions when he did use them, he knew what he was doing. His use of them was carefully thought out. There was nothing wrong with Simpson using drugs on the rare occasions that he did, he insists, as every cyclist used them in those days. A box of drugs was found in the Great Britain team car, acknowledges Beurick: they were said to belong to Simpson but, he asks, were they really Simpson's or did they belong to someone else in the race? His arguments are not those of a man who is trying to hide the truth, but they give the impression that he has spent three decades building his own version of events.

Beurick is equally hazy about the question of responsibility for Simpson's death. He speaks angrily about the doctor who treated him, the late Pierre Dumas, who was the chief of the small medical team at the Tour de France in 1967. After mouth-to-mouth resuscitation failed, Dumas had Simpson taken to hospital in a helicopter. Being flown off the mountain and high into the sky caused him to die of brain damage from oxygen deprivation, Beurick tells the audience. He clearly wishes to absolve his friend of any responsibility for his own death but, in spite of this, he, Denson and Butler all agree on one thing: Simpson was perfectly capable of riding himself to death without drugs in his system. He 'became twice the man' when he pulled on the Union Jack jersey, says Denson, and was prepared to ride himself 'into unconsciousness' for his country.

Simpson is far from being the first public figure to die a controversial, partially explained death. Parallels can be drawn in his case with the bitter arguments over Scott of the Antarctic, George Mallory and perhaps Ayrton Senna. They have one thing in common: the issue of how they died and what can be deduced from it has put their achievements in the shade.

There are other unsolved issues. For example, we have just watched footage of Simpson winning his world championship in 1965. It was the most important win of his career, taken with a glorious mix of courage and cunning. There is lengthy, elaborate speculation among the panel as to whether a deal of some kind was made with the rider who finished second, Rudi Altig, and the various ways in which it could have been done. It is rumoured, says Denson, that Simpson paid Altig 100,000 French francs to let him win.

Up comes another thorny question: what really happened the day after Simpson's death, when his teammate in the Great Britain squad, Barry Hoban, won a stage dedicated to his dead leader by the rest of the field. A touching image of solidarity, you might think – and so thought everyone at the time who was not immediately involved. But Beurick and Denson claim that Denson was appointed as the man who would win, and that Hoban knew of the deal, but robbed him of the stage win. Hoban has always denied that this was the case.

Petty it may seem, but there appears to be something of an underlying turf war over who was Simpson's best friend, with the reflected glory that comes with the status. Hoban was given that title by the press, largely because that was a convenient way of explaining the victory; Denson says Simpson was 'like a brother' to him. Beurick makes the same claim. He gets angry when he recalls the fact that Hoban has always had credit for the victory and calls the rider 'a prick', a 'young upstart', in front of 200 people. Denson seems embarrassed by the situation, as well he might. It's all rather complicated, and the whole question is muddied further by the fact that Hoban ended up marrying Simpson's widow Helen.

As an illustration of the deep-rooted and messy legacy that Simpson has left behind him, it has been a telling couple of hours. Several things strike me. First, there is the enduring hero worship of a man who died when I was still in nappies. The film itself is the product of that hero worship, which has persisted through most of Pascoe's 60 years. Then there are the fans. More than three decades since the cyclist's death, 200 people are prepared to come here, in many cases from far outside London. They have come to see a film some of them probably own already, to hear again a story which they already know, to hunt the bookstall in the foyer for postcards and old magazines.

The persistence of the old men's enthusiasm is touching. It's a measure of the status Simpson must have enjoyed during his life and a reminder of the lasting impact of his untimely death. The organizer, a tall, reed-thin veteran cyclist and author, Charlie Woods, is another Simpson fan. He has run these sessions before; this one has sold out, in the biggest turnout he can remember. Clearly, affection for Simpson is not dead: cycling fans of an older generation have fond memories, and they want to know more about him.

The presence of Beurick and Denson is undoubtedly a draw. For the ageing fans, who seem to hang on their every word, it is a way of being transported back in time to connect with their hero. Denson and Beurick knew Tom, they rubbed shoulders with him. And they seem to like the celebrity which rubs off on them.

Just as surprising as the enduring affection for Simpson were the unresolved issues and the degree of anger and conflict caused by this man's death. All of this was to spring up in my face when I began researching this book, but they were already there in the open at the Riverside Theatre on that January afternoon. Why did Simpson die? Could the doctor who treated him have been responsible? To what extent could Simpson's death be called self-inflicted?

Everything stemmed from the fact that Simpson died

while using banned drugs. This brought back the same thoughts that had kept me awake for 20 nights in a row in July 1998. Then, my mind had worked overtime as the Tour de France descended into chaos in the days after the Festina team was busted for drugs, a scandal which made newspaper front pages all over the world, and which called into question the validity of the entire sport of cycling.

The questions surrounding the Festina incident were basically the same as those over Simpson. To what degree is an athlete who takes performance-enhancing drugs at fault for his actions? How heavily do we weigh the fact that an athlete has taken drugs against the magnitude of his achievements and his status? How far up and down the sporting food chain does the responsibility extend? Does it go as far as race organizers, who devise the courses? Team managers who want their men to perform? The press and the fans who love to watch the spectacle?

In July 1998, I was asking these questions about living men, with whom I had, in some cases, developed close working relationships, and whom I had presented to the cycling public as heroes. They were questions which you tend to steer away from if you work in the professional cycling world and I had managed to avoid asking them until the Festina scandal thrust them in front of me. But Pascoe's film was a reminder that they were old questions, that they were not properly addressed at the time, and that was all too familiar. During the Festina case, the unwillingness of cyclists and the cycling world to confront their demons was only too apparent. In the way people had reacted to Simpson's death – and still reacted to it – that same unwillingness could be seen.

The drug questions had lain dormant since the late 1960s. Then, suddenly, the Festina scandal thrust them into centre stage. The difference was that, in Simpson's case, they stemmed from a man's death, which broke hearts and turned lives upside down. From the moment when I began

8

to wonder why Simpson had died, as those on stage at the film show still seemed to, I ran headlong into these bigger issues like a train going into the buffers.

Since his death, Simpson has played an occult role in British cycling: influential by his very absence. In Italy, Fausto Coppi holds a similar position, for similar reasons. Coppi magnetised the Italian public in the 1950s with a series of spectacular world championship and Tour de France victories, and indeed was Simpson's great hero. He lived a controversial life and died tragically at the age of 40, apparently from malaria although speculation over whether he may have been poisoned made headlines in Italy over 40 years later. Coppi's picture is still to be found behind the counter in Italian bike shops. He remains the benchmark against which all Italian *campioni* are measured.

The Belgians, on the other hand, do not have to wonder what might have become of the greatest cyclist of them all, Eddy Merckx, winner of 445 professional races, including five Tours de France. The all-conquering 'Cannibal' is now overweight and unhealthy. He remains an imposing presence but without the mythical aura of Coppi or Simpson.

The Briton is a hard act to follow. It took 32 years before Chris Boardman became the second British cyclist to wear the yellow jersey in the Tour de France. Simpson won the world professional road title and four of the one-day Classics: Tour of Flanders, Milan–San Remo, the Tour of Lombardy and the now-defunct Bordeaux–Paris. These are the cycling world's equivalent, in terms of prestige at least, of tennis's Grand Slam tournaments, and no Briton has won any of them since. Only one man, Robert Millar, has finished higher in the Tour de France, fourth to Simpson's sixth. No Briton has repeated Simpson's greatest stage race win, the Paris–Nice 'Race to the Sun'.

Like Banquo's ghost at the feast in Macbeth, Simpson is

still there in spirit. Every talented British cyclist since he died has been touted as a possible successor: Graham Webb, Derek Harrison, Bill Nickson, Graham Jones, Robert Millar, Joey McLoughlin and David Millar. Only the two Millars have come close to matching Simpson's achievements.

Graham Jones remembers being frequently compared to Simpson after turning professional in 1979. Jones had great talent. Like Simpson, he had a prominent nose. He rode for Simpson's old team, Peugeot. He even wore the same jersey as a professional – the black and white chequerboard of Peugeot had been left unchanged since the 1960s – and, like Simpson, he had gone to France with his bike and his bag to seek his fortune. But Jones would be the first to admit that he lacked Simpson's killer instinct.

The continuing British fascination with Simpson so many years after his death could be seen throughout 2001 in *Cycling Weekly* magazine. This is the bible for hard-core British cycling fans, widely read by the older generation of cyclists. An editorial on Boardman's retirement late in 2000 declared that he, not Simpson, was Britain's greatest cyclist. It sparked off a passionate, if spasmodic, 10-month-long debate in the magazine's readers' letters pages. Most who wrote in had a clear favourite. On the one hand was Simpson, with his all-round record: a single Olympic medal, a professional road title, a top-six finish in the Tour, four single-day Classics and massive star status at home and abroad. On the other was Boardman, the short-distance specialist. He had been an Olympic and world champion on the track, had won the prologue time trial at the Tour de France three times, and had spent six days wearing the yellow jersey.

For a Mr Denny of Bury St Edmunds in Suffolk, however, there was another issue. No matter how good Simpson's record, he had been shown to have taken banned performance-enhancing drugs. Therefore he was a cheat. It was 'completely inappropriate', he felt, to suggest Simpson was the greatest; therefore Boardman, who was known to be 'clean', had to be the better of the two. Clearly relishing the emotions which the controversy aroused, the magazine then decided to bring it back to life at the end of 2001. It ranked the top 50 British cyclists of all time, announced that Boardman was better than Simpson and put him at number one, then provided extra letters pages for the readers to have their say.

If it is surprising that cycling fans are debating Simpson's merits 35 years on, still more surprising is the way the man's death can stir the emotions of professional cyclists of today, even those born long after he died. When the 2000 Tour de France visited Avignon, I sat down with David Millar in the start village, the cluster of sponsors' tents where cyclists and the press gather before the stage begins. Millar had worn the yellow jersey at the start of the Tour and had raced up Mont Ventoux past the Simpson memorial for the first time the day before. He was fiddling with a limestone pebble which he had been given by Simpson's daughter Joanne, who had picked it up next to the statue. She had seen Millar throw his racing cap at the memorial as he passed, as a sign of respect. 'Simpson was one of the first stories I heard when I got into cycling,' says Millar. 'It's moving every time you go up there.' The stone stayed in Millar's suitcase for the rest of that Tour, and he still has it. In spite of the fact that Simpson had died almost a decade before he was born, Millar knew whose ghostly wheel marks he was following.

Where Simpson definitely surpassed Boardman and all other British cyclists since he died was in the impact he made on European hearts and minds. I lived and raced in France in the mid-1980s, almost 20 years after his death. People would often say 'ah, I remember Tom Simpson', or 'ah, like Tom Simpson', when they learned that I was an

English cyclist in their country. The affection could still be felt. Simpson remained the reference point.

The epitaph on Simpson's monument on Mont Ventoux, 'a sporting ambassador', is utterly appropriate. As the first cyclist from outside mainland Europe to achieve true stardom, he was a sporting pioneer, blazing a trail which leads, indirectly, to the achievements of Lance Armstrong today.

Simpson was not the first Briton to race in Europe. Brian Robinson paved the way four years earlier and his achievements as the first Briton to make any impact on the Tour de France are often overlooked. But Simpson was the one who made the great breakthrough, in his results and in the status he attained. His successes were the first step in a long process of opening up the Tour, which would eventually turn from a relatively insular European bike race into the world's greatest annual sporting event, with a truly international field.

The Tour de France's official historian, Jacques Augendre, a stooping, bespectacled man with the studious look of a university professor, was a journalist when Simpson first rode the Tour. He made this point to me 34 years on, as Armstrong rode to his third Tour win: 'When English riders arrived at the Tour they gave it an extra dimension, broadened the race's international appeal. Simpson's winning the yellow jersey [in 1962] was a turning point. Today, Armstrong's victories stem from all that. It was a long evolution but Simpson was a pioneer of something which ended with Greg LeMond and Armstrong. The Tour de France was Flemish and Latin, now it belongs to the Anglo-Saxons as well.'

For those who want to go and find physical reminders of Simpson, the possibilities are few and far between. There is the much-visited memorial at the spot where he died on Mont Ventoux and a bust in the Sportpaleis in his adopted home town of Ghent. Until recently, however, there was nothing in Britain, despite that when he died he was riding for his country and wearing the Union Jack. There was only the gravestone in his home village of Harworth, where he lived as a boy, although his jersey, shorts and gloves could be seen in a cycling museum in, of all places, Llandudno. Perhaps the lack of a memorial in Britain reflected the confusion that surrounds him, the question of whether he is hero, villain or victim. Should he be celebrated officially, or quietly forgotten? This rather sorry state of affairs was finally put right in August 2001 with the opening of a small museum in the Harworth and Bircotes sports and social club, a one-storey timber-framed building in the shadow of a pit heap and great concrete lift towers. 'Museum' is perhaps something of a grand term: the display is a single, large glass case in the entrance hall filled with memorabilia which had previously been scattered to the four winds.

The centrepiece is Simpson's white Peugeot bike, with its intricate chainset and complex centre-pull brakes, and the jersey and shorts which he was wearing when he died. The white jersey with Union Jacks crudely sewn on the shoulders is surprisingly small and stained, with the Peugeot stickers removed for some reason; the shorts are thick wool from another era, when Lycra was unheard of. There are other jerseys – the blue and red Great Britain strip he wore to win the world championship in 1965, and the rainbow-striped jersey he won on that day. There are special issue magazines, race programmes, and newspaper articles, including his ghosted, overblown 'revelations' from the *People* in September 1965, which were the source of great controversy at the time. There is even the race number plate which he carried on his bike, which I had seen unearthed at the house of his former mechanic Harry Hall.

Much of it looks like the kind of material which fans hoard away in boxes and it's none the worse for it. I had seen a lot of it before. When I visited Simpson's friends, teammates and family in search of the essence of the man, an identical ritual took place at least a dozen times. The envelope or cardboard box was opened, the cuttings, pictures, letters and souvenir magazines poured out onto the table. I know what these hoarded papers represent to the people who give them up to go on show.

The crowd assembled for the museum opening is similar to that at the film show seven months earlier: veteran cyclists in the main. Most have been riding the Tom Simpson memorial road race, which has been organized in or near the village since Simpson's death by his friends George Shaw and Dave Marsh. To maximise the turnout, the informal ribbon-cutting ceremony has been planned to coincide with the race, on this occasion combined with the national over-40s championship. The television comment-ator David Duffield, who can talk about Simpson – or anything else – until the cows come home, has come all the way from Bath. Another voice of Eurosport, Mike Smith, is doing the race commentary. As the rain drives down, the voluble Smith gets a little emotional as he recalls the same weather on a dark July day in 1967 when a larger, more sombre crowd gathered to bury Simpson half a mile away.

The president of the British Cycling Federation, Brian Cookson, has driven over from Preston to do the presenta-tions. Like most of those present, he has his treasured Simpson memory – seeing him riding his last race in England, on the seafront at New Brighton in June 1967 – and he still has his copy of Simpson's autobiography, *Cycling is My Life*, autographed on that day. The enduring fascination goes to the very top of British cycling.

There are others in Harworth who remember Simpson with less reverence. While delivering flyers for the event, Dave Marsh bumped into a local woman who remembered being courted by the great man before he disappeared in search of fame and fortune. There was no happy ending: 'He came round to my house at midnight, and I told my dad to tell him to bugger off, because all he could talk about was bikes.'

The tone at the opening is upbeat, with a team from local television adding to the sense of occasion. 'As far as I'm concerned, Tom will never die,' says his widow Helen. The museum may be extended, depending on funds, local politics and what other memorabilia comes in. More substantial, however, are plans for a purpose-built, one-mile cycle-racing circuit around the building, costing £750,000, and, of course, bearing Simpson's name. It's the sort of facility which is rare in Britain, and sorely needed: nowadays, if a teenage Simpson were living in Harworth, itching to ride bike races and emulate his heroes, he would have a frustrating start to his career. Increased road traffic has led the British cycling calendar to contract in recent years. If those wanting to emulate Simpson can do so here in future without the risk of being run over, there could be little better tribute.

To complete the circle – or, as the French say of the Tour de France, to 'buckle the buckle' – Ray Pascoe had driven up from London, with copies of *Something to Aim At* to sell from the boot of his car. The book and souvenir stall was the same as in January as well. Beurick and Denson were there too, among the group of teammates and family.

In much the same way that you could work out who was in favour in the Kremlin by watching the parade of Politburo members, the guest line-up was worth examining. As well as Denson, two of Simpson's other teammates from the 1967 Tour, Barry Hoban and Arthur Metcalfe*, were in attendance. The fourth team member who had been present on the 13th of July, Colin Lewis, was absent. He had been invited, but did not make the long trip from Devon. Lewis was aware that he had been *persona non grata* with both Helen and Barry Hoban since the appearance of an article in the *Sunday Times* about Simpson two years earlier. The interview with Lewis by the award-winning

* Sadly, Arthur Metcalfe died in December 2002.

sports writer David Walsh dealt with Simpson's drug-taking in some detail. It had prompted an outraged response from Simpson's widow. Lewis is a straightforward man, whom I'd visited at his bike shop in Paignton, and he was clearly hurt.

This was not the first article about her former husband to arouse Helen's ire. The chief cycling historian at the French newspaper *L'Equipe*, Philippe Brunel, is a devoted Simpson fan, and he wrote what he considered a definitive profile of the rider in 1997. This provoked an angry letter from Helen which has left him bemused and insulted. There is nothing in his article which is contentious, but he clearly accepts that Simpson used drugs. Helen was utterly welcoming to me in my research, unstinting with her time, but the experience of my two highly regarded colleagues indicated that the family defends Simpson's reputation closely.

This impression was strengthened a few days before I went to the opening of the Simpson museum when my publisher received an email. It came from Chris Sidwells, Simpson's nephew, and the author of the Simpson biography *Mr Tom: The True Story of Tom Simpson*, and it fell into two parts. First came an apologia for his own book, which he admitted had largely ignored the drugs issue, the complexities of Tom's personality and other issues. This was followed by the suggestion that Yellow Jersey should reverse my commission, and instead get him to write what he described as "a sort of 'Tom Simpson Unplugged'", because I was being poorly informed by my sources, virtually all of whom, he believed, had telephoned him to tell him what they had told me and what they had not told me.

Apart from conjuring up a hilarious vision of the phone lines of Britain humming with the people I had interviewed reporting back to base, Sidwells' email raised an important point. Only a member of the inner circle, it implied, was qualified to explore the Simpson myth. But the question and answer session at the film show seven months earlier had led me to feel exactly the opposite. It was high time for an account of Simpson's life written by someone who had no particular axe to grind. Time to go beyond the emotional baggage which has overwhelmed the story.

Of course, I should confess that I come to this story with my own baggage. His was the first name I heard in connection with cycling and the Tour de France. I came out of school on the afternoon of July 2, 1978. My father, who was a big Simpson fan and was responsible for stirring my interest in cycling, was sitting in the car waiting for me and my brother, his ear bent down to the car radio. It was tuned to a French station, Europe 1, to pick up that afternoon's live Tour coverage. When I got to the car, I asked Dad what he was listening to, and he told me 'some English guy is in the break. They say he could be the next Tom Simpson.' The rider on that occasion was Paul Sherwen; since then, like so many other English cycling fans, I have waited for the next Simpson, and have subconsciously measured any British cyclist of talent against the standard he set.

If you are an English cycling fan, it is hard to escape the man, hard not to feel his breath on the back of your neck at times. Six years on, when I wanted to race in France and wrote to various clubs to request a place in their teams, there was a little thrill when I opened a reply from the Club Olympique Briochin in Saint Brieuc, Brittany. They would be delighted, their president wrote, 'to welcome me as they had welcomed many *Britanniques*, including the late lamented Tom Simpson'. Simpson's old club! I still have the letter.

Financial need overcame sentiment and I chose Normandy because the club there found me a job. Even so, when I got on the ferry there was still the feeling that I was, in my own small way, following the Simpson trail, going to France with my bike, my bag and a few quid to see what might transpire. 'Living in a flat with no hot water and thinking you're going to be a pro', as one cyclist who went on to become a professional would say to me a few years later.

Back in England, my French adventure long over, I happened to be driving south down the A1 and turned into Harworth, eager to pay tribute in some way. I couldn't find his grave though. I couldn't even find the churchyard – and the gravestone is not there in any case, but in the cemetery. Despite that, just being in the village where Simpson had lived as a child meant something to me.

The little frisson came again when I saw Mont Ventoux for the first time – and thought the limestone on the top was snow. I felt it again in 1994, when I followed the Tour de France over the mountain. Then, the anticipation began mounting several days before, and the adrenaline grew all the way to the monument. The sensation has come each time I have driven or ridden up it, giving the mountain a hallowed feel.

It would be fanciful to say that Simpson's presence could be felt everywhere I went when researching this book, but just as the film gave him colour, mannerisms, an accent and a pedalling style, he was brought back to life for me by the people I visited with a succession of cherished mementoes and memories. Everyone I met on the Simpson trail has their own 'Tom', 'Tommy' or 'Mr Tom', that they carry with them like a monkey on their back: mine is a metal plate with the number '49' on it, a tiny 40-year-old recipe book, a sheet of foolscap listing 'tonics and medicines', a teenage boy's scribbled letter, and the image of a young doctor reaching into the pockets of a white checked woollen jersey.

'Something to Aim At'

Melbourne, Olympic Games, December 1956
Tom Simpson is slumped in the middle of the oval, banked,
concrete track, his head in his hands. Among the hustle and bustle
of bikes, cyclists and blazered officials, he is a small, sobbing figure
in his white jersey with the red and blue stripes and Olympic
rings. His three teammates, Mick Gambrill, Don Burgess and
John Geddes, and the British team manager, the avuncular,
rotund Benny Foster, have gathered around him. They are saying
the same things: 'Don't worry. It wasn't your fault. We can still
get the bronze.'

Simpson is inconsolable, convinced he has just lost his team the
gold medal in the team pursuit. It had been going so well. They
had qualified strongly, beaten the Russians in the quarter finals.
Then came the semi and the Italians, who the young British team
had already beaten when warming up in Russia. The Britons
were flying round the velodrome pursuing the Italians, who had
started on the other side. When they reached the banking at either
end of the track, one of the four would move sideways, slightly up
the slope, swinging back down to join the string.

After one of his turns at the front, Simpson could not catch up.
Just as Geddes was pushing up the speed at the front of the line,
the youngster went too far up the banking. Geddes had no idea
what was happening, and kept accelerating. There was no way
back, and the British were down to three men. Qualification for
the final was a formality for the Italians.

Simpson is the youngest in the team. He turned 19 just six days
before the Games opened. He is the most ambitious, and feels the
pressure more than the others. It's his first season racing at
international level. He has been away from home for 10 weeks,
warming up here amidst the adulation of the expatriate Britons,
who will applaud the quartet when they win their consolation
bronze medals.

Before the five-day flight here, at the Lord Mayor's banquet in
London, the team had to fill in forms stating their future goals.
All four had the same aims: Olympic pursuit champion, world

pursuit champion, world road race champion. Only the youngster, so angry at his own failure in Melbourne, will reach his objective.

CHAPTER TWO

'You Don't Have to be Mad to Go Up the Ventoux, But You're Mad if You Go Back'

Provençal proverb

On the second floor of his neat half-timbered house midway between Manchester and the Peak District, Harry Hall has a small office where he keeps the records of his career. Hall, a tall, slender, white-haired man in his late 60s, ran the biggest bike shop in Manchester for over 30 years. He was a veteran world cycling champion and worked as mechanic on Britain's national cycling teams in the 1960s and 70s. He was also one of the last men to see Tom Simpson alive.

The office is a neat yet disordered glory hole, an organized chaos of newspaper cuttings, photographs and race manuals. Among the piles are several small notebooks. They are Hall's diaries from his races with Great Britain, in which he meticulously recorded the work he carried out every day on each rider's bike: a tyre replaced here, gear ratios changed there.

Hall was mechanic for the British team on the 1967 Tour de France when Tom Simpson died. That year's notebook is small, red, and unlabelled, and he has had a struggle to find it for the first time since he put it away after returning from the race. On page after page the names Tom, Barry, Colin, Arthur and Vic are written: Simpson and his Great Britain teammates Hoban, Lewis, Metcalfe and Denson, whose name Vin was usually changed to Vic. The notes tell the story of the cyclists' Tour, as well as Hall's work each evening: 'fit silk tyres', 'change forks with spare'. His charges' form can be read in the gears they choose – lower than those of their mates if they feel bad – and their

21

fluctuating morale is indicated by the days on which Hall glues lighter tubular tyres onto their wheels, their misfortunes in the roll-call of punctured tyres and parts damaged in crashes.

Delving into the cupboards that morning, Hall has just rediscovered a road-stained metal number plate, three inches square and drilled so it can be bolted over the top tube of a bike. On either side, painted in white on the black background, is the number '49'. It is Tom Simpson's race number from the 1967 Tour, which was on his bike the day he died.

There is a deep symbolism about cycle race numbers. For all cyclists, putting one on for the first time is a moment of passage in their first race. For most, each time they pin one on their backs for a race there is a little rush of adrenaline. It is always said of the most competitive that their character changes 'when they pin a number on', and Simpson was surely numbered among these. In the Tour de France, a cyclist is always referred to by his number, or *dossard*, when he is mentioned on the race's short-wave radio as having punctured, crashed or broken away. If he is in a break, it is his number which is marked on the motorbike marshal's blackboard which keeps competitors informed; Simpson would have been *le dossard quarante-neuf*. In a certain sense, the man is the number.

The bitterest moment for any competitor in the Tour is if he has to abandon the race and his number is taken off his back and unbolted from his bike. Simpson's number is still in the little plastic bag where Hall placed it on the evening of the tragedy. The image comes freely to me: Hall outside the British team hotel on the evening of July 13, 1967, undoing the little screws which held the plate on Simpson's white bike, unfolding the metal. He would have been working like an automaton, going through the motions of his evening routine of cleaning and adjusting the bikes. What to do with the number?

Initially, the plate lived in the toolbox that Hall took with him to races. Then it went missing. When it resurfaced, it went into the drawer, but Hall did not like to take it out. If he came across it while rummaging for something else, he would push it under some papers, not relishing the memories it prompted. It was, he felt, 'the last bit of Tom'. There it lay now in front of us on the desk, a slightly scuffed souvenir of the fruitless fight to save Simpson's life in the desperate minutes after Hall had heard him whisper his last words – 'on, on, on!'

British cycling is a small world; before working as Simpson's mechanic, Hall had known him for several years from a distance as a young prodigy from Nottinghamshire, a 19-year-old, pigeon-chested slip of a lad. He competed with him at track meetings on the Fallowfield velodrome in Manchester in the 1950s, when stars like Reg Harris would draw crowds in their thousands.

After a meteoric rise, Simpson had disappeared to seek his fortune in France in 1959. Hall rode with him in his last race in England, then over the next years he followed his progress from afar, like the rest of the British cycling public. Simpson had gone to a distant world, with an aura of romance born in part from the scarcity of information about it. Only the biggest races were mentioned in the newspapers. There was one English magazine covering the major races, *Sporting Cyclist*. French magazines such as *But et Club* and *Miroir-Sprint*, with pages of black and white reportage, were bought in a certain shop in Manchester by the fans Hall knew and passed around like samizdat in the USSR.

Like so many others, Hall listened with his mates to a crackly Radio Luxembourg when Simpson became the first Briton to win the world professional road race championship in 1965. He couldn't understand the French, and, like all British cycling fans, he could barely believe it when the journalist Charlie Ruys turned to him and said, 'He's won, the bugger's won.' He saw Simpson return as a star to the Manchester track where they had raced together. He watched him banging a leathery steak on the side of his plate at breakfast and complaining lightheartedly about what he was being given to eat before the 270-mile London to Holyhead classic, which, of course, he won.

Then when Hall travelled with Simpson to the 1967 Tour, it was largely unknown territory for the mechanic, as it was for the majority of the British team. The manager, Alec Taylor, was taking time off from running his car-hire business in south London. Hall, and the driver, Ken Ryall, both ran bike shops; his fellow mechanic, Ken Bird, was working in one. For his efforts over the four weeks, Hall was paid the princely sum of £110.

Simpson designated Hall as the man who would look after his bike; he knew him a little, had seen him at other races. The British leader was particular about his equipment – 'what he had, where it had come from and how it was dealt with'. Having the best components on his bike and the right man working on it was all part of getting an edge over the opposition. Whether by instinct or design, Simpson was clearly canny enough to realize that the better his relations with the man who was looking after his bikes, the better his machines would be kept. He had a similarly close relationship with the team's chief *soigneur*, the Belgian Gus Naessens, who looked after his diet and physical preparation.

Simpson had Hall glue his tyres on with special white cement made by the Italian Pastelli company. They were lightweight tubular tyres he had bought himself from the manufacturers, Clément, in Paris. He had wheels built by a young British mechanic in Ghent. His shoes were hand-made by a Belgian specialist. He rarely rode the bikes he was given by his sponsor, Peugeot, but had instead bought himself a hand-built machine, like the other top professionals rode, from the Masi company in Italy. It was then painted in Peugeot colours. It's a small deception, but one that frequently occurs in professional cycling, when a star cyclist feels that his team's cycle sponsor is not able to produce the goods quite as he wants them.

Simpson had even devised his own saddle by gluing foam onto a plastic shell, and adding a leather cover made out of one of his wife's crocodile handbags. 'It wasn't perfect, because he tried to stick down the edges and they kept coming loose. It was a bit tatty, but he liked it. He was probably the first person to think of it,' Hall notes. In fact, Simpson was 30 years ahead of his time: virtually all racing bike saddles are now made in this way, comprising a thin leather cover, foam padding, and a plastic base.

When the brief details in the notebook from the 1967 Tour jog Hall's memory, Simpson's obsessive competitive drive springs back to life. On the rest day early in the race, Hall changed all three of Simpson's bikes from five- to six-speed – gear changers, sprockets, spare wheels and all. It was a long job and he worked late into the night in the market square at Belfort. The story behind the day's work speaks volumes about Simpson's urgent need to gain any advantage, however small, in any way he could. The British leader had been annoyed 24 hours before when the 1966 winner Lucien Aimar 'ripped his legs off' on the first big mountain of the race, the Ballon d'Alsace. Aimar had six gears, which gave him an extra ratio, lower than that ridden by the others. He could continually change pace, accelerating, waiting for the others to catch up, then accelerating again. It gave him a huge psychological advantage.

That evening, Simpson contacted a friend in Belgium, who brought the parts to Belfort immediately for Hall to work on the very next morning. He told Hall as he worked: 'If anyone comes snooping around, hide it [the bike] away.'

He added: 'I can get the buggers back. When they sit on my wheel I'll blow their brains out. I'll get the bastards.'

Simpson had worn the yellow jersey of Tour leader for one day in 1962. He was the first Briton to pull the most coveted prize in cycling over his shoulders, and deservedly made headlines. However, he had lost third place that year when he crashed, and finished only sixth overall. That was to remain the best British finish for 22 years but in fact it was neither nowt nor something: good enough to permit him to hope for better things, but not convincing or lucrative in the long term.

The Tour of 1967 was a 3,000-mile loop, starting in the Loire valley and heading east through Normandy, across northern France and into Alsace for that first rest day. South it went through the Alps to the Ventoux, and across to the Pyrénées, before the run north through the Massif Central for a stage finish on top of an extinct volcano, the Puy de Dôme, then up to Paris for a final time trial. The day before that Tour, which began in the town of Angers, a ballot was held among the journalists on the race to predict the possible winner. The verdict was brutally clear: they rated Simpson only 11th, with a mere nine votes, compared to 54 for the 1965 winner, Felice Gimondi of Italy.

The Tour had frustrated Simpson for the five years since his single day in yellow. He had never won a stage. In 1966 he had abandoned in tears while wearing the rainbow jersey of world champion. His all-or-nothing bid for victory in the Alps had backfired when a dramatic attack on the Col du Galibier was followed by a spectacular crash on the descent, which left him unable to hold the handlebars.

Simpson's other Tours were tributes to his ability to drive himself beyond his physical limits. In 1965, he rode himself to a standstill with a blood infection, caused by a septic hand which had debilitated his entire system. The year before he had struggled through for 16th place while weakened by a tapeworm, and he had finished an exhausted 29th at his first attempt, in 1960. As well as the press, some of his fellow cyclists doubted whether Simpson had the stamina to last through the Tour. If he had doubts himself, he hid them, and he made no secret of what he wanted to do. When his wife Helen put him on the train for Angers at Ghent's Sint Pieters station, his final words to her were 'see you in Paris with the yellow jersey'.

Hall was the only person Simpson would allow to work on his bike, and in the evenings he would sometimes come and talk to the mechanic as he stuck on tubular tyres, altered gear ratios and washed off the day's grime. Simpson seemed relaxed, but he was playing for high stakes. 'He said to me' – and the memory makes Hall laugh – 'I've got to win a lot of money. I've put down a deposit on a Merc in a showroom in Ghent, and when I come back I'll buy it, so I've got to earn some good money.' This is the 'something to aim at' of Pascoe's film.

To the young mechanic, he came across as a man 'whose mind was always one step ahead', who felt keenly the need to profit to the full from a career which had a limited span and could be cut short at any moment. 'He was a bright lad, commercially. It was quite simple: "you've got to make money, because how long do we have?"' recalls Hall.

Four days before he died, as he lay on his bed in a hotel room in Metz, Simpson summed up his position to Geoffrey Nicholson of the *Guardian*. He could only get a better contract, he said, 'if I can prove I'm a Tour man, prove that I can be a danger, and I've never done that yet ... I've got no more excuses. I can't say next year I'll be better. The only person I'd be kidding is myself.' A good Tour, he said, meant finishing in Paris in the top three, or holding the yellow jersey for five or six days, or winning a couple of prestigious stages and finishing in the first 10. Nothing less would do.

Simpson would also explain his strategy for the race to

Hall. It was dictated by the weakness of his team. A potential Tour de France winner needs eight or nine strong support men, or *domestiques*, around him. They can offer spare wheels or give up their bike if a tyre punctures, pace him back to the field after a toilet stop, offer their slipstream if a rival goes ahead, or simply give moral support by their presence.

For most of the Great Britain team, the Tour was a matter of survival rather than helping their leader. Of Simpson's nine teammates, five had not ridden the Tour before. Three were not even racing full-time as professionals. Simpson was riding his own race. 'His idea was that the lads were fine, but they weren't a support team,' says Hall. 'All he expected from them was to see a few faces around him, a few voices in the bunch, maybe a wheel or a bike change. If he was going to do anything, it would be an individual effort.'

As Hall describes how Simpson approached the 1967 race, he suddenly switches, in the middle of the flow of words, into the first person. The effect is uncanny. Is he quoting his dead leader verbatim, from memory, or is it as if, in mulling this over for more than three decades, he is paraphrasing several different conversations he had with Simpson? ' "The plan is, and it sounds daft, I want to try and win the Tour, but I haven't got the advantage of the strength some teams have. The plan is to pick one or two points in the race where I'll really attack it, critical points where time can be won and lost. I don't want to be in the [yellow] jersey, but I don't mind what position I'm in as long as I'm within three minutes at the time trial [the final stage]; I can win it." That was his belief: "I can take three minutes out of any of these buggers." That was his whole plan.'

Simpson had three target stages: the Alpine stage to Briançon, over the Col du Galibier, stage 13 from Marseille to Avignon via Mont Ventoux, and the leg through the Massif Central to the top of the Puy-de-Dôme, three days from Paris. Each included one of the hardest mountain climbs in the race at or near the finish.

Alongside Taylor in the British team car, Hall watched Simpson's progress each day. After a strong first week, he was handily placed in sixth overall when they went into the Alps, but that was as good as he would get. The first of his 'hit days', over the great Galibier pass, with its one in eight slopes, its snowdrifts and desolate scree slopes, did not go to plan. Simpson's health problems were brought home to Hall after the stage, when he cleaned Simpson's bike: it was 'covered in shit'. The British leader had been unable to keep his food down, he had diarrhoea and stomach pains. The mechanic and Taylor sat behind in the car as Simpson stopped at the foot of the Galibier to evacuate his system and then spent 15 miles of ascent chasing the leaders.

'When he got back to the field the leaders had gone, so he rode all the way up on his own. You could see them in front, you could see he was catching them, but the top came too early. He did go hell for leather down the other side, took a few chances' – on the same descent where he had ruined his Tour the previous year – 'but he ran out of steam and lost time,' remembers Hall.

Simpson was convinced that, had it not been for the stomach trouble, he would have stayed with the leaders according to his plan, rather than dropping to seventh overall. Perhaps this was true, but stomach trouble on the Tour is simultaneously a symptom and a cause of weakness: it drags the body down into a spiral of gradual decline. His teammate Vin Denson also noticed Simpson's physical troubles. 'I remember when we finished [one stage] in the Alps we had to carry him up the stairs. He was ill and couldn't eat. I was telling him "have some soup, some broth"; he just said "I'm going to be sick" but the next morning he was as bright as a button.'

Three days later, Simpson was at the foot of the Ventoux, a sick man with minimal team support, but driven on by his intensely competitive mind and his need to make money. The consensus from those in the team is that he was strung up, but outwardly relaxed. He still had the stomach trouble: he had had a bout of it the previous evening, and talked then of seeing the race doctor about it the next morning.

Hall prepared Simpson's bike meticulously that night, wrapping new tape round the handlebars – an old mechanics' trick to boost a rider's morale: when he looks down, he sees a bike which looks new. In the little red notebook, Hall listed the extra low gears he fitted on the bikes of what remained of the team: Denson, Colin Lewis, Barry Hoban and Arthur Metcalfe. By now, the other five team members had abandoned. He tinkered with Simpson's machine until one o'clock in the morning outside the team's hotel in Marseille. When he took it out for a test ride he was stopped on a deserted backstreet by the old port by a gendarme who thought he had stolen the bike. Then as now, the words 'Tour de France' can work wonders, and Hall was quickly let off the hook.

For most of stage 13, Hall, Alec Taylor and the driver, Ken Ryall, went through their usual daily routine in the Great Britain team's Peugeot 404 saloon. After the early morning start in Marseille, they followed the main bunch of riders. They listened to Radio Tour, the short-wave radio station which provided news of what was happening up ahead, and were on the alert to deal with punctures or any mechanical trouble. They overtook the field before the feeding station in the town of Carpentras, where the race was to finish after a loop up the thirteen-mile climb to the top of the Ventoux and down the other side. The heat was intense, the air filled with the high-pitched whirring of the cicadas, the little grasshoppers which are everywhere in Provence. The whole field was feeling the heat. Liquid food in the cyclists' bottles curdled and they regularly dived into bars and ran to roadside fountains to get drinks.

In Carpentras, Hall, Taylor and Ryall handed the riders their *musettes* – cotton bags with food and bottles of water – and then they drove hard to catch up the peloton again. Shortly after they got back behind the main group of riders, by now on the lower slopes of the Ventoux, Hall saw the first of a number of things that would later strike him as peculiar. Hall liked to make home movies of the major races, which he showed to his cycling clubmates in the winter, and he knew Simpson 'was destined to do a ride that day'. So as they rolled slowly along the lower slopes of the Ventoux in the blistering heat, he was sitting on top of the car getting his cine-camera and film ready. 'It was just before we started the Ventoux, an area where you are going through some trees, beginning to climb quite steeply. We got onto a quiet stretch of road and all of a sudden I saw Tom's bike in the grass on the right. I said to Alec, "Hang on, that's Tom's bike," and Tom came running out of a wooden hut. He was just banging the top of his bottle to put the cap on.

'I remember what I said to him. He came round the back of the car, got on his bike, and I said something like "Hey, Tom, that's naughty, you shouldn't be doing that," and he just winked at me and put his bottle in his cage and pedalled off.' Afterwards, Hall was told that Simpson had put cognac in his bottle; a *commissaire* – race referee – who witnessed the incident, Jacques Lohmuller, confirmed this.

The incident would not have been notable had it not been for the tragedy which was to follow. Until the 1970s, *la chasse à la canette* – the hunt for water – was common on the Tour on baking days like this when the riders would soon exhaust the two small bottles they carried on their bikes. They were not permitted to take bottles from the support cars, as they do today, so they would grab water from anywhere they could.

Hall went back in later years and tried to work out where the building was; it was no longer there. But what he had seen was another ingredient being added to the fatal cocktail swishing around the British leader's system. Simpson had already emptied two of the three tubes of amphetamines in his back pockets and he had already drunk part of a bottle of brandy grabbed by his room-mate Colin Lewis in another café raid earlier in the stage.

Simpson's 'guts were queer', he told Lewis. He had not been able to drink the liquid rice which Naessens usually gave him in his feeding bottle and had thrown it away. To one teammate, Vin Denson, he 'looked as if he was grimacing, pulling his face, rolling his head a bit, as if he was trying too hard'. Clearly, when he arrived at the mountain and saw the observatory 5,000 feet above him to his left, he felt he needed a second dose.

Hall and Taylor stood in the front seats of the cut-down car, looking up the mountain as they went past the also-rans being spat out on the first section of the climb, through the Bedoin forest. They could just make out what was going on at the front of the race, a couple of hundred yards up the slope, and occasionally glimpsed the white-clad figure of Simpson, who escaped early on but could not hold the pace set by Julio Jimenez, one of the finest climbers in the race. Simpson slipped back, to be overtaken by five other riders four miles from the top, where the road swings left past the café at Chalet Reynard and across the mountainside on the final approach to the summit. One of the five, Lucien Aimar, noticed that Simpson was in a peculiar state. 'I offered him a drink but he couldn't hear me. His look was empty. The bizarre thing was, he was trying to get away from me. He got about two and a half metres ahead and I said, "Tom, stop fooling about," but he didn't answer. His behaviour was completely bizarre.'

About one and a half miles from the top, Hall captured the start of the drama on his cine-camera, as Simpson began to zigzag, first almost going over the edge and down the scree to the left, then coming close to falling up the slope to the right. 'He was out of control for a moment or two. I thought he was going to go over the edge – if he'd gone over the left side he'd have gone and gone. He pulled himself up a couple of times, jerkily,' Hall recollects. Initially, the mechanic was worried about how Simpson might fare on the descent. 'I said "he's not going to get down", or something like that, because he was losing his control.' Taylor realized that Simpson's chances of winning the Tour were slipping away and shouted to him to concentrate.

When cyclists are at the point of exhaustion, any minute physical peculiarities in their riding style – a weak shoulder, a slightly bent knee – will become exaggerated as they fight the bike. Simpson's head had twisted towards his right shoulder at an angle of 45 degrees, like a bird with a broken neck. This was the posture he automatically adopted when he had one of his *jours sans*, as the French call a day when a cyclist is drained of physical strength.

This is where Hall's home movie ends – the moment when he realized something was horribly wrong. Part of the brief sequence is on *Something to Aim At*. So too is Hall's footage of Simpson making his way back up to the bunch on the lower slopes after his café stop. Hall speculates ironically on what he might have made in royalties. But he felt the same about the film as the number plate: it was 'a thing I didn't want to look at for years and years'.

Simpson fell for the first time roughly a mile from the summit. 'It isn't like it is now,' says Hall. 'It was a narrower road, with no room for a car to pass, cut into the bank with quite a drop down onto the grey-white stony stuff. I thought he'd just blown. He fell more or less against the bank.'

When Hall jumped off the car, he thought Simpson had

simply overdone it. 'He [Simpson] was leaned up against the bank, and I undid his toe straps and said, "Come on, Tom, that's it, that's your Tour finished." I was going to help him off, because he was just leaning against the bank, still on his bike, then of course he started protesting, "No no no no no, get me up, up." He was a bit incoherent but he knew what was going on. "I want to go on, on, get me up, get me straight." Alec had stopped the car and he came over. I said, "He wants to go on, Alec," and Alec said, "If Tom wants to go, he goes." So I just pulled him off the bank, and we wobbled him into the middle of the road, between us we were pushing him, and he said "Me straps, Harry, me straps", so he knew that his toe straps were undone. So I had to quickly tighten them up for him, and we pushed him off.'

Here, Hall's reaction to the events seems to change. He was now being taken beyond anything he had ever experienced. He had seen riders pedal themselves into a state of exhaustion or hypoglycaemia before, but of Simpson collapsed against the bank telling him to put him back on his bike, he can only say, 'At that moment I don't know what I thought. I just don't know.' What Hall does know is that Simpson's last words were murmured, in a rasping voice, just as he was pushing him off: 'On, on, on.' He could have been exhorting the mechanic, or telling himself to keep going; Hall seems to think it was both. This probably explodes the idea that Simpson's final words were 'Put me back on my bike.' Hall does not remember Simpson using the expression at any point.

Credit for 'Put me back on my bike' should perhaps go to the *Sun*'s man on the 1967 Tour, the late Sidney Saltmarsh. The writer used to claim to fellow journalists that, after Simpson's death was announced, he was asked by foreign colleagues what his last words were, and he told them 'Put me back on my bike.' He uses the quote in his report of the stage in *Cycling Weekly*. Saltmarsh used to say that he made the quote up; if he did, it was a good guess. Equally, he might have asked Hall, Taylor or Ryall what Simpson said, and recieved the reply 'He told us to put him back on his bike.' Then, he simply translated their paraphrase back into direct speech.

Taylor and Hall felt that Simpson might still make it over the climb. It was, after all, only just over a mile to the summit. 'We got back in the car, we said "he's managing now", he was going quite straight, quite steady, bobbing away. He went straight for maybe 500 yards, it seemed a fair way. We thought he might just get over the top, if he gets to the top he'll be OK.' Suddenly, Simpson started to wobble again. Aware of what was coming, Hall and Taylor jumped out of the car and ran forward to catch him, and Simpson began falling as they got to him. Taylor supported Simpson on the left, Hall to the right, with three spectators also trying to keep him moving and upright as he zigzagged across the road

Taylor and Hall, in their shorts and T-shirts, stumbled as Simpson's weight pushed them across the road to the left, almost into the gutter. Then the three men veered to the right, with Simpson now completely unable to support himself as he was laid down on the roadside. The fight to keep him upright barely lasted a few seconds but Hall describes it as he might a process which took several minutes.

'He was on his side,' says Hall. 'I was undoing his straps. I'd lifted him up. I'd slipped my body under his. I was trying to put him on my back and get him off the road, as you're always aware that there's stuff [the other cars and cyclists] coming and you've got to get out of the way, whatever you're doing.'

Now the long pauses between words begin, as if Hall is still trying to get a grip on the tragedy, still can't quite figure out how to describe it. Thus far, he has looked me in the face, but his eyes now have a faraway expression. He no longer seems to be entirely in the same room. 'The last terrible thought I had was . . . he wouldn't release the bars. He was hooked on the bars. I had to say to Ken Ryall, "Get his hands off" and Ken had to peel his fingers off so that I could let the bike go and carry him.'

Simpson's fingers were locked on the bars as if in rigor mortis, which has convinced Hall with hindsight that by then he was dealing with a dead man. Simpson, he feels, died somewhere between the moment when he was put back on his bike, and his second fall. There was no sign of life when he was carrying him off the road: like a sleeping child, Simpson was not supporting himself. He was a dead weight.

They laid Simpson on the stones, with his legs in the road, with 'a bit of a wet tea towel or something under his head', and his bike thrown down any old how on the rocks between the bumpers of two cars parked up on the slope. Hall loosened his jersey and began mouth-to-mouth resuscitation with one of the nurses from the Tour's medical team, taking it in turns to apply pressure to the lungs and do Simpson's breathing. Taylor and Ryall had gone to watch for the team's other riders, to ensure they did not stop and see their leader dying.

Again he searches for words. 'He was a sort of a yellowish colour . . . He was . . . It was hard to understand what was happening, because you were getting air into him when you were pumping him, and the air was coming out again.' Gruesomely, he mimics the sound the air made as it left Simpson's lungs: a drawn-out slobbering bubbling, like the tail end of a deflating balloon. Hall cannot remember how long his part in the fight for Simpson's life lasted. He has no idea how many cycling fans had rushed over to watch. 'I was taking no notice. You're in your own little world. There was a load of people, it was a matter of [saying] "Keep back, keep back, give him air." You're thinking "He's dead", "No, he can't be."'

Standing on the car, a breeze had kept Hall cool, but as soon as he got down, the heat struck him: merely breathing in the air was uncomfortable. 'It was terrible, very glaring, because it's all white stones it just seemed to intensify the heat. It's the stillness . . . When I carried him to the side of the road it was oppressive, hot, like being in a cauldron, no air at all.'

As he leans forward in his comfortable armchair in his sitting room, Hall can make a little pit form in the bottom of your stomach as you share in some of the adrenaline, feel the totality of the involvement. He can still see Simpson's face. 'He had a yellowy transparency – my lasting memory is of his eyes, just staring eyes. There was no sweat on his face. The sweat had gone. It had a waxy transparent look, with no colour on the top of his skin.'

They had to leave Simpson there. The tour's doctor, Pierre Dumas, had just brought an oxygen mask when Taylor, who wanted to get to the finish, came up to Hall and dragged him away. In the car, as they went through the steep succession of hairpins on the Ventoux's north side, Hall, Taylor and Ryall were stunned. 'You're in a bit of a daze, wondering what's going to happen. You think, well, maybe they can save him. You're telling yourself, "Perhaps he isn't [dead], perhaps there's something they can do, perhaps they can give him an injection in the helicopter, he's in good hands." ' And so down the mountain: hoping against hope, but knowing inside.

The British team were staying in the village of Malau- cène, on the descent from the Ventoux observatory to the finish in Carpentras. Taylor had to go to the race headquarters to find out what had happened to Simpson. Hall was left to deal with the team in the Hôtel du

Ventoux, a three-storey building among the main street's lime trees and shady squares.

The two *soigneurs*, Naessens and Rudi Van der Weide, got drunk, locked themselves in their hotel room on the hotel's first floor, and would not come out. Hall will not say what he said to calm them down: 'I got to them eventually and what happened then is between me and the lads.' Naessens had been close to Simpson for several years and regarded him as a son. He had looked after Simpson before this and other major races, and now, as well as being devastated by the shock, he probably felt responsible to some extent. In the light of their close relationship, it is almost certain that he knew that Simpson used drugs, although it is perfectly possible that he did not know precisely what Simpson was using and in what quantities.

The race finished at about 4.30 p.m. in the tree-lined centre of Carpentras. Simpson's absence had passed almost unnoticed. When the announcement had been made that no more riders were left to finish and he had still not arrived, the three British journalists on the race tried desperately to find out what had happened. No one knew what had happened to Simpson beyond the fact that he had fallen.

The Tour's press room that evening was the chapel of the Collège des Garçons in Carpentras. The building is an imposing, domed, 17th-century Jesuit church, built of honey-coloured limestone in a backstreet close to the old centre and used today to house art exhibitions. At 6.30 p.m., the communiqué written and signed by Dumas was read out by Félix Levitan, the editor of the *Parisien Libéré* newspaper, a dapper little man who jointly directed the race with Jacques Goddet: 'On arrival at the hospital in Avignon, Tom Simpson was in a state of apparent death. Specialist services at the hospital continued attempts at reanimation, without success. Tom Simpson died at 17.40. The doctors concerned have decided to refuse permission for the corpse to be buried.'

Simpson's body was placed in cell 3 of the hospital's morgue, where a few reporters went and found him to pay their last respects. 'The trolley glided slowly, the white sheet seemed endless,' wrote *Miroir-Sprint*'s man on the race, who seemed to find the business gruesomely fascinating. 'At last his face appeared. Tom looked to be sleeping. He seemed peaceful, his lips pink, his eyes half-closed. His half-open mouth still seemed to be gasping for air. The sheet accentuated his tan.' One journalist hid his face in his hands but a photographer kept shooting away, saying 'I'm sorry' after each exposure.

Hall did not know that three tubes of amphetamines had been found in Simpson's jersey and handed to the police; only the Tour organizers and the police were aware of it. 'We knew there was going to be a hoo-ha about drugs, knew we had to keep that side of things quietened down,' he says. To add to the feeling of unreality, Taylor, Naessens and Van der Weide spent the night in the police station in Malaucène answering questions. The following day the hotel was searched, more drugs found, and Hall too was arrested, in farcical circumstances. Together with his fellow mechanic Ken Bird, he was taken to the police station in Sète, where the stage finished, and the British car was impounded. They were in a panic, but eventually the two of them merely waited for the gendarmes' attention to be diverted, and then jumped in the car and drove away. That was the last Hall heard from the French police.

The Tour has a strict daily routine: eat, race, eat, sleep. Sticking to it is a prop in adversity. This was how it was for Hall and the team. He recalls the remaining 10 days of the Tour as a matter of survival, of numbly going through the motions. Members of the Motorola team in the 1995 Tour said the same thing about the days after the death of their team member Fabio Casartelli. Hall has no memory of what was said at meals between the riders and staff. He does not even remember meal times 'although we must have had them, and I must have been there as there wasn't much work to do'. Taylor did his best to keep the team together: Hoban, who had won the stage the day after Simpson died, tried for a second victory; and Lewis and Metcalfe struggled through. 'We said we'd get to Paris whatever, for Tom.'

Hall's race notebook also offers insights into the demands on this numbed little group of men. It records how they had to dispose of their dead leader's possessions, even while they were coming to terms with his loss, coping with an emerging drug scandal, and of course competing in the world's most demanding cycle race.

In the back pages is an inventory of Simpson's kit and a list of the people who came to take it away: three pairs of lightweight 28-spoked wheels, around 40 tubular tyres, including the ones he had had specially made in Paris by the Clément company, four bikes. Glued onto one page is a receipt signed by a representative of Peugeot who was sent to take the bikes back. Another page towards the end of the notebook records that Simpson's suitcase with his belongings has been put in a certain lorry, and that two wreaths for the funeral have been organized on behalf of the team.

The tragedy affected Hall far beyond the point when he went home and laid flowers at Simpson's grave in Harworth. Taylor and Ryall are now dead, so journalists or film makers now come to Hall's door whenever they want a first-hand account of Simpson's death. As with so many involved with Simpson, one way in which Hall came to terms with the trauma was to ride up the mountain. He did not steel himself to return for a quarter of a century, but then rode up it twice in one day. He found it tough: 'The second time I said, "Come on, Tom, you'll have to move over."'

In his dreams, he would have flashbacks of his team

leader dying in front of him. He was disillusioned with cycling for several years after Simpson's death due to the revelations about drugs: 'I wasn't going to do the job again. I didn't want to go abroad on professional races, the continental scene ... that it could end in someone killing themself for it.'

Hall had seen where the sport he loved could take a man if he was desperate enough: 'You always know other people that could be that way. There's a report from a London polytechnic which says that cycling and rowing are the two most dangerous sports for that. The individual is pushing a machine which doesn't know when to stop. It always asks for another pull of the oars, another pedal stroke.'

Not everyone shared this view of the dead champion as a victim of an implacable machine, however. Hall still remembers Taylor's words when the manager came back to the hotel in Malaucène. Taylor had spent the brief trip tuning in the car radio to stations across Europe, all discussing the death of the man he had hoped would win the Tour de France. 'He [Taylor] came in and said "he's dead" and then he said "the stupid bastard." '

Saint Brieuc, August 2, 1959
A baking day on the 'pink granite coast', the sumptuous seaboard of northern Brittany. The holidaymakers have left the beaches in force to cheer the cyclists in the Tour de l'Ouest as they pedal along the cliffs and through the fishing villages. At the front of the peloton, Tom Simpson is puzzled. He is wearing the leader's jersey in his first stage race as a professional. Two days ago, in Quimper, on his first day riding for the Rapha-Geminiani squad, he won. He was trying to tow his team leader, Pierre Everaert, to the front of the race, but Everaert could not hold his pace. So Simpson kept going, across to the lead group and on to the finish, arms raised in the air, the other five cyclists yards behind.

Yesterday, just to make the point that he is the strongest here, he won the afternoon time trial around Brest. 26 hilly miles in under an hour. Everyone was tipping Jean Forestier, who has won the Paris–Roubaix and Tour of Flanders classics, but he was almost two minutes slower. Two wins in two days: not bad for a 21-year-old in his first pro race.

Today, though, something funny is going on. There is a group of cyclists ahead, but the Rapha team won't make the pace, to keep that group within reach, so that the peloton can catch up by the finish. They keep telling Simpson the front-runners will slow down, but that's not how it looks to him. 'Job Morvan's in there,' they keep saying, 'so we have a rider from the team in the group.' By the finish, Morvan and his little group are five minutes ahead, and Simpson has lost his leader's jersey.

Later, Simpson will learn how he has been betrayed. Morvan is a local rider. He is retiring at the end of the year. He has tried to win the Tour of his home region five times. It's a bigger story for the local press, more exposure for the sponsors. Even if he is not a worthy victor, the team would prefer a Breton to win, rather than an unknown Briton.

It is Simpson's first lesson as a professional: being the strongest in a race carries no guarantees.

CHAPTER THREE

'PS I'm 19th Overall Now'

The letter is dated February 28, 1957. The address is 4, Festival Avenue, Harworth, Nottinghamshire. It is nothing more than a note from one 19-year-old boy to another. Both are cyclists, and the note is to arrange their weekend's training ride. The writer can't manage a ride on Saturday but, all other things being equal, they will meet at 9.30 on Sunday morning and ride to Nottingham and back, a distance of some 50 miles. If the letter had not been written by Tom Simpson, it would be merely a piece of flotsam left over from the youth of his training partner, George Shaw, which had somehow happened to survive in a drawer in his Sheffield home. Shaw himself cannot quite work out why he still has it, together with another 25 letters and postcards from Simpson. 'You have thousands of letters in your time. You tell me why I saved a letter from another young lad in February 1957. I can't explain it,' he says.

Brief it may be, but certain things stand out. To begin with, the letter is a reminder of the added complexity of organizing life in the age before everyone had a telephone. It reveals a little of the writer. The handwriting is careful, curlicued and ornate, reflecting the fact that he is learning to be a draughtsman. And he is a cyclist who is motivated and focused enough to be thinking ahead, both in the short and medium terms. It clearly matters that he gets that training ride in: it matters enough for him to write a letter to make sure it happens. He recognizes the need to have a companion. He already knows what he is doing on Saturday – taking a pair of wheels to a bike shop to be rebuilt. He is clearly well organized, which is far more than can be said for many adult cyclists.

Shaw was born three months before Simpson in 1937, and lived in Sheffield, some 20 miles away from Harworth. The first he knew of him was at a regional junior championship in 1955 when the man helping him out told him: 'Watch Simpson, he's been winning everything.' After they were both selected for the North Midlands Division team for the national junior road race title later that year, the friendship blossomed. Before car ownership was wide-spread, racing cyclists would spend the whole weekend on their bikes. George and Tom would ride to their races and head off with their mates to a café in the Peak District afterwards – Over Hadden, near Bakewell, was the favour-ite. They would sit there yarning and stagger into their homes at nine o'clock at night.

At the time of writing that first letter to George in 1957, Tom had already been competing on a bike for 16 years, according to his mother, Alice. She recalled Tom racing on his tricycle, aged only three, already trying to keep up with the older children. 'They would send him away,' said Alice Simpson. 'But he would get off his bike and say "I'll show you buggers who'll make a cyclist."' He is unlikely to have used precisely those words as a three-year-old, but clearly Alice had already seen unusual determination in her son.

Shortly after Tom's death, Alice Simpson and her husband, Tom senior, were interviewed by Ray Pascoe for his first film about their son. A small clip appears in *Something to Aim At*. Pascoe lent me the uncut version, on which Tom senior can be heard sucking on his pipe throughout. Time after time Alice sets her husband right, with more than a hint of her son's sharpness of mind. Both have kept their lilting north-eastern accents in spite of 20 years spent living in Nottinghamshire.

In a photograph taken at the first Memorial Race in Harworth after their son's death, the couple look every inch

the retired miner and his wife: Tom senior, broad-shouldered in his braces and floppy sun hat, his stomach curving
over his outsize trousers; Alice slight and nervous-looking
in her floral dress. Tom senior was a large, outgoing,
generous man. 'Whatever money he had he would give
away, he'd shout the bar, tip the taxi driver,' says Harry,
Tom's elder brother. He would perform comedy mono-
logues for the family. Both traits would be passed on to
Tom junior. The resilient, intense Alice managed the
money; Tom junior would inherit her determination.

Alice and Tom senior had six children in Station Street in
the Durham mining village of Haswell: Tom was the
youngest, born on November 30, 1937. He was not to be
the only sportsman in the family. When Tom senior was
not down the mine – his job is given on the birth certificate
as 'conveyor worker' – he had been a sprinter on the north-
eastern semi-professional running circuit.

As a child, Tom junior was good with his hands. 'There
was not much he could not take to pieces and put together,'
says Harry, Tom's elder by a year and 10 months. In the
future, Tom would be fixated with his equipment as a
professional, even to the extent of making his own saddle.
Young Tom was 'determined and obsessive, [he] would not
be denied' and was 'always on the lookout to make a dollar',
recalls Harry. Both these character traits would combine to
fatal effect on July 13, 1967.

After the war, as new coalfields opened up, the family
moved to Harworth, a north Nottinghamshire village
dominated by its vast pit heap – the biggest in Europe, it
was said at the time – and the winding gear of the colliery.
The Simpsons' home was in Festival Avenue, among the
rows of 1930s houses which were built in the fields,
between the pit and the old village centre with the church
and the cemetery where Tom was to be buried. Number
Four is still there, a brick end-of-terrace house in a quiet
estate. It doesn't smack of riches, nor of hard times: it is

modest but must have been a step above the family's house, with outside toilet, in Haswell. The family were not exactly poor, but they were not rich, and poverty would only have been one piece of ill fortune away.

Fortunately, Alice was a good manager. Mashed potato and gravy were the typical staple foods. Harry can remember only two family holidays, to Redcar and Seaton Delaval. Tom senior would say that, for a pitman, moving on was the only way to get on; for young Tom, cycling was the way on, up and out.

Tom and Harry raced around the block on the clunky old bike which they shared, but it was Harry who was the first to take cycling seriously, although he never became a true fan. He joined the Harworth and District Cycling Club, winning schoolboy time trials, and passed on the cycling bug to his younger brother.

Harry was 'always kicking a ball against the wall'. He went on to play schoolboy cricket and football for Durham and Sunderland, and later non-league football, getting as far as a trial for Blackpool United. Tom, on the other hand, had 'ball skills bordering on the inept', according to his brother, who, to his irritation, would be asked to take Tom along to play cricket and football even though he was 'hopeless'. Harry turned his hand to most sports; Tom followed him into cycling and, straight away, found a sport that he could do and stuck at it.

Young Tom covered the walls of his little boxroom with pictures of the cycling heroes of the late 1940s: Fausto Coppi, Ferdi Kubler, Hugo Koblet. 'He devoured the stories of the greats, he read them and read them,' recalls Harry. Tom pasted their photos into his schoolbooks, and said to his mother, 'I'm going to be one of them.' Later he would tell the readers of *Cycling* that there was nothing wrong with hero worship: he had been through it himself.

Most British cyclists start their racing with a local time

trial, over five or 10 miles: at the age of 13, Tom was no exception. Riding the butcher's bike he used to deliver meat for a local shop, he covered the five miles on a course close to Harworth in a relatively slow time of 17 minutes and 50 seconds. Then, showing the nose for a deal which was to be a hallmark of his adult life, he painted his heavy clunker red and swapped it for a sports bike belonging to a local miner.

So the scrawny youth entered cycling club life, a world of evening time trials, weekend grass track races and long club runs, when the Harworth and District would slog in an orderly crocodile to a café in Cleethorpes, a round trip of 120 miles, or into the Peak District. Tales are still told about older members attempting to burn off Simpson on the steep hills in the Peaks, and always finding him with them at the top. Harry Needham, the club secretary, nicknamed the youngster 'four-stone Coppi', because of his slight physique: 'A referral he readily accepted,' says Harry Simpson. John Noble senior, one of a whole family involved in the club, was one early mentor: he took young Tom under his wing, according to the current club secretary, George Morris, and Tom would often go to his house for help and advice.

The money Tom earned on his delivery round 'was put to the purpose of purchasing frames, wheels, gears, anything', says Harry, to feed his drive 'to be not only competitive but always first'. It was winning that mattered, as Tom's friend and rival Lenny Jones could testify: Tom would not speak to him if he, Jones, won a race. Once, after losing to Jones, Simpson was so desperate to avoid having to acknowledge him that he took off into a ploughed field and walked behind the hedge, pushing his bike for a good 200 yards.

At Worksop Technical College, which he attended from the age of 13, Tom Simpson stood out from the crowd, recalls one schoolmate, Peter Parkin. It was partly down to his Geordie accent, partly his liveliness, he explains: 'He was always taking the mickey out of the teachers, he used to like telling jokes. He'd have us in fits.' Parkin recalls walking to the school bus in Worksop and going past a butcher's shop where Tom opened the door and shouted 'Have you got any sausages left?' 'Yes, plenty,' said the butcher. 'Serves you right for making too many,' came the answer. Most of all, however, it was Simpson's obsession with cycling which set him apart. 'He talked about very little else, where he'd been, what he was going to do,' says Parkin. 'He was a rum kid.'

By 1954, as he approached 17, Simpson had matured enough physically to compete with the seniors in the Harworth club. The 20-mile daily cycle ride to his work as an apprentice draughtsman at Jenkins, an engineering company in Retford, must have helped. By the end of the year, he had grown out of the club.

In his autobiography *Cycling is My Life*, Simpson recalled 'shouting the odds' about winning a local time trial, which made him unpopular in the club. His obsession with road racing, European-style, had led him to propose that the club join the breakaway British League of Racing Cyclists, which ruffled feathers. Simpson was more than just a highly competitive teenager, however. He also realized that, if he wanted to progress, he had to move on. He was sure that he would be able to beat the rest of the Harworth club soon, and needed 'to find a club where I was a rabbit again and try to beat the other members'. That club was the Scala Wheelers in nearby Rotherham – the rather incongruous Italian name showing its loyalty to the BLRC. Ever the individualist, Simpson began his own team within the Scala. There were four of them. George Shaw was one: 'I don't think Scala Wheelers ever knew it [the team] existed. Tom got Italian national champions' jerseys made up, red, green and white, which simply read "Scala" in a band on the chest. Tom just wanted to be an Italian pro.'

By the time they were racing as juniors, Shaw could see the difference between Simpson and the other lads such as himself. 'When it really hurts, that's when most of us drop off the pace. Tom never dropped off. We read the magazines, or rather we looked at the pictures because we couldn't translate the French. We all wanted to ride the Tour de France, but really he wanted it and we dreamt it.'

Something else about Simpson struck Shaw. 'Even when he was a junior, he would push himself over the edge. From a young lad, he either won, or blew up, or he crashed. You would never see him without bandages. There was always a bandage on his elbow or whatever.' The rest of Simpson's career would follow a similar pattern.

As juniors, Shaw and Simpson would ride races in the Derbyshire hills which were open to all categories, from 16-year-olds to the top amateurs of the time. Simpson did not respect reputations, and would sprint up the road ahead of the bunch time after time. His aim was always to win, when for his contemporaries merely finishing with the best over-18s would have been an achievement. 'He was so aggressive, right from the word go,' says Shaw. 'He would take them all on, some of the best guys in the country.' However, the slender junior would often overestimate his strength. He would be out front with a clear lead, looking a likely winner, but would suddenly find he had nothing left and his legs had turned to jelly. Another fellow cyclist, Pete Ryalls, remembers a race in the Peak District, the Burbage road race, in which Simpson led from the start until the final climb, where Ryalls and the others passed him walking, exhausted, and close to tears.

Simpson was already prepared to drive himself beyond the bounds that are usual for most people. Peter Parkin worked alongside him at Jenkins after secondary school. 'He came in one Monday morning, he'd been riding a race on Sunday. It was the middle of the summer, and he'd taken his top off. He rolled it up and showed us: the sunburn was like raw meat. He couldn't bear anyone to touch it. I've never seen anyone burnt so badly.' Parkin says that Simpson could get into such a state of exhaustion that his body gave out. 'He would race all weekend, then would ride to work on his bike, work a full day, and train in the evenings. It wore him out. He had a problem; eventually it dawned on him and he got a job in Harworth. One day he just collapsed at work and was taken home in a car.'

Like many others, Shaw links Simpson's death firmly to the obsessive courage he saw in his teenage contemporary. 'He knew there was an opportunity and he was going to take it. In his early days he was not the best climber, but he was a fearful descender – he would drop off and catch the rest on the descents. He probably just tried to stay with the climbers for too long. I can imagine when he got to the Ventoux, he got carried away with the emotion.'

Shaw was not the only person the young Simpson wrote to. As a teenager Simpson had no inhibitions about seeking help from, among others, the runner Gordon Pirie, the boxer Terry Downs and the great French cyclist-turned-manager Francis Pelissier. He had a thirst for any information which might help him progress on his bike. He wrote to Pelissier on November 22, 1954, nine days before his 17th birthday, after Simplex, the cycle components company, invited letters to the great Frenchman. Cyclists from all over Britain wrote, and the journalist Jock Wadley had the task of dealing with the letters. He rediscovered Simpson's a few years later and printed it in his magazine, *Sporting Cyclist*. It shows that young Tom is precise about his time trial placings – '11th, 8th, 15th, 7th' – and cannot resist mentioning that he is the fastest 16-year-old over 25 miles in England that year.

Simpson is looking for simple information – he wants to know if it is advisable to combine road racing, track and time trials, and the maximum distance he should race. He is also more sceptical than the average 16-year-old about what he is being told. 'I have been told that if I race often I will burn myself out, and will be no good when I get older. Do you think this is true?'

Another letter put Simpson in touch with his first trainer, the naturalised Austrian George Berger. Simpson's choice reflects the clarity of his vision: Berger had learned all he knew in France, which made him one of the few points of contact in England with the European cycling world Simpson wanted to enter.

Berger travelled from his home in London to Harworth and found an ungainly youth with boundless potential. He changed Simpson's position so that he was sitting correctly on his bike, and advised him to take up pursuiting on the track – an intense, short-distance discipline which is where Simpson's great hero Fausto Coppi had begun. Berger's plan was that, as the young rider turned from junior to senior, Simpson would develop the pedalling speed which would enable him to win road races later in his career. He was to be proved correct.

In his first year at the discipline, 1956, Simpson began to earn notoriety in Britain by defeating the reigning world champion Norman Sheil in the semi-final of the British championship. Still aged only 18, he followed that with a bronze medal in the four-man team pursuit at the Melbourne Olympics the same year. 'Five days in a plane is really trying,' he wrote to George and Marlene, on a postcard of a Constellation airliner.

Simpson had his setbacks on the track. A brace of punctures in the final cost him the national title in 1956. A disastrous crash put him out of the 1958 world championship. His sheer youth showed on the way to his bronze in Melbourne: he went through a crisis of confidence beforehand, and was unable to keep up during a vital semi-final. His attempt on the world amateur hour distance record on the Oerlikon velodrome in Zurich in November 1958 was overambitious. 'Thank you for the invitation to your house,' he wrote to George Shaw, 'but I will be away. I am going on the 28th Nov to attack the record on the 29th, I am 21 [years old] on the 30th. The present record stands at 45km587m, or 28.335mls, so I am going to have to motor it to make it.' He did not 'motor' quite fast enough, missing out by 300 yards.

The defeat which hurt him most, though, was a narrow loss to Sheil of the gold medal in the 1958 Empire Games in Cardiff. 'Even when he was a pro, he always said to me that that was the one race he regretted not winning,' says Sheil. But the blistering turn of speed which track racing gave Simpson was to be invaluable on the road. He was never able to sprint with the very best but his pedalling style retained the suppleness of a track racer, which gave him the ability to finish rapidly. Superior speed in a two-man sprint won Simpson three of his biggest victories: Milan–San Remo, the Tour of Flanders, and the world title. Berger's advice kept paying dividends long after Simpson had left Britain behind.

Simpson's spell in track racing had another long-term effect on his career. It was while racing on the now defunct track at Fallowfield in Manchester that he found a second mentor, Cyril Cartwright, who had won the silver medal in the individual world pursuit championship in 1949. If Berger had pointed Simpson in the right general direction, it was Cartwright who did much to show him how to proceed, by instilling in the youngster the principles of nutrition which he had taken years to formulate. Cartwright believed that you are what you eat. This was perfectly understandable: he had recovered from rheumatic fever to win his medal with the help of a diet based on fresh vegetables, vegetable juices, nuts and lightly cooked meat.

His ideas were to stay with Simpson, who was obsessed with diet throughout his career.

When Cartwright offered to train Simpson in the spring of 1956, the young man showed a remarkably clear-headed approach. In spite of Cartwright's record, the 18-year-old was not bowled over and did not commit himself. Instead he went away and found out more about his prospective coach before giving his answer: a wholehearted 'yes'.

Simpson returned from a two-week stay at Cartwright's house in Manchester in the spring of 1956. With typically brutal honesty, he told his mother Alice, 'You're not feeding us right,' as she recalled it. 'I used to make him a plate of salad. I had a job to feed him.' So much so that she went out to work in order to earn the extra money it took to buy the fresh fruit and vegetables. In the interview with Ray Pascoe, Alice reels off the list – bananas, apples, grapes, sultanas, pears – and reveals how preoccupied she was with paying for it: 'When he was eating it I said, "Do you know how much that plate of salad cost me, boy? Seven and threepence." He would say, "I've made you a lot of work, mother."' Harry Simpson would eat his meat and two veg and tell his younger brother that he did not know what he was missing.

Like many younger sons, Simpson seems to have been the apple of his mother's eye. It is said that his premature death hastened hers. In Pascoe's interview, she cannot resist the temptation to underline the extraordinary nature of the back-up she gave her son, relating how another of his little cycling circle, Bobby Womack, came into the Simpsons' house and saw the salad. 'He said, "Who's that for?" "It's for Tom." "That would serve us a week in our house."' Alice adds that Bobby almost got to be a better cyclist than Tom, but 'he liked going dancing and didn't keep up with the training'. You can almost see the maternal breast swelling with pride.

Even at that age, Simpson had a clear idea of where he

wanted to go and had the dedication which was going to get him there. His mother would tell him, 'You lead the life of a monk,' and he would reply: 'I'm not doing it for nothing.' In the interview, his mother repeats, like a mantra, this phrase: 'He put his heart and soul into it.'

He would come into the house on Festival Avenue after training in the evening, and the television would be on. After his bath he would come into the room in his dressing gown and would ask when the programme would finish. On hearing that, for example, it would be over at 9.30, nine times out of ten he would say 'I need nine hours' bed' and would be on his way upstairs.

The anecdote closely resembles a tale told by the Belgian family who looked after another English-speaking great, Sean Kelly of Ireland, in the early 1980s. Herman and Elise Nijs could not work out why Kelly went to his room at nine o'clock every evening – was he writing letters home, reading a book? One evening they peeped through the bedroom door, and Kelly was lying there sound asleep.

George Shaw's plastic folders of letters in that ornate handwriting show that Simpson was no ascetic, however. I spent most of my two hours with Shaw laughing. During 13 years of correspondence, Simpson comes over as raunchy, vulnerable, funny, deadly serious, naive and worldly-wise. His mind jumps rapidly and busily from subject to subject. People and topics are jostling for space. He goes well beyond the immediate focus of the next race, the last race, the next training ride.

Simpson, and his wife Helen, continued writing to Shaw and his wife: Shaw has kept the entire correspondence. Set out in order by date, the letters and postcards chart Simpson's rise. Notes arranging training rides as a teenager give way to letters from Brittany as Simpson makes the breakthrough in Europe. There are letters from the Tour de France and postcards from holidays on the beaches of Corsica and the ski slopes of the Alps.

There are glimpses of the detail behind major events in Simpson's career: a postcard from the Melbourne Olympics, the news of his professional contract, his first training camp with a pro team, his first Tour de France and the broken leg that ruined his season as world champion. But mentions of major turning points in his career are overwhelmed by requests for news from home, inquiries about the Shaws' welfare, and commentary on the letters he has received. Simpson never brags about his own achievements, and he never seems to dwell on his failures.

Strikingly, there is not a single excuse in the correspondence, never a 'might have been' or an 'if only'. There is barely a word of complaint in any of the letters or postcards, other than an admission or two of homesickness, and the mention of a puncture here and a crash there. These are traits which go far towards making a champion athlete. Little things stand out as well: immersion in French enters Simpson's subconscious after a year in the country, when he spells 'modern' in the French style, with the final 'e'. There is his ordinariness: like every other British bike rider I have known, Simpson refers to the magazine *Cycling and Mopeds* – now *Cycling Weekly* – as *The Cycling*, reflecting the magazine's status as an institution within the British sport.

The letters show him uncut, unedited for public consumption, but they confirm that, in private as in public, he is far more than a man who can merely ride fast on a bike. Simpson is as uninhibited on paper as he was in his racing style. These are an extrovert's letters, conversational in style, packed with sly asides, in-jokes and self-deprecation. Read them at speed, and you can imagine what it might have been like to talk to the man, why his contemporaries all agree that there was rarely a dull moment when he was about.

Running through the letters is an intriguing in-joke. Tom has a soft spot for Shaw's wife Marlene. 'He used to tell me that he would have married her himself if I hadn't got there first,' says Shaw. 'If I come to [the race at] Wentworth it will be to see Marlene not you,' Simpson writes rather brutally on March 21, 1957. Two years later, he writes from Brittany: 'So all the best to you George and to you Marlene (my heart throbs when I say the name), all my love, well nearly . . .'

After George and Marlene marry in 1958, most of the letters are addressed 'Dear Both'. Simpson would sign off to both of them and would send Marlene a special inverted pyramid of X's at the foot of the letters. 'All the best, yours Tom; love Marlene, half yours, Tom,' ends a letter in 1960. Sometimes, he imagines Marlene's reaction to his raunchier comments with bracketed asides – 'Thinks Marlene: "the dirty dog".' Nor is he above sending a smutty seaside postcard from training camp with the Rapha-Geminiani team in the south of France in early 1960: the buxom silhouette of a lady in a beach hut with a queue of gawking men. He teases George and Marlene about what they got up to on honeymoon – 'I bet you did a lot of walking, ha ha.' Soon after their marriage, he warns her that 'married life can do terrible things to a woman'.

Among his fellow bike riders, Simpson had a reputation as a man with an eye for the ladies. 'They just used to throw themselves at him. It was like that with all the big stars,' says Alan Ramsbottom. Simpson's letters bear this out. In its crudity, a comment on June 20, 1960, is worthy of *Loaded* magazine – 'Well mate if you see that Barbara again, just tell her I found one that <u>did</u>, one that doesn't is no good is it?'

Clearly, Simpson did not always live the life of a monk, whatever his mother might have thought. Besides Barbara, who lived near Harworth, other girlfriends' names appear in the letters: Fay, who worked with Shaw, and Bobby, a bridesmaid at George and Marlene's wedding. Fay apparently went with Simpson to a track race in Manchester just before he left for Brittany, and he wrote to Shaw from there: 'She may go to more [track races] and if I do well here I may get contracts to ride in England and ?' The question mark makes his intentions clear.

As well as spending weekends on their bikes in the summer, Tom and George partied in the winter, following the rhythm of cycling club life at the time. 'In those days, everyone raced from March to October, then they stopped,' explains Shaw. 'Come October it was what was called the social season, when there were loads of parties all over the place, then on January 1 everyone got serious again.' Simpson clearly liked to let off steam, something which was not in the least incompatible with living the life of a dedicated athlete for the bulk of the year. On September 1, 1960, a few months before he was married, he wrote to Shaw: 'Well mate, the season is nearly finished, start getting that social season prepared. Any dolls up your way for when I can get away from mine? See, I'm starting already to rake back my wicked ways.'

Before his first training camp as a professional, at Narbonne Plage in the south of France, he seems to have overdone it: 'I don't think I will come to any more partys [*sic*], I am still tired, I never seem to get enough sleep,' he groans in a smutty seaside postcard written in early February 1960.

Even at his peak, and when married, Simpson did not completely calm down. Two British amateur cyclists were once settling down to sleep in a hotel room in Spain when they heard a clicking of high heels and a loud screaming from the corridor. They opened the door and saw a half-naked woman, a member of a coach party from Lancashire. 'Quick, quick, hide me,' she said. 'That Tom Simpson is chasing me.' This was two nights before Simpson won the world road race championship in San Sebastian.

Simpson saw no alternative but to go to Europe to further his cycling career: at the top of the tree in Britain it was possible to glean a living, but little more. Pursuiting would never bring in a great deal of cash, and it had been merely a means to a greater end: success in road racing. Like all the other British pursuiters, Simpson had successfully mixed his track racing with races on the road, but had stayed away from the longer, hillier events which would have blunted his speed. He had also won time trial after time trial, and had taken the BLRC's national hill climb championship. Yet all this meant nothing if he could not get a contract with a professional team in Europe. Winning the world pursuit title might have earned him a place, but he had missed out in 1957 and 1958 owing to crashes at the wrong time. His attempt to gain attention by challenging the amateur hour record in November 1958 was unsuccessful, and cost him dear. 'Just a line to wish you a Merry Xmas, I don't think I'll have any money by then,' he wrote to George.

After an abortive attempt to make a living on the track in Ghent, he returned to Harworth early in 1959 with half a crown in his pocket. At 21, he now had to begin his cycling career again – Olympic Games, Empire Games and national title medals notwithstanding. There was one step open to him: move to Europe and earn his contact by winning enough races to get noticed. His move to Brittany in April 1959 was not quite the last-chance saloon, but it was next door to it. 'Shit or bust,' he told a fellow cyclist.

The opportunity came through the Murphy brothers, friends of a friend. They were French, but of Irish descent and ran a butcher's shop in the Breton fishing port of Saint Brieuc. Simpson caught the bus from Harworth to Doncaster and the train south in April 1959 with £100 (enough to live off for a few months), a suitcase, a haversack and two Carlton racing bikes. His mother remembered his words as he went: 'I don't want to be sitting here in 20 years' time, wondering what would have happened if I hadn't gone to France.' As in his racing, his inclination was to take the risk.

Among those who competed in Simpson's final road race in Britain was Harry Hall, the mechanic who would, eight years later, desperately fight to save his life on the Ventoux. He and the other competitors asked the organizer to give Simpson all the prize money, as he was off to France the next day and he would need it. The other lads made do with the puncture repair outfits, tyres and bike shop vouchers which typically made up prize lists in those days. Clearly Simpson's move was common knowledge, and his fellows were supportive: he must have been well-liked.

It was a hurried departure, partly because of Simpson's need to avoid the draft. Doing National Service would mean putting his professional career on hold. Simpson knew the call-up could come any time that spring: 'He said that if the letter from France came before the National Service forms, he would go,' says a Harworth contemporary. His papers came through the Festival Avenue letterbox the day after he departed. His father was not keen on him missing the draft, and their parting was tinged with rebuke.

As a draft-dodger his future visits to England would be brief; for the next couple of years he would be dodging the Military Police. On one occasion, he cancelled a racing trip after it was rumoured, correctly, that they would be waiting at the airport. Simpson wrote to Shaw on September 1, 1960: 'This winter I won't be home for long 'cause I don't want to get nabbed, St Raphael are paying me more next year. So my social life will be spent in France where I don't have any army worries.'

Simpson wrote long letters from France, sometimes up to four pages, and Shaw was by no means his only correspondent. He asks George and Marlene to write longer letters: 'You write the progress of the races, George, and Marlene you write some juicy bits, I'm a right one for a bit of the local news.' He was clearly homesick, a problem born of his inability to speak French. 'It can be very lonely at times, in the four-day [race] I spoke with only one man who spoke English for about a quarter of an hour,' he wrote on May 12, 1959. 'I live a pretty silent life, you can understand that this doesn't agree with me. I am not one of the silent types.' Six years later he would be fluent enough to make puns in French which would put a native to shame.

In 1959, France was still sufficiently unfamiliar territory for the English to prompt Simpson to reassure Shaw that 'the food is almost like in England'. The fishing port is one of Brittany's less attractive towns, but clearly it compared favourably with the Nottinghamshire coalfields – 'very beautiful', wrote Simpson that April.

Not that it was comfortable. Soon after arriving at his digs above the Murphys' butcher's shop at 15, Rue de Rennes in April 1959, Simpson wrote: 'The only problem is that housing is a little behind in modern fittings such as baths, hot water, carpets on the floor, paper on the walls and clean toilets, otherwise it's just the job.'

Brittany was, and remains, a hotbed of the sport. It served Simpson's purpose well: the racing in the area was of a high standard, and there was cash to be made. Money was Simpson's preoccupation. In the letters, the amount of prizes he won always takes precedence over the wins themselves. Presumably, winning races was nothing new; the novelty was in earning £35 a time for doing it. 'Oh boy, this is the place for me, when I have built my house I shall expect to see you,' Simpson's first letter concludes – after a lengthy exposition of the cash on offer.

Nowadays, a talented cyclist such as David Millar will spend at least a full season proving himself as a top amateur before landing a place in a professional team, but Simpson's apprenticeship was remarkably brief. On July 9, 1959, within three months of alighting in Saint Brieuc, Simpson wrote to Shaw: 'I have been very lucky recently, and have had two [team] contracts offered me, with Mercier and Rapha Geminiani. I will probably ride with Rapha.'

The 'very lucky' is sheer modesty. In getting a professional contract, a rider makes his own luck: Simpson won his second race within a week of arriving in France; within five or six weeks he had won five races. His progress up the ladder was rapid, as it had been in the world of English pursuiting, and as it would be when he arrived at the Rapha squad.

Rapha included Brian Robinson, the Yorkshireman who had already made the breakthrough Simpson was seeking. Mercier were a smaller squad with less money, but with several Breton riders who had doubtless seen Simpson in action. Robinson, Simpson and the Rapha manager Raymond Louviot met when the Tour de France visited Rennes on June 29, and agreed terms: 80,000 old francs (£80) a month. This was exceptionally good money for a debutant; more than Rapha were paying Robinson, who had a Tour stage win to his credit.

A first professional team place is a momentous breakthrough in a cyclist's career; even better, Simpson had two teams competing for his services. It was a major achievement, but typically, he deflates it: '. . . my first race will be the Tour [de] l'Ouest with [Jo] De Haan & Co. (oh I do like to be a water carrier).' The aside indicates, modestly, that he thinks he will be a mere *domestique* or team worker – the French term is literally *porteur d'eau*. In the event, he nearly won the race.

Considering the momentous nature of the first pro contract, one would expect him to be bursting to break the news. Instead, he spends the first page and a half of the letter pondering Shaw's achievement in finishing the Tour of Britain, contemplating the fact that, contrary to an arcane British rule about sponsors, Shaw lists his trade sponsor, Ovaltine, before his bike supplier, Alp.

You can imagine him sitting at a table with Shaw's letter in front of him, replying to what his friend writes before adding his own news. 'Well you finished the Tour [of Britain], that is something many couldn't do, I read in *The Cycling* that it just about killed everybody but [Bill] Bradley . . . I'm glad to hear you are winning the team prizes (Ovaltine Alps eh), have you had a comic letter from the BCF about the Ovaltine before the Alp, you naughty boys you.'

In the same letter, Simpson reveals something which has lain hidden until now. After winning the final stage of the Route de France amateur stage race that June, he was offered a place in that year's Tour de France with the international team. This included several Britons, of whom Robinson was one. 'I turned down the chance to ride the Tour, I'd had enough,' Simpson wrote. 'Maybe in a couple of years I will ride the horrible thing.'

It was a year later, in fact, in July 1960, that a letter which Simpson had headed 'Equip [*sic*] Grande-Bretagne, Tour de France, France' dropped through George and Marlene's letterbox in Wilson Street, Sheffield. Simpson was in the middle of his first Tour de France, but travel arrangements for Marlene to visit Paris the week after the race fill the letter, down to the cost of the taxi and bus fares. 'It's a hell of a fast race,' is as much as he offers. The letter ends 'PS: I'm 19th overall now' with no explanation of how or why, causing one of those moments when George and I both laugh out loud. The note of anticlimax empitomises Simpson's ambition. For most people, lying 19th in the Tour de France would be worth shouting about. Clearly, it was incidental to him: he almost took the yellow jersey earlier in the race and 19th was probably something of a disappointment.

The same side of his character is seen on an undatable postcard from Genoa – 'Yesterday the Milan–San Remo, did not win.' It sounds like irony, but Simpson would have begun the race thinking he could win; that he did not was noteworthy. The only thing he seems to take seriously is money, a constant theme through the correspondence.

Reading Simpson's spidery writing – which gets increasingly ragged as he gets older and leaves his draughtsman's training further behind – it is impossible not to warm to him as Shaw, and many others, clearly did. His interest in his friend's affairs, his modesty about his own achievements, and his self-deprecation all help to explain his popularity. Even so, Simpson's confidence shines through. It may be bravado, but apart from his admission that he was 'lucky' to get a team place, there is no indication anywhere in the letters that what is happening to him is any more than he expects. In fact, sometimes he consciously downplays a major stepping stone, as in this *double entendre*: 'Next week I've got my first race with the pros (no the bicycle riding type)'.

In a similar vein, when he turns independent in May 1959 – the first stepping stone to a professional licence – he laughs it off by putting it in the context of the campaign among sports officials at the time to do away with the status: 'I am now inde. [*sic*] so I have now joined the ranks of the untouchables.' He is not one for dramatic flourishes. That vital life event, his marriage, is mentioned as a brief footnote. 'Oh, by the way, I'm going to get married I hope', he wrote from Saint Malo after stage five of the Tour de France on June 30, 1960. Sleeping in the same room as his boyhood hero, Fausto Coppi, during his attempt on the world hour record in Zurich was treated equally coolly. 'At the track I shared a room with Coppi, [Rik] van Looy and Batiz* but I didn't get the magic touch,' says the postcard of the Alps he sent to George and Marlene.

* Jose Batiz, an Argentine sprinter active on the professional track circuit at the time.

63

At times, despite his flippant tone, the fatigue creeps through. On July 9, 1959, Simpson writes: 'How did you find the mountains [in the Tour of Britain]? I had my taste at the Route de France, oh boy did I suffer.' The stress can also be felt during Simpson's third Tour in 1962: he bought a postcard in Saint Malo, but clearly he had no spare time to write it until he reached Bayonne, five days and 600 miles of racing later. 'It's the fastest Tour ever till now, and it's very hot. This is written in bed, I'm trying to prepare for the mountains but at the moment feel b—— [*sic*].' It is easy to imagine the scene. The young man is lying on his hotel bed, following the advice of senior pros and attempting to save his energy by lying down rather than sitting in a chair. While he writes, he thinks for a few moments about life away from the race. A day and a half later he will pull on the yellow jersey and win his place in cycling history.

'PS I'm 19th Overall Now'

Roubaix, northern France, 26 June 1961
The group of about 80 cyclists is strung out in single file as they speed towards the finish of the second stage of the Tour de France. White eyes peer out from faces black with coal dust which has been sprayed over them by the day's rain. Mud is caked on the torn, dirt-stained jerseys and bleeding elbows of those who have fallen in the day's huge pile-ups on the cobbled roads.

Tom Simpson is at the end of the string, eyes fixed on the back wheel of the cyclist in front. It keeps moving away from him as the group accelerates. He can't hold the pace. Since his crash on these same roads in April he has been out of form: the knee injury, the little illnesses, the food poisoning, the rash. Some have said he's just lost it because he has got married and has been spending time with his wife instead of training as he should.

Why the knee pain won't go away, he does not know. He's rested it, kept it warmed up, rubbed in the lotions the doctor gave him. It's wrecked his season. He didn't dare train before Bordeaux–Paris because of the pain, then he couldn't even start. No contract money. He shouldn't be here either, but there's always the chance it might go away.

Pete Ryalls has been behind him for the last 20 miles. Every time that wheel in front pulls away, Pete puts a hand on his backside and pushes him towards it. If one of the guys in front can't hang on, and sends him backwards, Pete pushes him round so he stays in the shelter. He's grabbed his arm a few times when he's slowed down, and slung him back to that wheel like a cricketer bunging a ball.

He's known Pete since they were juniors, now Pete's here in his first Tour, and has been told to push him, keep him in the race. Why won't Pete leave him alone? Why can't he just stop pushing? The decision is made: Simpson slows down, mutters 'there's no point, just leave me to it', and watches the peloton disappear into the distance as the convoy of support cars passes him. Defeat is accepted: tomorrow he will go home.

CHAPTER FOUR

'Unstable Dynamite'
Benny Foster, England team manager, on Simpson

In an evening of laughter with George Shaw, there was one wintry intervention of grief: a two-page letter from Helen Simpson postmarked October 2, 1967. She is writing partly to thank George for selling Tom's remaining team kit on her behalf: 'It breaks my heart really but there is no point in keeping them, only to keep in the cupboards.' The house, Helen writes, is 'very quiet now without a house full'. The people who have come to support her since the death have left – Tom's parents came for a fortnight, her mother for a few days. She must be newly aware of the hours passing, because she writes the time, 3 p.m. Saturday, on the letterhead. Her earlier letters are not even dated.

In her letters and postcards written to George and Marlene on Tom's behalf, Helen is more formal than her husband, more conventionally matter-of-fact, with no hint of Tom's chatty style. Now, it seems, the freshly bereaved widow is writing at least in part to externalise her feelings. She now feels prepared to 'face up to the long years ahead of me, which at the time [of her husband's death] seemed unbearable . . .' There is an undertone of quiet desperation in the letter. 'Sometimes I feel so depressed and lose all courage . . . One doesn't seem to realize how much one depends on the other in marriage. Even though we were only able to live six years together, it seems too hard to understand why he had to go so young and leave me alone.'

Meeting Helen was an intense experience, and left me feeling drained. It was not, however, for the reason I expected, which was that I was worried I would say the wrong thing and end up feeling embarrassed. I felt that talking to someone who had lost a husband in such a painful way was beyond me. If I ended up exhausted, though, after a long afternoon with Helen and her second husband, Barry Hoban, the feeling of being constantly on my guard was only a small part of it. The root cause went back 40 years: to the intensity of the six short years Helen spent with Simpson. For all its brevity, the marriage has left her with a densely woven tissue of memories.

I had grown to like Simpson myself in the few months I had spent hearing and reading about him; it was impossible not to react as Helen's memories spilled out one after the other. As she told her story, I would recognize elements that I had discovered elsewhere. I would make the link to a different anecdote and this would prompt further memories from Helen. So we spiralled from digression to further digression for several hours, in what at times felt like an emotional form of memory ping-pong.

There is emotion but no unease at revisiting the past. Helen has the tone of a woman who has faced up to her loss and embraced it, rather than cutting herself off from her past. I mention 'closure' at one point and she responds sharply: 'Why would I ever want to close the book?' And so we opened it again.

In April 1959, Helen Sherburn was working in Saint Brieuc as an au pair when she was told about an English cyclist living a few houses down the same street, Rue de Rennes. She set off to find him. Simpson was sitting in the garden when she arrived at the Murphys' and asked, in perfect French, if this was where the young Englishman lived. Assuming she was merely an inquisitive Frenchwoman, he replied 'Bugger off.'

In spite of this inauspicious start, the pair found they had much in common. Helen was 19, Simpson 21. Both were abroad for the first time; this in a period when travelling abroad was rare and living abroad rarer still. Helen's parents farmed in the Yorkshore village of Sutton, close to Doncaster, 20 miles from Simpson's home on the other side of the Yorkshire–Nottinghamshire border. They were amazed by the coincidence.

Simpson was homesick, so the Murphys had actually told him about Helen and he had already tried to visit her. He had got as far as knocking on the door, only to realize that if one of the French family opened it, he would not know what to say to them. He had run off down the street like a small boy.

Helen's first impression? 'Dishy', she says, as a 19-year-old girl might have in the late 1950s. And 'determined'. The pair talked for hours, or rather Simpson did most of the talking, telling Helen of his plans. 'After a few minutes, I could see he knew what he wanted in life.' Cycling, however, was something completely new to her. Her father was mad about cricket, but she had no idea it was even possible to make a living from racing a bike. 'I decided it was something I could cope with,' she says wryly. She would walk past the Murphys' house when she took her family's children to school in the morning, and would stop to talk to Tom when she came back.

Helen was struck by Simpson's avid desire for information about his chosen profession. He read every magazine from cover to cover. As a professional, Simpson was constantly asking his colleagues questions. He is the only cyclist I have ever heard of who would visit libraries to get the books he needed. Most would simply not bother.

Helen moved to Germany after just two months, but she and Simpson kept in touch, and in 1960 he drove over to see her in his new Aston Martin. She took the train to Paris to meet him when he finished his first Tour de France that year: 'a wreck, his face covered in blisters', she recalls. By the end of June 1960, a little over a year since they had first met, Simpson was already planning to marry Helen, or so

he wrote to George Shaw from the Tour de France. Over
40 years on, this is news to Helen; when I told her, she
could only say, 'He probably hadn't mentioned it to me!'

The couple holidayed in the Black Forest in November
that year – 'we have a beautiful country house (all to
ourselves)' says the postcard, addressed to 'Shaws'ouse' –
and were engaged that summer. They intended to marry in
October 1961, when the racing season would be over, but
what followed on January 3 was that most romantic of
events: a spontaneous, unplanned wedding.

'It was typical Tom – don't hang around, don't mess
about, do it now,' says Helen. They were standing on
Doncaster station when he put the idea to her; she was 'not
fussed' about having a big wedding. She went with her
mother to Sheffield, bought a dark green fitted suit, and
they had a small family wedding. 'We had a Christmas cake
that hadn't been cut, so we scraped the decoration off and
used it as a wedding cake. It was magical.'

It was a shock for those around them. After the decision
had been made, they visited Helen's aunt, who did not
know about it. Simpson could not resist loudly humming,
'I'm getting married in the morning.' The aunt failed to
take the hint. Simpson showed the wedding ring to his
teammate and mentor Brian Robinson at a dinner the day
after the ceremony, and the stolid Yorkshireman was
convinced it was a joke. Shaw too was convinced it was
another Simpson prank.

Helen Simpson's new husband was a mercurial character,
with a hunger for new experience, a man of dreams. 'One
ambition [of Tom's] was to buy a train, do it up and live in
it, a train with a carriage. He talked about it so many times.
He was going to have a boat, a plane as well.' Simpson was
planning a house on his land in Corsica when he died: it was
'to have a tree growing through it'.

He was a man quick to fall in love with places. Within

days of moving to Saint Brieuc he was writing to George Shaw about building a house there. A year later, he was talking of buying a hotel in Normandy. A racing trip to New Caledonia in 1964 prompted him to talk about moving to the Pacific islands. Initially, however, he and Helen shared a sparsely furnished flat with Brian Robinson in the Paris suburb of Clichy, moving to Ghent in October 1961. Helen stayed on in Belgium after Simpson died, moving to mid-Wales when her second husband, Barry Hoban, ended his long career as a professional cyclist in 1980.

Helen is tall, imposing, with fine features. Together, the Simpsons made a glamorous couple. The magazine photographers of the time often snapped them together out on the town: Helen with her butterfly glasses and beehive hairdos in the finest 60s style, atop a delicate set of cheekbones, and Tom with his sharp suits, sparkling eyes and laughter lines. 'He was avant garde with his fashion, and obsessive about his clothes,' recalls Helen, who remembers her husband shopping for clothes in the boutiques on the Champs-Elysées. 'There was a mandarin-collared suit with brass buttons, a pair of black leather trousers,' she adds. Later, there would be the bowler hat and the umbrella.

The quick-fire wedding epitomised Simpson's impulsiveness, his belief that it was better to act at once than wait and see. This was seen constantly in his racing, but spilled over into all areas of his life, whether it was heading off for Saint Brieuc to make his fortune, or his decision to ride from Harworth to London and back in two days to be fitted for his Olympic uniform in 1956.

'Sometimes he didn't think,' says a fellow professional, Michael Wright. 'The ski accident [in 1966] came just when he could have started to make serious money, but the start of that season was ruined.' Simpson would surprise his colleagues in other ways. Robinson, for example, recalls

Simpson's choice of a first car: 'He said, "I need some transport now," so I gave him the address of a Peugeot agent round the corner so that he could get something which would "just do for now",' says Robinson. 'I came home and there was a fucking great Aston Martin – "a second-hand DB2 from 1953", according to Simpson – parked outside. I said, "Oh Tom, what have you done now?" "It's lovely," he said, "half the price it would be in England." He shipped it home and it stood in his wife's parents' barn for a long, long time. It was typical Tom.'

It wasn't just cars that caught his eye. 'Went out and spent a fortune on furniture the other day,' Simpson wrote to George and Marlene after moving to Paris. 'Real old-fashioned stuff, you'd just rave about it Marlene, don't believe in this trashy moderne [*sic*] stuff.' Helen still wears the diamond ring he bought her for one birthday.

Cars were an obsession with Simpson, just as they have always been for many professional cyclists. He bought a 1913 Peugeot, which he drove around the streets of Ghent for a Belgian TV documentary, sitting upright in his suit and bowler hat. The car was kept in the showroom of a Peugeot dealership. In April 1964 he went shopping for other vintage cars – getting particularly excited by an 1898 Benz dog-cart, but not clinching the deal.

After the Aston Martin 'there were the Mercedes, Jaguars and BMWs,' recalls Helen. He would 'fling 'em and flog 'em'. Another dream was to have a Jensen. 'I used to get so worried, because I never knew what would come up next.' As well as putting down the deposit on the Mercedes in Ghent as 'something to aim at', before he died Simpson had apparently ordered an E-type Jaguar, which turned up at the house in Ghent and was sent back.

You only have to sit in a car with a cyclist at the wheel to be aware that they tend to push the envelope when driving, just as they do when flying down mountain descents on their bikes. It's partly the fact that cyclists spend many hours at the wheel, partly that racing a bike breeds the ability to read a road and its surface at speed. Many professionals have a touch of the toad about them. A disproportionate number die in fatal car crashes. The most celebrated victim of the 1960s was one of Simpson's heroes: the *pedaleur de charme*, Hugo Koblet. More recently, the 1998 Tour de France and Giro d'Italia winner Marco Pantani wrote off a succession of sports cars and four-wheel-drives, just at the point when his career had plumbed the depths. Happily, the only casualty was his bank balance.

Cyclists are not more macho than other sportsmen. It's more that risk-taking is part of the sport, and top cyclists tend to be impatient, and competitive. Simpson was typical. 'Driving through the West End of London at 60 mph' was nothing, Helen says. Norman Sheil, for one, says he would never get in a car with him.

Simpson had more crashes than most. From the back seat, he forced Helen into a head-on collision on the way home after his disastrous 1965 Tour de France. Helen was driving him back from hospital after the operation on the septic hand which had put him out of the race. 'He kept saying, "Put your foot down and let's get home." ' They lost control and spun into another car. 'If we had not been in a Mercedes, I would not be here now.'

On another occasion, George and Marlene Shaw were travelling with Simpson to a track race in Brittany in June 1960 when he went off the road in a hired Renault Dauphine, rolled the car three times and wrote it off. Marlene broke her collarbone. They were hauling the little car back onto the road when a lorry driver stopped and said to Shaw, 'Simpson, eh?' '*Oui, oui*,' he answered. The man in the *camion* tapped his head Obelix-style and said, 'Ah, they're all mad.'

Later, writing to the Shaws about the incident, Simpson shrugs it off. 'I am honestly sorry, but you didn't seem too bad in France, did you?' George Shaw was convinced that Simpson would die driving and indeed Simpson did not behave as if he was aware of his own mortality. He dreamed of the future, but focused on the present. He lived fast; he would die young.

The cars also provided a perfect symbol of the Simpsons' social ascent. The contrast with what Simpson left behind was apparent when he and the family revisited Harworth in their Inspector Morse-style Jaguar, which had anti-static strip trailing underneath to stop the children being sick. 'People would come up and say "Hey, missus, there's something hanging from back of t'car",' says Helen. 'They used to look gobsmacked.' As well they might: merely owning a car was not universal in Britain at the time, let alone having a Jag.

Helen still remembers the slightly unreal feeling of hobnobbing with stars of cycling such as Jacques Anquetil, who cut a glamorous figure with his wife Janine. When Simpson was an amateur racer in Saint Brieuc in 1959, almost two years after Anquetil won the Tour de France, she and Tom would look at Anquetil's picture in cycling magazines; that status had seemed unattainable. 'We were in awe of people like them; the wives like Janine seemed like film stars. When we went to a race there was always a hotel *en route* where they would have arranged to eat. We'd be eating, in would come Anquetil and he'd sit at the table. It was unreal. At the finish of the Tour one year, Janine and her daughter came and stood and chatted with me, and I thought, "Am I dreaming this?"'

On a postcard of Mont Blanc dated January 10, 1966, she writes to George and Marlene Shaw from the Hôtel Relax in the ski resort of Saint Gervais: '[We] were out till four with the Anquetils, it was Jacques' birthday.' The skiing holiday again symbolised the couple's movement up the social and economic ladder. 'Just a few words to make you envious,' she writes.

Benny Foster, Norman Shiel and Simpson (left to right) ponder Shiel's narrow victory in the pursuit of the 1958 Empire Games at Cardiff, a defeat Simpson resented for the rest of his career.

Racing through the snow in a time trial stage on the 1962 Paris–Nice 'race to the sun', in which Simpson finished second overall.

Playing up to the camera was key for the profession cyclist: in autumn 1963 Simpson turns on the cha with a hula girl to publici a series of circuit races in the French Pacific colony New Caledonia.

Victory beckons in th 1963 Bordeaux–Par motorpaced Classi the motorcycle rid Fernand Wambst (righ checks Simpson's progre as they tackle the hills i the Chevreuse Valle

Glory day: Simpson and
Albert Beurick (in Great
Britain hat) force their way
through the crowd after the
Briton's victory in the world
road race championship in
August 1965.

In the world champion's
jersey, Simpson (centre)
leads the Italians Massignan,
Motta and Poggiali on the
Intelvi pass en route to a
crushing victory in the 1965
Tour of Lombardy.

Helen Simpson rarely saw Tom race, but she was at the finish in Como to savour that win in the 'race of the falling leaves' as Lombardy is known.

Simpson's world title earned him lucrative contracts on the winter indoor racing circuit in events such as the Brussels Six Day, which included motorpaced events such as this.

A gold medal on the wall, a vast picture of the world title podium as a reminder – and time to treat the press to a little music in winter 1965.

Keeping fit in the off-season would include sessions of weights and circuit training, such as at this 1966 Peugeot training camp. The 1967 Tour winner Roger Pingeon is to Simpson's right.

Simpson forces the pace, and the young Eddy Merckx struggles to hold him as they escape together in the 1967 Paris–Nice; the Dutchman Lute is fading and will soon be left behind.

The 1967 Tour was hotter than usual, as Simpson and his team mate Barry Hoban (right) amusingly attempt to illustrate.

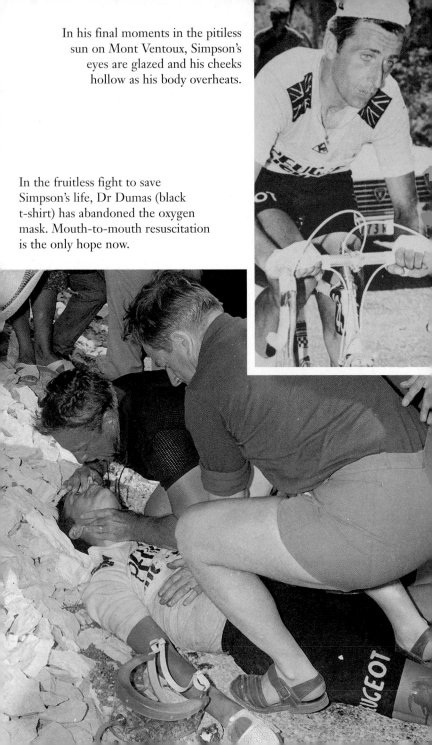

In his final moments in the pitiless sun on Mont Ventoux, Simpson's eyes are glazed and his cheeks hollow as his body overheats.

In the fruitless fight to save Simpson's life, Dr Dumas (black t-shirt) has abandoned the oxygen mask. Mouth-to-mouth resuscitation is the only hope now.

There were soirées with pop stars of the time such as Petula Clarke, with whom Tom got on particularly well, and Sacha Distel. And Simpson met the Queen when she was on a state visit to Brussels. 'She talked about the Tour and how hard it must be climbing all those mountains.' Simpson, never one to resist the chance to joke about a solemn event, would later tell journalists that he had refused to meet Her Majesty as she wouldn't pay his expenses for the trip.

In Ghent, where there was a sizeable community of English-speaking expatriates, about 300-strong, Helen became secretary of the British Colonial Association. She kept herself busy organizing cocktail parties and ladies' lunches for the wives of employees of multinational companies such as ICI and Monsanto.

The Simpsons' social ascent was typical in a decade of class flexibility. This was a time when opportunities for status and wealth were opening up for those with talent and drive, and when barriers were breaking down. It no longer mattered where you had come from or gone to school if you had charisma and were the best in your chosen field. If David Bailey, the son of an East Ham tailor, could become a society photographer and, in August 1965, marry Catherine Deneuve (with Mick Jagger as best man), what was to stop a Durham miner's son becoming a world champion, driving an Aston Martin, and rubbing shoulders with pop stars? After all, just a decade before, Simpson's great hero, Fausto Coppi, had begun life on a hill farm in Liguria and had gone on to grace the salons of the Italian Riviera.

Despite the fact that Simpson's visits home were limited owing to his fear of the Military Police, he kept in touch with his past. Older members of the Harworth and District Cycling Club recall how he would accompany them on the Christmas club run for a traditional dinner at the café at Edwinstowe, where Robin Hood is supposed to have

75

married Maid Marian. The abundance of letters and postcards in George Shaw's collection testifies to the rider's need to keep in touch with fellow cyclists back home: Simpson even managed to get him a postcard signed by the entire 1960 British Tour de France team.

In early 1960, 10 months after he left England, Simpson was writing to George Shaw from his team's training camp in Narbonne that 'behind the hotel is a hill like Fox House', a hairpinned climb 10 miles outside Sheffield which is an obligatory part of every club run returning to the city. That reference could be mere homesickness, but it also shows an affection for what he left behind, something which Shaw saw when Simpson returned to race on the Isle of Man in 1961. 'He was the star, and we went with him to a presentation after the race, in the casino,' Shaw recalls. 'People kept talking to him, and eventually he came to us and said "quick", and we nipped over the road to a pub. It was full of all the guys from the Rockingham, the Harworth, the Scala, and all the local guys from cycling clubs around this way, and we spent all night with them.'

Simpson's attachment to his roots came through in another way: his patriotism, which can only have stemmed from his working-class background among the coal-mining villages. 'He was like a man possessed when he put the Union Jack jersey on,' says Denson. Shaw concurs: 'He was so patriotic it was untrue. He was *absolutely* proud to be British.' This did not just mean riding hard when wearing a Great Britain jersey; Simpson also felt passionately about cycling in his homeland, so much so that he regularly promoted the idea of a British professional team in his ghosted articles and he eventually began a subscription fund to set up a squad. (The idea, intriguingly enough, was to be emulated some 30 years later by a team in the Basque Country, Euskadi, which made it as far as riding the 2001 Tour de France.)

These are the reasons why Simpson lies buried in the

cemetery at Harworth, in spite of the fact that, had he lived, he would probably have ended up making his home in either Corsica or Ghent. 'He wouldn't have gone back,' says Helen. She wrote to George and Marlene Shaw after her husband's death: 'I feel it's so far away but I know that Tom would have wanted to be there in his dear old England.'

The man Helen Simpson married in January 1960 was as utterly meticulous and focused in his approach to his cycling as he was impulsive and mercurial in other areas of his life. Inevitably, Helen's marriage and her family life were moulded by Simpson's goals, which were 'to look after himself and win races'. The best example of this was his obsession with diet. It had begun young, after the pursuiter Cyril Cartwright taught him his secrets. Helen still largely sticks to the principles which Tom followed, and lunch when I visited would have pleased the finicky Cartwright: fresh vegetables predominated.

I had heard that Simpson took a diet book written by the French nutritionist Raymond Dextreit with him everywhere he went. 'Of course,' says Helen and, in one of those moments when past and present elide seamlessly, nips into the kitchen to get it. *Les Cures du Jus* is a small, thin, orange book which deals with 'the problems of nutrition studied in the light of science and naturalist experience'. 'It won him the world championship, Bordeaux–Paris and the Tour of Lombardy,' says Helen.

Dextreit goes through the various healing properties of all vegetables and fruits, and, for easy reference, lists physical problems together with the vegetables to cure them. This presumably is why Simpson travelled with it, as it could be looked at in case of need. If, for example, you had insomnia, Dextreit would tell you to take lettuce and mandarin.

Simpson was obsessed with carrot juice. He believed it

would ward off illness and boost his haemoglobin levels: as he said to one teammate, 'You never see a rabbit with a cold.' He would get through '10lb a day in winter', according to Helen, which liquidized down to about a litre or a little more. It is a massive quantity and the carrots all had to be peeled, which would take at least half an hour a day, every day. Helen would buy the carrots in bulk at a market in Ghent. Her hands would go yellow from peeling them and the Simpson house would end up full of piles of orange sawdust. 'I remember one day I thought I'd get ahead of myself so my father and I peeled two sackfuls and bottled them and put them on the floor in the kitchen in sealed glass jars. They fermented.' She was understandably heartbroken.

Pigeons were another fetish of Simpson's 'because they were very good for the digestion. The cleaning lady kept them and used to deliver them ready-plucked. I used to cook them very lightly in a pressure cooker.' Her husband had acquired other dietary quirks, a mix of old wives' tales and good science: duck and trout skin, for the vitamins they contain, for example. He was also a great man for his herbal teas, particularly blackcurrant, for its Vitamin C, and also raspberry leaf, for its muscle-toning properties. He ate 'garlic in copious amounts', for its antiseptic and blood-thinning qualities. Simpson was, incidentally, not the only cyclist to believe in garlic: in the early 1980s, Sean Yates, who would go on to wear the yellow jersey in the 1994 Tour, disgusted his flatmates with his garlic consumption in an attempt to ward off colds.

The time when meals were eaten was critical – 'never late at night', to ensure proper digestion. Sometimes Simpson would fast for about a week at a time; at other times he would go through cycles of carbohydrate starvation and super-compensation, to stimulate his body to burn its fat and to enhance his ability to absorb energy.

Any great athlete builds his or her own support network.

In Ghent, Simpson had his soigneur Gus Naessens; his doctor at the Gentse Wielersport club, Vandenweghe; his wheelbuilder Ted Wood; and training partners such as Vin Denson, Alan Ramsbottom and Barry Hoban. Helen played a critical role by ensuring that, in the build-up to a major goal, all her man had to think about was training, eating and sleeping. 'He used to set his goals every year, for example winning Bordeaux–Paris, or winning the Tour that year he died, and when preparation time came he had to be very strict. He would get very concerned about his diet and sleep, so I would see he had nothing to worry about apart from the bike.' Helen would pack Simpson's case, making sure that tiny but vital items such as shoelaces were not forgotten.

Helen would deal with everyday household chores, such as paying bills, in addition to looking after the couple's two children: Jane, born in April 1962, and Joanne, who arrived in May 1963. Tom's heavy woollen cycling jerseys and shorts, soiled daily on the road in training, had to be washed by hand – 'a nightmare'. She would also deal with extraordinary jobs too, such as selecting her husband's choice of records for his appearance on Desert Island Discs in 1965, as Simpson was not a great music fan.

Most curious of all, perhaps, was the job of sewing 'sausages' of cloth into the backsides of Simpson's shorts. These were for the winter six-day races, which included 'madison' relay events. In these, the team of two cyclists would change over by grabbing the backside of the other rider's shorts and 'throwing' him up to race speed. The 'sausage' gave better purchase as the smooth woollen shorts were grabbed.

Simpson was a person with 'only black and white in his life, no grey areas', and this was reflected in their home life, which was one of highs and lows. 'When he prepared for races I'd be hoping and praying that nothing would happen, no falls. If he fell and hurt himself it would put him back however many months or weeks. If he became ill, I would worry. Was it the food he'd been eating, or had he not done something the soigneur told him to do?'

Life *chez* Simpson was not normal, Helen now reflects, principally because a constant eye had to be kept on anything that might affect Simpson's performance, whether he was racing or not. 'Even in winter he had to be careful because every kilo meant an extra 100 miles that had to be ridden. Social life [as a couple] was non-existent. I often used to think it would be really strange living a normal life, going out and having a meal with people.'

A professional cyclist is more often absent from home than present, which leads to a lack of routine. When he is present, the husband has to be the centre of attention; when he is not, there is little support for the wife running the household. Simpson's schedule of appearances was some-times so packed that he would drive past the end of the road where they lived in Ghent, *en route* from one race to the next, and would be unable to stop. 'All his races are in the evening which makes it late every night before he's home,' Helen wrote to George and Marlene Shaw on July 18, 1963. Joanne, their youngest daughter, was eight weeks old. The combination of a new-born baby and a husband coming home late at night and having to get his sleep must have been explosive. 'It would worry me if the children cried in the night. We had a bedroom on the top floor, and if they had a disturbed night Tom would go there.'

Before telephones were ubiquitous, keeping in touch was difficult. Helen and Tom wrote long letters to each other every day. Helen would post hers to the *permanence* – the headquarters – of whatever race he was riding. Sometimes the letters would follow him around Europe, and arrive home after he did. Even today, she still automatically writes her address on the back of any envelope. On one occasion, when Helen wanted to find out how her husband was faring on the Tour de France, she had to send a telegram requesting a phone call. Simpson learned about Jane's birth from a newspaper.

The unstructured lifestyle did have its rewards, however. Simpson won one of his biggest victories, the motor-paced 350 miles from Bordeaux to Paris, just six days after their second daughter, Joanne, was born. He had to leave immediately after the birth and, when he did get back, 'it was very special,' recalls Helen, 'because I was still in hospital and he didn't come back to Ghent until midnight, so they opened the hospital door especially to let him in.'

Simpson, it has to be remembered, was a man who was frequently under pressure, which made life tense at the house in Ghent. There was no time, for example, to celebrate his world title. 'When he came back [from the world championship] he was very short, I don't think he realized what it entailed, [or] all the reactions of people. It was a combination of being tired . . . he came home and said "I've got to get ready, go to a presentation or something."

'We used to live on a knife-edge. He used to take it out on those closest to him, he would get so worked up and cross about it. You had to be careful what you said [when he was racing]. He was a different person when he was not racing. I used to say to the girls, "Be careful what you say, because he's under a lot of pressure." I could read him like a book, I knew when to talk, when not to talk.' Simpson was, in the words of his early trainer, Benny Foster, like 'unstable dynamite': liable to explode when you least expected it.

Helen had no inkling that her husband was pushing himself too hard. After all, this was not a time when people were given to analysing the way they lived and worrying about its effect on their health. 'He would come back [from training and racing] physically totally exhausted. It was 110 per cent all the time. He was overambitious, he put mind over matter. [But] I never thought he was not capable of recovering. His recuperation was second to none. It never worried me at all.'

As well as nursing Simpson through his fatigue, Helen had to support him during the low periods in his career, which were at least as numerous as the victorious times. His withdrawal from the 1965 Tour, the knee injury which wrecked much of his 1961 season after the win in the Tour of Flanders, the skiing accident at the start of 1966 which lost him half the months he should have spent racing in the world champion's jersey. Here, the couple's attitude was pure Yorkshire, for all that Simpson was actually a Nottinghamshire boy by way of Durham. 'It was up and off and get focused again. He wouldn't dwell on it. You dust yourself off and start again.' It is in this way that she seems to have dealt with her husband's untimely death.

On July 13, 1967, Helen was sunbathing in the Corsican resort of Pianotoli with the children and Blanche Leulliot, the wife of the French journalist Jean Leulliot, who organized the Paris–Nice 'Race to the Sun'. She had brought the children in the Renault Four, nicknamed 'Puff-Puff', which her husband won in the Brussels Six Day. It was Leulliot who had introduced Simpson to the island, where the family had holidayed for the past two years; it was Leulliot who had helped him buy 11 hectares of scrubland which Simpson planned to develop into holiday chalets. The family's holiday house on the plot, with its view across towards Sardinia, was almost finished. Tom had not yet seen what was perhaps the ultimate symbol of his rise from an anonymous house on an estate in a mining village. A place in the sun after a childhood of grey skies.

Helen was listening to the radio following her husband's progress on the Tour de France: suddenly the announcer reported that he had fallen off. This was nothing new. Tom often fell off. Then it was reported that he had fallen again, and that he had fractured his skull. The two women were more worried. It would be a good idea perhaps to go to the café at the head of the beach to call the *permanence*.

The operator took 15 minutes to get through; a little group of villagers had gathered around the telephone. Blanche spoke to her husband, limiting her answers to '*Oui . . . oui . . . oui*'. She did not break the news then, but took Helen to the house where her father was staying. 'Daddy came into the room, and his face was that colour,' Helen says, pointing to a white china mug on the table.

The next day, Helen and her father took the first flight to Marseille. In the airport, 'heaving with journalists', she was met by Jean Leulliot, who broke the news that stimulants had been found in Tom's bloodstream. In the morgue in Avignon – 'of course I wanted to see him' – she found a card from Tom's brother Harry. It bore the words, 'His body ached, his legs grew tired, but still he would not give in.' They are now inscribed on Simpson's gravestone in Harworth.

She was in shock as she was given her husband's wedding ring, his clothes and had to make the instant decisions: choose the coffin, decide 'in a flash' whether and where he was to be buried. 'My first reaction was "Why have you gone and left us here?" You can't eat, you can't drink, your mind wanders. I kept thinking about the girls, then I'd come back to reality and it was real. I read it in the newspapers.'

Her father shared the hotel room in Avignon with her that night: there were fears that she would 'do something silly'. The funeral was 'horrendous' and in a couple of days she was back in Belgium, sorting out their affairs, when she collapsed with a burst ovarian cyst. Two weeks in hospital, with no visitors, followed. There were reports that she had had a miscarriage due to shock. By the time she saw their daughters again, a month had passed since she had left them in Corsica.

Simpson died intestate: as a man who lived intensely for the day, his own death was not something for which he was ever likely to make plans. His financial affairs were complex: he owned property in three countries, he was living in Belgium on an English passport and earning money in France. He and Helen had managed the properties together, but tying up the loose ends took her years.

Matters were not helped when Helen's assets were frozen, as happens automatically under Belgian law when there is a death, and she had to borrow money. 'Many times I've said to him "If you could see me now",' says Helen, half-angry, half-laughing as she looks skywards. There are reports that Helen had to take legal action against his life insurance company, which is said to have refused to pay out on the grounds that his death was self-inflicted: she is adamant that this did not happen.

As we looked through the letters of condolence which had arrived at the house in Mariakerke while Helen was in hospital, we came across the last letter she sent to her husband, written on the morning of July 13, 1967, and posted 'express' from Corsica to the Great Britain team's hotel in Sète. Helen does not read it all to me. There is a mixture of encouragement at his fourth place on the previous day's stage – 'I'd have pushed you if I could', wifely advice ('try to be pleasant with all the supporters') and reflection on how happy her holiday is with the children, who are learning to swim. There could be no more poignant illustration of a life on the cusp between bliss and tragedy.

Helen first saw the Ventoux a year after Tom's death when she went up the mountain for the unveiling of his memorial close to the summit. 'I had to do it. I wanted to see where he drew his last breath. It had to be done.' She cannot explain what she felt. Her face works a little and she chews her nails, but she cannot say more except that when she is there, she feels the need to be on her own. With her, at the unveiling, was Barry Hoban, a member of the small British cycling community in Ghent, who had won the stage across the Midi dedicated to her husband's memory the day after he died. In December 1969 they were married and Hoban moved into the house that the Simpsons had built in Mariakerke.

Hoban, who was to win a further seven stages in the Tour, clearly felt in the shadow of Simpson, his former rival and role model. He had lived not far from Harworth, had raced with Tom as an amateur, had been his rival as a professional. Just how friendly the pair were is a matter of some debate in the British cycling world. But Hoban respected Simpson, supported him when he took his world title, and kept the British flag flying in Ghent for another 13 years after his death.

After Hoban retired from professional racing in 1980, he and Helen returned from Ghent to Wales, where Hoban briefly marketed a range of Barry Hoban bikes for Coventry Eagle. In their factory in Newtown, a vast photograph of Simpson stood behind the counter in the reception area. One area of their house is devoted to the mementoes of the two professionals with whom Helen has spent her life. There is Tom's world championship medal; the certificate giving him the freedom of the town of Mariakerke; Hoban's race numbers, and a photo of Hoban, Simpson and an Australian, Nev Veale, larking around with an umbrella in a rainy San Sebastian in the run-up to the 1965 world championship. 'If Tom isn't mentioned every day in the house, he is thought about,' says Helen. 'He is part of our life and our children's. He gave me two beautiful children. It would be nice if he were here, but I feel blessed that I had him for six short years.'

Revisiting the site of a bereavement is widely believed to help the healing process. This seems to have been the case with Helen, who now wishes she had had Tom cremated so that his ashes could be scattered on his mountain. Helen and Barry pay an annual visit, and clear away the piles of offerings left by fans at the memorial close to the summit before they rot and get blown away – three and a half bin liners full in *2001*. She has recently been organizing the renovation of the memorial, which is now becoming unstable due to poor drainage and erosion.

'When you see the amount of people going up there, it touches you,' says Helen. 'They drop something [on the memorial], say a prayer. I went on July 13 [2000], which was the anniversary, and met someone who said they had been up there every year on that day. We walk, collect flowers, have a picnic and sit with Tom. I like going up there.'

Col de Peyresourde, July 5, 1962
'Allez Seemson' shout the crowds in the chilly, drizzling rain, 5,000 feet up on the green slopes of the Pyrenees, as the gaggle of 25 cyclists struggle up the hairpins. The race announcer, travelling just ahead of the lead group, has told them the news: Tom Simpson is about to become yellow jersey of the Tour de France.

When this first mountain stage of the Tour began in Pau – 'the belvedere of the Pyrenees' – Simpson was lying third, but now race leader, Willy Schroeders of Belgium, and the man in second, André Darrigade, are both lagging behind, unable to stand the pace set by the wafer-thin, curly-haired Spaniard Federico Bahamontes. The 'Eagle of Toledo' has bided his time for 11 days as the Tour circled France from Nancy in the east to the Atlantic seaboard. Now, at last, he is in his element – the mountains. Spain is just eight miles away, over the snow-capped summits to the left, and he can make the flat-landers suffer.

As race leader 'on the road', all Simpson has to do is follow the rest, and ensure that he loses no time to the Dutchman Ab Gelderman, who is 30 seconds behind in the standings. He has done the groundwork in the last 11 days, by staying at the head of the race; today Bahamontes has unwittingly helped him by tiring out Schroeders and Darrigade, and whittling the front group down to the 26 strongest men in the race.

Straightforward today's task may be, but it's not easy. Already, they have climbed the Tourmalet, which rears up like the side of a house out of the little spa town of Barèges, and ends at 6,000 feet above sea level on the freezing shoulder of a great amphitheatre of cliffs. They flew down through the avalanche tunnels at 60mph, and straight up the next col, Aspin, with its dark pinewoods leading up to impossibly sloped hay fields. All Simpson has to do now is finish the job, by staying in this group for the 30 miles to the stage finish in Saint Gaudens, where he will pull on the yellow jersey with his sponsors' names – Leroux, Gitane – hastily stuck to a panel on the front. No Briton will repeat the feat for 32 years.

CHAPTER FIVE

'Roule Britannia'
headline, *L'Equipe*, 1962

A hard-as-nails Belgian weeps in the front seat of a team bus: a fellow cyclist has just died in front of him. A normally ebullient Italian stares into space on the start line. A Swiss vents his anger on photographers who took pictures of the corpse. Black ribbons on sunburnt arms. A teammate points his fingers at the sky to tell the world that he has won a race for a dead man he saw every morning at the breakfast table, yet barely knew. A mass of cyclists promenade in a brightly coloured cortège of grief, too bewildered to compete.

Scenes at the death of a Tour de France cyclist. I remember them when I hear the name Fabio Casartelli; similar things are recalled by those I spoke to about Tom Simpson's death. Casartelli, a young Italian of 24, riding his first Tour de France, died in 1995 of head injuries after a high-speed fall. No one was left unaffected by the event.

What I felt was nothing abnormal in the face of sudden tragedy: confusion, a desperate search for sketchy information, an unease about intruding on those who were close – in this case teammates and personnel. The worst part was the questioning: was something as frivolous as a cycle race – my livelihood, our livelihood – a worthwhile exercise if a man could die for it? Afterwards came other emotions. There was resentment at anyone who did not understand what had happened, such as the local guests at the next morning's start, bent on having a good time. The cyclists they had come to see were so shaken they could barely speak. There was a shared, overwhelming sense that the final days of travelling through France should end as quickly as possible. The party was bereft of any festive ambience, but we all had to go through the motions.

I felt this way in 1995, but I had never met Casartelli and would have had trouble recognizing him. I never had time. By 1995, the Tour was a sprawling monster comprising 4,000 people spread over a huge area. In contrast, the race was relatively small when Simpson died, with perhaps 700 people in the caravan. It was so intimate that, the night before he died, Simpson bumped into four English journalists in the street outside his hotel in Marseille and treated them to a show of bargaining with a street pedlar.

Death on the Tour is uncommon, despite the speed at which the cyclists descend mountains and the frequency with which they fall off. In fact, the biggest risks are run by the spectators among the motorcade. Only three Tour cyclists have died on the race: the Spaniard Francisco Cepeda, in 1935; Simpson; and Casartelli.

Simpson's death was a rare tragedy, in a small event, in an intimate sport. But there was another reason why the shockwaves were far more intense in 1967 than in 1995. Casartelli, for all his Olympic title and worthy talent, was still on the uphill slope towards celebrity. Simpson was established on the plateau, one of the select group at the top of the sport who needed no further introduction.

Simpson's fellow cyclists found an unprecedented way of expressing their feelings: they chose not to race. The senior riders in the race – Simpson's colleagues in the elite – met before the start and decided that that day's stage across the baking roads of Provence to the town of Sète should be a tribute to the dead man. Vin Denson was the man the elite chose to win the stage, according to their leader Jean Stablinski, the stocky little Polish immigrant who had been world champion in 1961. With Simpson gone, Denson was the senior rider in the British team.

Instead of Denson, another Briton, Barry Hoban, rode ahead and crossed the finish line first. The dispute about whether or not he had been designated the winner before the start misses a more important point. His victory struck an emotional chord across Europe and was the strongest possible illustration of the grief and respect felt for Simpson. Nothing similar would be seen again on the Tour until the death of Casartelli.

The 1967 Tour de France riders were in a state of shock. In the British team, Denson felt 'numbness and disbelief. I was like a zombie.' On the road to Sète, Denson and his teammate Colin Lewis both imagined that they were seeing their dead leader whenever a white jersey came into view, as did Jean Stablinksi. Denson wanted to go home there and then. So too did the 1965 winner Felice Gimondi. As the riders stood for a minute's silence on the start line among the plane trees of Carpentras's Boulevard Albin-Durand, the Italian Gimondi was so strung out that Dr Dumas had to calm him down. The man who was to win the 1968 race, Jan Janssen of Holland, also needed the doctor's attention.

The senior cyclists who decided that a Briton had to win that day were a close-knit bunch, no more than 15- or 20-strong. They were the men who made the headlines, personalities with massive public profiles. Two of them, Jacques Anquetil and Raymond Poulidor, divided the French nation's loyalties. They fought it out for the victories in the great Tours and one-day Classics, in which they formed their own little alliances; they shared the same trains, planes and cars and attended the same soirées. Simpson had been part of the group.

They were tied together in ways which transcended teams and nationalities. The defending Tour winner that year, Lucien Aimar, for example, was owed £300 by Simpson. It was Aimar's contract money from a race in the Isle of Man, which had been presented to him in a sterling cheque. Aimar could not change the cheque, so he had given it to Simpson, who had put it in his suitcase. Every time they saw each other, they mentioned it: Simpson was going to give Aimar the cash on the Tour's rest day, two days after the Ventoux. He never received the money.

Today, Stablinski still does not find it easy to explain their collective grief. He can only manage to repeat this phrase two or three times: 'We were so traumatised.' He prefers an anecdote, to illustrate why Simpson was popular, to show how he was one of the boys – the big boys: 'We rode a criterium at La Rochelle: Poulidor, Anquetil, Rudi Altig' – the German Simpson beat to win the 1965 world title – 'everyone. I knew a restaurant there, Chez Jean. We ate there, and were pretty stirred up. We stayed until two or three in the morning. I remember leaving the restaurant, and Altig, who was a bit of a joker, walked out on his hands.

'Tom wanted to do the same, but he was all over the shop. He kept trying, putting his feet on the wall and so on, but he had loads of small change, keys and papers in his pockets and it all went everywhere. So there he was in the street on his hands and knees picking it all up, but he couldn't find all the stuff. And the next day he kept saying "I've lost this bit of paper, this contract", and one of us would pull out what he'd lost and wave it at him.'

The image is endearing: the highly paid, celebrated elite of cycling – a five-times Tour winner in Anquetil, world champions in Simpson and Altig – getting drunk, and then scrabbling on their hands and knees to pick lost change out of the gutter in a deserted street in a French provincial town. And Simpson is in his niche, among the best in his sport.

It was not just the best cyclists who felt sick at heart on July 14, 1967, the day after Simpson's death. The man who organizes the Tour de France today, Jean-Marie Leblanc, told me why. Leblanc raced modestly as a professional and met Simpson just once. At a race in the south of France early in 1966, Leblanc sat down on a bench to put on his racing kit. 'Simpson, the world champion, sat down beside me. "Bonjour," he [Simpson] said. "What's your name?"

"Jean-Marie Leblanc." "Who do you ride for?" "Where do you live?" and so on.' Even now, Leblanc can hardly believe that the world champion showed such interest in a colleague of his lowly status. He can't help but think of Simpson as a nice guy, a man who liked to communicate, who could hunt with the top dogs and spare time for the underdogs. The French word Leblanc chooses to describe him comes from Simpson's England: '*un gentleman*'.

Simpson's position among the cycling elite had been earned on merit. To win his status, he had achieved results and celebrity far beyond those of any other English cyclist: five victories in the toughest single-day races on the cycling calendar – the world championship, plus four of the one-day Classics. There were many more near misses. On a good day, Simpson was capable of combining leg power, cunning and killer instinct in a way that was irresistible. His racing was a delight to watch, and there was little the opposition could do about him. Such days were not common in the Englishman's career, but his surprising world professional road race title win, less than two years before his death, exemplified his style at its best.

The English team leader was not expected to win when he broke away with the German Rudi Altig 26 miles from the finish at Lasarte, near San Sebastian in the Spanish Basque Country: Altig was known as a faster sprinter. But Simpson used his experience and his ability to read a race and a rival. Early on he had not hesitated to race across from the main field to the large lead group which was to dominate the event, and he showed similar sang-froid in dealing with Altig in the final miles when the pair had broken clear. They came into the finish well ahead of the chasers and Simpson launched his sprint just as Altig was changing gear, in the split second when he could not readily respond.

There is no evidence to support the claim that Simpson

'bought' Altig, as has been rumoured. Unless this is proven, the world title will remain a testimony to Simpson's self-belief and lucid thinking after seven hours in the saddle. By this point in a race, clarity of thought is directly related to how much energy a cyclist has left. If you are tired, you can't think as quickly as the other man.

Altig later revealed that Simpson had 'played dead', telling him he had no strength left and luring him into a mistaken feeling of security. Such tricks were all part of the game, and the German seemed impressed rather than aggrieved with Simpson's cleverness. He made it clear that Simpson was no fluke winner.

Simpson's cunning is frequently overlooked. It won him his first Classic, the Tour of Flanders in 1961, less than two years after he had turned professional. He was up against a faster and vastly more experienced man, the Italian Nino Defilippis, in his 10th year as a professional, with seven Tour de France stage wins to his credit. Defilippis was outwitted when Simpson pretended to sprint for the finish and stuck his tongue out to give the impression that his legs were fading. Once the Italian had made his effort and overtaken him, Simpson attacked on his blind side, to win by inches.

Defilippis, is clearly still frustrated 45 years on that he did not win, and claims that Simpson pretended he was struggling (as he did with Rudy Altig in the 1965 world championship). 'He said to me, "don't drop me Nino, you can get 10 metres on me in the spirit."' The Italian also claims that the finish line was moved 100m after the pair crossed it to begin the last lap. When he crossed the line Delilippis thought he had won, and Simpson agreed, the Italian claimed, although this is not borne out by the Briton's face in photographs of the finish sprint.

What is clear is that Simpson out-thought the Italian, and he showed similar saugfroid in dealing with the French icon Raymond Poulidor at the finish of Milan-San Remo in 1964. Poulidor was slower than Simpson on paper but three years earlier he had won this race, which the Italians call *La Classicissima*, the Classic of Classics. Simpson manoeuvred him into the windy side of the road and kept in the shelter. The killer instinct ensured there was no mistake.

Simpson's single day in the yellow jersey in the Tour de France of 1962 best illustrates the obsessive way in which he would pursue a goal. In this case, the target was the prestige, high public profile and lucrative appearance contracts which would go to the first man from outside mainland Europe to lead the great race.

A cyclist with a speciality – time trialling, sprinting or climbing – can use his particular skill to win the *maillot jaune* by targeting, say, the first time trial of the race. This tactic would win Chris Boardman the jersey in 1994, 1997 and 1998. For the non-specialist such as Simpson, however, there is only one way to earn the *maillot jaune*: attack, and gain time on the rest. Then repeat the process if necessary. It is physically tiring because of the repeated efforts on a daily basis, and mentally stressful because there is no time in the race when the yellow jersey hunter can relax.

Early in his debut Tour, 1960, Simpson had missed the yellow jersey by a single stage placing: one day he finished third, when second place would have sufficed. Two years later, 12 stages passed before he took the race lead in the first mountain stage at Saint Gaudens in the Pyrenees. That equates to some 1,500 miles of making moves, following moves, watching the other contenders to make sure none steals a march, and doing daily arithmetic: how many minutes do I need? How many seconds can I lose or gain here?

Simpson wore the yellow jersey for a single day, but that barely matters in the broader context of his place in cycling history. The impact reached as far as his home town of Harworth: his mother recalled the postmistress coming to the house in order to tell her: 'You must send him a telegram, because he's the first English boy to do this.'

*

95

Each of Simpson's big wins had its place in the record books: his historic day in the yellow jersey was followed by sixth place overall, making him the first man from outside cycling's European heartland to come close to the podium in the Tour. He would be the first to win both the world professional road title and one of the great single-day Classics, in the modern era at least.

In the context of what had come before, it was sensational. When Simpson turned professional in 1959, only once had a British team even started the Tour de France: the Hercules squad in 1955. Only one of its number, Brian Robinson, had made the breakthrough into the European circuit, in winning a stage of the Tour in 1958. Of the single-day Classics Simpson won, only Bordeaux–Paris had previously fallen to an Englishman – but that was in the heroic days of the *belle epoque* 60 years before.

Here too, Simpson captured the imagination of fans in a new way: cycle racing as he understood it – the world of the Tour de France and the great European single-day Classics – had no roots in Britain. When he turned professional in 1959, the only other Englishman on the circuit was Robinson, who was more self-effacing than Simpson on and off the bike. Only the Australian Hubert Opperman, who finished 12th in the Tour and won the Paris–Brest–Paris marathon in the early 1930s, had come from outside Europe and conquered the cycling world in similar style. But no New Worlders followed Opperman's trail, as other British cyclists would seek to emulate Simpson.

The Briton brought more than novelty value with him. The 1960s were the time of world-beating British exports such as the hovercraft and the Mini, when pop culture was centred on Carnaby Street, when the Beatles and the Stones were shooting to stardom. For all his working-class roots and down-to-earth nature, Simpson brought a small part of the aura of 'swinging London' to cycling.

Europe's affection for the English interloper also had its

roots in the Second World War and the Liberation, still recent events in the early 1960s. Simpson was quickly nicknamed Tommy, with all its connotations of the plucky British soldier fighting on a foreign shore. (Ironically, he actually preferred Tom, a name handed down through his family.) *L'Equipe*'s headline after an early Simpson near-miss in the 1960 Paris–Roubaix was explicit in its D-Day reference: 'The landing of a Tommy', using the same word, *debarquement*, as referred to the Normandy invasion. His Churchillian V-sign after winning the world championship was greatly appreciated, as was the fact that he shared his birthday with the war leader.

At a time when Britain was regarded as insular and aloof, people appreciated the gesture Simpson had made in crossing the Channel to immerse himself in a very un-British sport. Antoine Blondin's article in *L'Equipe* on the day Simpson won his yellow jersey was headlined '*Roule* Britannia!' and made much of the fact that the Englishman was the Frenchman's 'beloved and traditional adversary'. But Simpson's adaptation to his chosen *métier* had to be total if he was to overcome the obstacles in his path. First, there was the language barrier. From inarticulate loneliness when he first moved to France, Simpson mastered cycling's three main languages. Initially with the help of his wife Helen, he quickly acquired fluent French: the first step in working out how the sport functioned. He later picked up adequate Flemish and Italian.

Simpson's best source of information early in his profes-sional career was Robinson, his flatmate and teammate at the Rapha squad between 1960 and 1961. Simpson would constantly ask questions, and sometimes Robinson would take advantage of him. 'Sometimes I'd fit him up,' chuckles Robinson. 'We were in a restaurant once with some French guys and he wanted to say "Where is the toilet?" so I told him "*Où est la chiotte?*" which means "Where is the shithouse?", and he yelled it out across the restaurant. Tom got his own back by telling the French lads "The English word for bottle is bollocks", so when they came over to the Isle of Man they asked for a "bollocks of wine, please".'

In French, cycling's lingua franca, he reached a level of fluency where he could earn the admiration of a Frenchman, in this case *L'Equipe*'s Jacques Augendre, who told me: 'In 1966 Tom broke his leg skiing, and it cost him a lot of money, so he needed to do a good Tour. "*Le Tour paiera la fracture*," he said: the Tour will pay for the break.' This is a pun on the wordplay between *fracture* and *facture*, the French word for bill. It would be sophisticated even for a Frenchman.

The unwritten rules of European professional cycling also had to be learned. These covered the full spectrum, from respecting the moments in a race when it was the convention not to attack – during a collective toilet stop, or at a feeding station – to accepting that in exhibition events the local favourite had to be allowed to win. Simpson had an impulsive nature, which he had to learn to master: early in his career, for example, he would fall foul of promoters simply for competing too enthusiastically.

One incident sums up both Simpson's shrewdness and the nature of the system he entered: during his first world road championship in 1959, only weeks after he turned professional, he was one of the winning break and was offered money by the eventual winner, André Darrigade, if he would assist the Frenchman. Simpson turned down the cash, knowing that if Darrigade won, as indeed he did, the Frenchman would owe him a favour. Two and a half years later, as his teammate, Darrigade would help him take the yellow jersey in the Tour.

Simpson's achievement in getting to the very top of cycling can be put in simple perspective. The sport was as distant and alien to the Harworth miners among whom Simpson grew up as Test cricket would be to a fisherman in

Saint Brieuc. Five years after welcoming him with *'Roule Britannia'*, Blondin summed up in his obituary the pleasure and satisfaction the Europeans had gained from watching Simpson's progress: 'He was our pride.'

There was far more to Simpson, however, than a whiff of Carnaby Street, *une belle gueule* (a nice face) as the French put it, a place in the history books and a set of results which for a Belgian or an Italian would have been worthy rather than exceptional. Where Simpson touched heartstrings among the press, fans, organizers and his fellow cyclists was in his approach to a race. As the French put it: 'He left no one indifferent.'

His tactics were straightforward and uninhibited: it was better to try to the utmost, fail and be visible rather than wait and hope. This had been his way even when he had begun racing as a schoolboy. Now, as a professional it guaranteed headlines, and made his public profile higher than that of Robinson, his early mentor. In one of his first one-day Classics, the Paris–Roubaix in 1960, for example, Simpson was a newspaperman's dream. He led for 25 miles and looked a certain winner until his strength deserted him three miles from the finish. The valiant foreign newcomer, cruelly deprived within an ace of victory, accepted defeat by murmuring the words 'I nearly got it'. He exemplified *le fair-play*, the quality so admired in the English. In terms of his public profile, it was a critical afternoon's work: this was the first race to be shown live on Eurovision, and a whole new audience watched the heroic near miss.

The press would sympathise so much with Simpson's approach, even if he was unsuccessful, that they sometimes painted him as the moral victor. Pierre Chany, the doyen of French cycling writers in the post-war years, certainly felt that way after the hilly Liège–Bastogne–Liège Classic in 1963. Simpson began attacking 60 miles from the finish, and was swept up within three miles of the chequered flag.

He should have won, but finished 32nd, prompting this from Chany: 'Sensitive souls will have shed a tear for Simpson, caught by an alliance of 30 adversaries when he deserved victory 100 times over. Fellow travellers such as ourselves can only pity the fate of this extraordinary battler, audacious in competition, generous in his efforts, and whose merits are never officially recognized. This man does not receive his due. He is the victim of a curse.'

Throughout cycling and, indeed, sporting history, fans and the press have always found it easier to empathise with a valiant, unlucky battler who gets the occasional big result than with a less charismatic winner. In the 1960s, Raymond Poulidor, who never won the Tour, was more popular than Jacques Anquetil, who won it five times. In the early 1990s, Claudio Chiappucci was preferred to the robotic Miguel Indurain. After his disastrous spring of 1963, Simpson earned the epithet *l'eternel malchanceux* – the eternal accursed. In cycling it is not a pejorative term.

On the other side of the Channel, there was pride aplenty in Simpson's achievements, but it was of a different order: he was the lynchpin at the centre of an entire sport. His funeral in his home town of Harworth was attended by 5,000 mourners, both ordinary fans and the elite of the sport. They stood shoulder to shoulder in a thundery downpour on the little knoll around the 12th-century church, listening via loudspeakers to a service which included Psalm 121: 'I will lift up mine eyes unto the hills'.

A vast procession of cyclists wheeling bikes followed the coffin through the village streets. Some 400 wreaths were piled outside the cemetery a little way away from the church. It could not match the crowd which covered a Ligurian hillside seven years earlier for the funeral of Simpson's boyhood hero Fausto Coppi, but it was a huge turnout for British cycling.

In his editorial in *Cycling*, Simpson's close friend Alan

Gayfer expressed the anguish felt by British cycling fans at his loss: 'Tom Simpson, our own Tom, is dead – what on earth shall we do without him? I am still trying to think straight, to conceive of a world of cycling without the lively face and straightforward comments of "Mr Tom" to guide and to lead.' The final two verbs are key. Simpson was a sporting ambassador for Britain when he was in Europe. In his home country he was both the figurehead and ambassador for the sport.

When Simpson left for Brittany in 1959 to begin his career in Europe, British cycling was just emerging from the internecine dispute of the post-war years between the proponents of road racing, the British League of Racing Cyclists, and the establishment, the National Cycling Union, who felt that large bunches of cyclists on the roads would alienate the police and the car-driving public. Road racing, European style, had been banned in Britain at the turn of the century: time trialling and track racing had developed instead.

In the early 1960s, British cycling was a genteel, pastoral world. As now, *Cycling* set the tone, for the majority at least, and at the start of the decade the magazine was little changed from the 1930s. Alongside editorials attacking 'road race madness' were touring articles by writers with pseudonyms such as 'Nimrod' and 'Centaur' with titles like 'A Day on Clare Island', or 'An Adventure for Two Lads'.

It was impossible for the establishment to ignore Simpson's spectacular achievements. He erupted into this tranquil milieu much as the Beatles and the Rolling Stones did into the wider world, making a whole generation of British cyclists aware that they inhabited a cycling backwater, cut off from the mainstream. Across the Channel lay money and celebrity: the success of Brian Robinson a few years earlier had hinted at the possibilities, but the level of Simpson's successes and his near-misses hammered the message home.

When he wore the yellow jersey in 1962, he was greeted in Paris, *Cycling* reported, by 'cheering excursionists from as far north as Teesside and as far west as Plymouth'. The fact that large numbers of British fans had gone to France was news in itself. 'Quite a few made an early start to the social season and for them dawn broke before bedtime', the magazine said primly.

Jacques Goddet was editorial director of *L'Equipe* as well as Tour organizer. He was explicit about the wider significance of what Simpson had achieved when he took the yellow jersey in 1962. Goddet wrote in his editorial that day that the English saw the Tour as 'a funny old thing, a typical invention of a country where they eat frogs', and called on his readers to 'rejoice in this historic date for cycling, which will widen its international appeal. Let's hope this will rejuvenate British cycling and make them consign their black alpaca jackets to mothballs.'

A few months later, Goddet and Simpson appeared at British cycling's gala night, the 'Champions' Concert', organized at the Royal Albert Hall by time trialling's governing body, the Road Time Trials Council. They were guests of honour among 4,000 cyclists, entertained by the Moulin Rouge-style Cavalcade Girls – 'lovelier than ever despite the scanty costumes' reported *Cycling* – along with jugglers and 'dare-devil roller skaters'. Resplendent in his yellow jersey, Simpson pedalled on a set of stationary rollers for a few minutes, 'amid a crescendo of enthusiastic applause'. Six years earlier such a scene would have been unthinkable, as British cycling fought its civil war and Simpson was banned under NCU rules for six months for failing to respect a 'Stop' sign.

The British fans would throng to see Simpson on the rare occasions when he appeared in the UK to race. His feats encouraged British promoters: in August 1964, there were queues a mile long as 12,000 fans turned up at Crystal

Palace to watch Simpson ride a circuit race. Two months earlier, the Herne Hill track in London had been packed for a meeting with Simpson and Jacques Anquetil topping the bill.

Simpson's successes and the sport's higher profile led to other spin-offs. Peter Clifford's book *Tour de France* sold out in 1965. *Cycling* magazine was prompted to organize trips to the Ghent and Antwerp six-day track races to watch Simpson; by 1967, the Sportsmen's Travel Club and a rival, Page & Moy, were organizing trips for fans to attend the fateful Tour de France, at 35 guineas a head. The Falcon bike company ran a successful 'Majorca training camp with Simpson' in 1966. This was a boom time in British cycling. No fewer than 33 foreign stars – including Stablinski, Altig and Anquetil – were flown to the Isle of Man for the Manx Premier race in 1962. Major sponsors such as Corona, Players and Fyffes entered the sport – the banana company specifically to back the ill-fated 1967 British Tour team. Even the London six-day track race was revived in the year of Simpson's death, on the back of his success.

Simpson brought a confidence to British cycling which it had never known before. This was best expressed by Alan Gayfer when Simpson won his world championship in 1965, a feat which had always seemed unattainable to British fans. 'We have waited 38 years for this moment, for the time when we could hold our heads up ... a young miner's son has proved that anything a Belgian or a Frenchman can do, we can do better.'

Simpson knew the importance of the home audience. A fellow professional, Michael Wright, remembers missing the plane on the way to ride a race in England with Simpson, Hoban and Denson. Simpson spent all their contract money on hiring an eight-seater to get them there. 'He absolutely wanted to do it so as not to let the organizer down. We earned nothing, because it all went on the plane.'

British cycling mattered to Simpson in a wider sense as

well. He encouraged any British cyclists who came over to his base in Ghent, and in 1964 he began campaigning in the press for a team sponsored by a British company to bring together the best home cyclists to compete in Europe – led naturally by him. By the time of his death he had founded, together with Albert Beurick and the writer Peter Clifford, a subscription fund which was to have supported the team. Simpson had other, wider ambitions as well. He seems to have been determined to restructure the entire sport in Britain after his retirement. Given the effect he had already had, plus his clout, his connections, and his determination, he would have had more than a fighting chance of pushing the sport to a higher level. What he might have achieved off the road, as well as on it, will remain British cycling's great might-have-been.

When Chris Brasher of the *Observer* went to interview Simpson in Paris in the early 1960s, he expected to meet a rough-hewn Durham miner's son. He found the opposite, he told me, a vision of continental sophistication which he would never forget: 'an impeccable Englishman in a Prince of Wales suit'.

'I asked if he knew a good restaurant; he did and it was Michelin-starred. I made notes on my paper napkins, brought them home and put them on my desk and the article just flowed, which was a tribute to Tom rather than to me. I don't know how many interviews I've done over 40 years, but that sticks in my mind. Tom had style.'

In Britain, Simpson's feats were in keeping with the times. Like the country's other sporting greats, he epitomised a brief period when Britain was riding high. This was the time of confidence which had led Harold Macmillan to declare in 1957 that 'most of our people have never had it so good'. In sport, Britain was still used to taking on the world and winning. In 1963, Jim Clark became the youngest Formula One world champion ever, and then, of course, there were the events of the 1966 World Cup. That a Durham miner's son could conquer a sport as alien as cycling typified a time when anything seemed possible for those who had talent and a dream.

The world championship in 1965 was Simpson's breakthrough into the wider world outside cycling magazines and sports pages. Classic wins and yellow jerseys were not easy concepts for the British media to deal with: a world title needed no translation. Simpson's three tabloid exposés in the *People* were only one way in which his profile was raised. The BBC had shot the half-hour documentary 'The World of Tom Simpson' earlier that year – and it was repeated.

As a world champion, Simpson won three separate 'Sportsman of the Year' awards: the BBC's 'Sports Personality of the Year', the 'Sports Writers' Personality of the Year', and the *Daily Express* 'Sportsman of the Year'. By 1967, five British newspaper sports writers were following the Tour de France to cover Simpson. Four of them drove together in an Austin Maxi, drawing amused comment from their European colleagues. The reports, in the *Guardian* at least, appeared near the top of each day's sports page.

At a time when coverage of all sports was limited, Simpson's attempt to win the Tour was allotted a large amount of space: at least as much as the cricket, and more, proportionally, than the Tour would be given now. Earlier in 1967, ITV's 'World of Sport' had covered the Milan–San Remo classic for the first time. This was the beginning of a 15-year connection with cycling through Simpson's friend the journalist David Saunders, which lasted until the demise of the independent channel's flagship sports programme.

Simpson's acceptance speech at the 'Sports Writers' award, delivered in the presence of the Prime Minister Harold Wilson, was the classic Simpson mixture of frankness and self-deprecating humour. Simpson noted that the PM was also 'in the saddle but I hope his bottom doesn't hurt as much as mine'. He went on to call for British industry to take note of cycling; he hoped that industrialists would wake up to the advertising potential of cycling teams, with the advent of the Common Market and proposals for a tunnel under the Channel. The latter, he added, would be a useful thing, because 'the kids are always sick on the boat on the way home'.

The speech was a little marvel of deadpan delivery and perfect comic timing, and it was also a perfect example of Simpson's ability to play to almost any audience. He was clearly aware of the importance of promoting himself in any way he could, in the places it mattered. Sometimes this backfired. In the same autumn that Simpson won the hearts of the British press, he also created a sensation by being one of the first top cyclists to 'kiss and tell'. In 1965, the new world champion sold his story to the *People*. It ran over three Sundays: September 19 and 26, and October 3.

All the features were in the first person; the first bore the headline: 'World champ but they call me a crook'. It dealt with the persistent allegations of race-fixing against Simpson; he revealed that he had offered the Irish rider Shay Elliott £1,100 to help him win the 1963 world championship, which Elliott had turned down, and that he had once taken £500 to help another team. Not noble acts, but these were relatively common practices in cycling.

'Nobbled by a secret doper', the following week, gave 'the whole story' about drugs. This amounted to little more than that Simpson had once thought he had been given a drugged bottle, and that he used 'tonics' provided by his doctors. 'Nobbling' was clearly a preoccupation of the paper's: alongside Simpson's articles that autumn was an exposé of greyhound doping, involving 'bent' races, crooked kennel girls and spiked sausage meat.

The final episode, 'I blew my top at the champ', referred to a scuffle between Simpson and a fellow rider, Henri Anglade. This article's gist, among the hyperbole, was that cycling was a no-holds-barred sport in which it was possible to make a lot of money. Not exactly news, and confirmation that the paper was doing its worst with relatively innocuous material.

Lame and overblown it may all have been, but in Europe, for any cyclist to talk to the press about selling races and the use of drugs was a major event. For the newly crowned world champion to do so was explosive. The articles appeared translated in full in European newspapers; the scandal and the fall-out made the front page of the French sports newspaper *L'Equipe* for several days.

Simpson's explanations were inconsistent. First he stood by the articles, then he said he had been misquoted and would sue. His motives were also unclear. His constant need for money had to be one, but he also claimed the exposés were intended to raise the profile of cycling in Britain. This is not as disingenuous as it sounds; the issue was a constant refrain of his, and he was quite capable of merely seeing the end and assuming no one else would disapprove of the means.

However, there was general disapproval. One French newspaper cartoon depicted the world champion as a bell, with bags of money where the clapper should have been. Simpson's team manager, Gaston Plaud, and his personal manager, Daniel Dousset, condemned his rash conduct. His sponsor, Peugeot, came close to sacking him. He received anonymous letters accusing him of being unworthy of the world champion's jersey, and was rumoured to have been cold-shouldered by his fellow professionals. 'Cycling will not pardon him' thundered a French Sunday paper's editorial.

Simpson donated the money to a cyclists' benevolent fund and won his pardon two weeks later with a simply stunning victory in the closing one-day Classic of the season, the Tour of Lombardy. It was a show of strength worthy of his hero, the Italian Fausto Coppi, or any of the greats. He escaped alone and had enough time in hand at the finish in Como to talk to the press before the second-placed rider arrived: a 'marvellous revenge' as the headline in *L'Equipe* put it. Only one man had done the world championship/Tour of Lombardy double before – Alfredo Binda in the 1920s. Any victory by a world road race champion is notable; wearing the distinctive rainbow-striped white jersey, the champion is a marked man whose every move can be followed.

His fellow cyclists' reaction to the *People* affair had meant that Simpson was doubly marked. It all made the story even better: the world champion gained several weeks of notoriety. For a man who made his living from appearance money, from drawing crowds to races, this was hardly a disaster.

Simpson's talent for self-promotion is best shown by his embrace of his alter ego, 'Major Tom'. The 'Major' first popped up after Simpson's surprise fourth place in his first professional world championship, at Zandvoordt in Holland in 1959. A headline in *L'Equipe* read: '*Les carnets du Major Simpson*' (the notebooks of Major Simpson), a reference to a popular book of the time *Les carnets du Major Thompson*.

The original is a gentle mocking of the French, seen through the eyes of a fictional expatriate English gentleman, written by Pierre Daninos, who also covered the Tour de France for the newspaper *Le Figaro*. Simpson was the embodiment of Major Thompson as he appeared in a caricature on the cover of the book: slender, sharp-featured, well turned-out, exuding a crisp 'English sense of humour'. It was a convenient way of pigeon-holing a British cyclist: Brian Robinson had also been compared to the ubiquitous major by the press.

'Major Tom' was born after Simpson's Tour of Flanders win when a journalist from *Miroir-Sprint* magazine brought a Thompson-style bowler hat and umbrella to the cyclist's Paris apartment for a photo shoot. Simpson already had the sharp suits. The idea had come from his manager Daniel

Dousset, a man with a keen eye for a new way of selling his protégés. Simpson was photographed selecting his morning *Times* from a bookstall and sipping tea in a café, and a minor legend was born.

British fans would have seen a resemblance to the sardonic, bowler- and brolly-wielding John Steed from *The Avengers*, which first screened in England in January 1961. The note of 'swinging London' played well on the Continent. Simpson was clearly touting his Englishness to the full to a willing Continental audience but it was merely an act: he always seemed perfectly at home in Europe. He eventually decided that the bowler hat had jinxed him, and stopped wearing it, but there was a final curious twist: after his marriage to Helen Simpson, Barry Hoban recycled the bowler and brolly by posing with them for a magazine in the guise of 'the gent from Ghent'.

Even after the bowler was abandoned, Simpson retained a sartorial edge over the opposition. Typically, he turned up at the start of the 1967 Tour wearing a blue blazer with a red rose embroidered on it. Equally typically, he quipped: 'I'm not going for stage wins, just the Most Elegant Rider and the Most Unfortunate Rider's prizes.'

To promote himself to his various audiences, Simpson did more than simply dress up: in the 1960s, double-page articles bearing his byline were a regular feature of *Cycling*. He gave his inside view of the great races, passed on his training tips, and expounded his arguments for the foundation of a British national professional team. The articles were apparently ghost-written by the editor Alan Gayfer, but they bore the indelible Simpson stamp of brutal honesty and wry humour. His inside view of victory in Milan–San Remo writes off some of the field as 'the most hopeless lot of cowboys you could ever meet'. In another, a few months before he died, he says of his failed hour record attempt in 1958: 'I learned nothing. I was too stupid to learn then.'

Simpson was happy to accommodate the clichéd French

view of the typical Englishman, but he also knew exactly what his home audience wanted. In his inside account of the 1962 Tour he delivers the perfect homespun touch: 'The only celebration I had [after taking the jersey] was my pot of tea and bread and jam in bed before my massage.' The thought of their boy putting away his jam butty in between battles with Johnny Foreigner would have melted the heart of any English cycling fan.

There was a serious purpose to all this self-promotion. As early as the 1960s, the trend for sportsmen to be as much entertainers as athletes had begun, something which would be most strikingly seen later in the decade with Muhammad Ali. As a younger professional, Simpson came across a cyclist called Roger Hassenforder, by then past his best but still legendary as the clown and prankster of the circuit; the man who would, for example, pedal around a velodrome sitting on his handlebars and facing backwards.

Simpson would have observed that Hassenforder gained more and better contracts than his somewhat meagre racing results merited. When it came to making money, a cyclist's profile and ability to draw a crowd mattered. Indeed, Simpson admitted learning much from him. He did Hassenforder-style stunts of his own, such as the time he grabbed a large stick out of the hedge and pretended to assault a fellow cyclist. 'He [Simpson] used to laugh and joke about, but it was more calculating than that. He'd see someone in the crowd at the start of a race, go and borrow something and act the fool,' recalls Alan Ramsbottom. 'He'd pick up musical instruments, hats and all sorts.' If the hat looked funny, Simpson would wear it, be it Stetson, bowler, or lofty traditional Breton lace coiffe. 'It was pure performance,' says Brian Robinson.

However, this was more than mere imitation of Hassenforder: Simpson was a natural comedian. He could spot the potential in a situation or a prop, deliver a joke's punchline with pinpoint timing, and come up with a quick retort when required. If he learnt these things anywhere, it was as a small boy, when his parents ran the working men's club in the Durham village of Haswell, and Tom and his elder brother Harry would lean out of their bedroom window to listen to the comedians working the audience in the evenings.

So quotable was Simpson that, after his death, one magazine devoted an entire panel to his witticisms from the 1967 Tour under the title 'Tom's Bons Mots'. On a teammate abandoning, probably reflecting his inner thoughts: 'That's a gentleman for you, he quit so there are fewer of us to share the prize money.' On the contrasting abilities of the British team, 'It's so absurd I love it.'

In this posthumous tribute to 'Simpson's humour', the picture in the panel of his *bons mots* is truly worth 1,000 words. Simpson is holding a huge block of ice on a fork and Barry Hoban has one corner in his mouth; Simpson is licking the other end, his tongue fully extended, his gurning grin a small, and vulgar, masterpiece in itself.

The ways in which Simpson managed to appeal to spectators and promoters were infinitely varied, and usually mischievous. At the Sportpaleis track in Ghent, he was riding a 'devil-take-the-hindmost', a race where the last cyclist in the pack is eliminated until the two fastest meet. In the end, Simpson was up against Giuseppe Beghetto, the reigning world sprint champion. Simpson had no chance of winning so, as Beghetto sped past him, he took one hand off the bars, leant over – travelling at 40 mph – and pretended to take a tow on the Italian's saddle. On another occasion in Ghent, he was part of a panel selecting 'Miss Sportpaleis' – and he persuaded the others to choose 'the roughest girl there', according to one witness.

Even on the morning of his death, Simpson was fooling around with Hoban in a rowing boat at the stage start in Marseille's Old Port, dipping his toe in the water for the photographers. This was before the most important stage of the Tour, on which his career depended. Today, prior to such a day, the Tourmen would be cocooned in air-conditioned buses. The notion of playing up to the crowd and the media would be the last thing on their minds.

For any public figure, the key to popularity is genuine emotional engagement. Simpson's death was a major event because he struck chords right across a wide range of audiences. He offered the complete package: success to attract the aspirational, the Dunkirk spirit for admirers of glorious failure, a humble background for those who liked the homespun, an aristocratic touch for the snobs, off-the-wall humour for fans of the peculiar, wider aims of his sport for the serious-minded.

For the French, Simpson could either play the stiff-backed English major, or the precise opposite: the Englishman 'who was not phlegmatic', as one journalist put it. 'He is ambitious like a Frenchman, selfish like a Spaniard, industrious like a German, talkative like an Italian and versatile like a Fleming,' wrote the professional cyclist turned journalist Jean Bobet. And there was a final, crucial element in the equation of stardom: a hint of self-mockery in Simpson which meant that he never looked as if he was trying too hard or taking it all too seriously.

In *Cycling*, Alan Gayfer compared him to the Formula One driver Mike Hawthorne, 'another laughing cavalier cut off in his prime', while two of the tributes in the magazine drew a parallel with Sir Donald Campbell, both 'killed while fulfilling their aspiration to put Britain at the top'. For Jacques Goddet, he was: 'A champion in his own style, a lover of the peculiar, ambitious to the point of imprudence and collapse.' For Chris Brasher, an Olympic gold medallist and still one of the country's leading sports writers, Simpson was more: one of the greatest figures in British sport in the 20th century.

All he lacked was the survival instinct.

'Roule Britannia'

Côte de Dourdan, May 26, 1963
The five small motorbikes putter up the dead straight hill out of the village in the Chevreuse valley, through the crowds lined three-deep. Old men in berets, Brylcreemed fathers, mothers and children in frilly Sunday dresses have turned out to watch cycling's longest race, the Bordeaux–Paris 'Derby of the Road'.

The 'dernys' are motorised bikes driven by fat men in dark glasses, cycling jerseys and shorts, who pedal slowly to help the engines; behind each one is a cyclist. They are wearing identical kit to the 'derny' drivers, but the similarity ends there: the cyclists are slender, athletic, their pacemakers corpulent and varicose-veined.

The cyclists left Bordeaux 14 hours ago, at two in the morning. They rode through the night in a silent, orderly crocodile with their police outriders and support cars, saw the sun rise at Angoulême and began racing near Poitiers, where the 'derny' drivers were waiting. The 'Derby', 348 miles long, 180 of those miles behind the 'dernys', is a throwback to cycle racing in the 1890s, when racers were paced by tandem cycles over inhuman distances; Dourdan, an hour and a half from Paris, is usually decisive, where the distance finally makes itself felt.

Tactics are dictated by the pacer; Tom Simpson's guide, Fernand Wambst, is a calculating man, chosen by the Peugeot team to master Simpson's impetuous instincts. He wants to make their move here. His gut wobbling under the black and white Peugeot jersey, he guides Simpson to the front of the little group and accelerates, with Simpson sprinting behind, eyes fixed on the back tyre of the 'derny'.

Only one man attempts to hold their pace: Edouard Delberghe, in the striped jersey of the Pelforth Beer team, and he is soon 100 metres behind Simpson. He races the final 42 miles to the Parc des Princes stadium with 'the ease of an English gentleman going to his daily bridge session', as one writer puts it. After a spring of frustrating near misses, his career is back on track.

CHAPTER SIX

'A Kind of Expatriate Dick Whittington'
Geoffrey Nicholson, 1967

Big, round tears roll slowly down the cheeks of the mountainous old man in a backstreet bar in Ghent. Albert Beurick is sitting at a table in the Kafe de Koninck talking, as he so often has, of his friendship with Tom Simpson, as he did at the film show back in January at the Riverside Theatre in Hammersmith. He sweats heavily, and occasionally wipes away the tears he has shed for over 30 years. This could be any bar in Belgium, with its red-brick walls, its ebullient off-duty army recruits in green fatigues, the old men sitting over unhealthily dark beers. It's afternoon, so the pinball machines are quiet and the 1980s hits on the stereo correspondingly loud. This is Beurick's café, but there is nothing here of the little world of 35 years ago centred around the quixotic Simpson and Beurick, his factotal Sancho Panza.

Beurick was at the finish when Simpson won his world championship in Spain in 1965, 'crying his eyes out in joy', wrote David Saunders in *Cycling in the Sixties*: 'I could hear him shouting "*champion du monde*" over the din, his well-filled stomach thrusting aside police, troops, and even metal barriers.' No sooner had Simpson crossed the line than Beurick fought his way through the dictator Franco's Guardia Civil to be with his idol, to pick him up, while still on his bike, and lift him in the air. But there's no sign of this 35-year-old passion in the Kafe de Koninck, where the only link with English sport is the ubiquitous Manchester United 'Red Devils' scarf pinned on the wall. The café could be a shrine to Simpson, but isn't. Beurick, I sense, is trying to move on. The tears, however, and his outbursts at the film show a few months before, imply that he cannot.

Asked to define the Flemish passion for cycling, one Belgian simply answered: 'It is a neurosis.' He pointed to the sky as if implying that, in the Dutch-speaking part of the country, the love of things two-wheeled comes from above: it is an implacable, innate fact of life rather than an acquired habit. The Flemish 'supporters', as they call themselves, are the most obsessive and driven of them all. For the Flemish supporters, going to races and screaming encouragement is a peripheral part of the business. What matters above all is the reflected glory of involvement, however marginal, in the sport. It may be waving a flag on a crossroads at a village race, dressing up in the same team strip as a superstar or domestique, or wearing a cap with a local cycling club name, but it is still about getting involved.

Only the Flemish seem to push fandom towards stalking. For the last 13 years, on every single stage of the Tour de France that I have driven – perhaps 200 – I have seen the same Belgian camper van pulled up on verges from Nice to Nantes, driven by a 75-year-old named Lucien Blio from a village in Flanders. It has always had the same flag on the back window, bearing an intricate, incomprehensible pun about the Lions of Flanders. Blio began following the Tour in 1974, and is as much part of the race's furniture as Lance Armstrong. It is admirable, but not normal and Beurick's devotion to Simpson has to be seen in this light. Some who lived in Ghent at the time say that Simpson exploited Beurick's support, that he ordered him around as you might a servant. Beurick would never see it that way. In his friendship with Simpson, Beurick achieved the ultimate dream for any Flemish fan: the champion came and lived with him.

Beurick was a wrestling fan when he bumped into the British amateur cycling squad at a track in Paris in 1958.

He offered his services as an unpaid team helper.* Simpson was one of the team; the two kept in touch. Simpson would stay with Beurick when racing in Belgium. It was Beurick who helped him find a place to stay for nothing when the English cyclist and his young family arrived in Ghent in October 1961, and Beurick who piled Simpson's furniture into a van and helped him move from Paris.

Soon, the city became the centre of a little expatriate British cycling colony. After Simpson, two other English professionals, Alan Ramsbottom and Vin Denson, moved from their base in eastern France. Denson and his wife Vi eventually opened a bar in the suburb of Gentbrugge. Barry Hoban came from his home just over the border in northern France. Keith Butler and Bob Addy were amongst others who came over from England too.

For a professional cyclist, the attraction was obvious: Ghent was a central location from which to travel to races in every part of Europe. If his team did not call on a rider's services, there were races aplenty, the 'kermesses' in the Flemish villages. 'You could race every day: there were prizes down to 30th and you could make a living just by coming 10th,' recalled Ramsbottom. Ghent had another enticing side to it: the tax bills were lower than in France.

Initially, the Simpsons lived in a small cottage. A year later they moved to Saint Amandsberg, a self-contained Ghent suburb across the railway line from the city proper, where they speak Dutch with a slightly different accent. Then they moved to Mariakerke, and settled at No. 87, Hugo Kouter Street for four years.

Mariakerke is quiet and affluent, with plenty of space between the large, neat villas and a big brick church. It's the

* Beurick's links with English cycling pre-date this encounter; according to one cyclist, Malcolm Smith, cyclists from England were living at and racing from, the Café Den Engel as early as 1957, while Beurick acted as Great Britain team manager at a race in Bruges in August 1958, in between Belgian national service duties.

kind of place where professional people live, and was an area favoured by Ghent's expatriate community. The move from St Amandsberg must have been an important step up the social ladder for a man who began life in a back-to-back Durham mining village. Early in 1966 the Simpsons began building a high-gabled house of dun-coloured bricks, 22 Vijverstraat. The house is still there. Tom was away racing when it was finished in 1967, and slept there for only a few nights before leaving for the Tour.

A quarter of a century after Simpson's death, Ray Pascoe happened to be passing while filming *Something to Aim At*. The lady who owned the house, as proud as a peacock of the building's association with the man who built it, invited him in. Simpson's name was there on the original plans she showed him; the kitchen was the one he had ordered from Italy from the Salvarani company. They were the sponsor whose team he was set to join in 1968.

After Paris, settling down in Flanders was easy for the Simpson couple, according to Helen: 'It was a good life. In Paris we were unknown because it is a big city, in Ghent you were somebody.' Living in the centre of Paris meant training was hard for Tom; the 111 stairs to the apartment in Clichy and the lack of a garden were not ideal for Helen, especially when she became pregnant.

Ghent took its adopted son to its heart: Simpson's victory in the 1965 world championship prompted a series of civic receptions. Most of the population turned out to watch him and Helen parade along a circuitous route in a horse-drawn carriage with the mayor.

Flanders is as steeped in cycling as the Welsh valleys are in rugby. Virtually every small village has its 'kermesse' and a local professional or former pro running a café or a bike shop. The history runs deep: iconic heroes such as Rik Van Looy and the great races, topped by the *Ronde*, the Tour of Flanders. Once word spread through the small, intimate world of British cycling – helped by Simpson's ghosted articles in *Cycling* magazine – that there was an English-speaking bridgehead in Ghent, one amateur cyclist after another would come over to indulge their passion. They raced the crowded calendar, rubbed shoulders with the British elite, took in the atmosphere, and visited the exotic bike shops. They would stay at Beurick's place, a café called Den Engel – the Angel – in the quiet middle-class Ghent suburb of Saint Amandsberg, or at another famous cyclists' boarding house, Mrs Deene's. Ray Pascoe was among them. He dates his passion for Simpson to a meeting with him in Den Engel, where he was taken to see the great man by Beurick. Simpson was seated in a chair, waiting to answer questions put to him by a group of amateur acolytes – but Pascoe clammed up and barely knew what to say.

Another to make the trip was Arthur Metcalfe, who was to be Simpson's teammate in the 1967 Tour de France. He put on his best suit for the occasion but got on the wrong train and ended up in Antwerp. He got the train back to Ghent, walked across a railway marshalling yard in the pouring rain with his bike and bag, and eventually arrived bedraggled and wet at Den Engel. He slept the night in a room with no heating. The following day he rode a race where the other cyclists went so fast he thought he'd been told the wrong distance, because there was no way he reckoned they could keep that pace up for 90 miles.

There were Australians as well, who lived in even rougher style than the Britons. The English-speakers would train together, hang around each other's houses, and share the travelling. 'I was taking the Australians to one race, and I ran over a big rabbit,' recalls Alan Ramsbottom. 'The Aussies jumped out of the car, cut its throat, skinned it, and they all came round the day after for rabbit pie cooked by my wife.' Sometimes, the British and Australians from Ghent would make up a little informal team in the kermesses, helping each other and splitting the prize money.

Back in the 1960s, Belgium was 24 hours travelling time from most parts of England, the same as Australia is now. For most of the British cyclists, coming to Ghent was the first time they had been abroad. Having someone like Beurick on the ground to look after you was vital. In this respect, the word 'supporter' meant more than a mere fan.

Men such as Albert and their families formed a little network of fixers and fetchers for the expatriate Britons and Australians – and today foreign cyclists living in the area are still warmly looked after. Ramsbottom's daughter was born in Ghent, and the supporters' club paid for his wife's private hospital treatment. When he broke his arm, fortunately the club had arranged the insurance. Like Helen Hoban, he has fond memories of Flanders: 'Cyclists can do no wrong there.'

Beurick put me in his Renault Espace, and we drove around the city, stopping off to visit a grandchild or three on the way. Den Engel is still there on Dendermonsesteenweg in St Amandsberg, a small, one-storey building set slightly back from the busy thoroughfare, with rooms built into the loft space – once a dormitory which could take 20 British cyclists. In European towns, a particular café always acts as a vital hub for any sport; Den Engel was the heart of the British cycling community in Ghent. This was where Beurick organized the Simpson supporters' club, with between 400 and 500 members, paying 100 Belgian francs (15 shillings) per year; here was where the fans met in the evenings to drink, and where the cyclists congregated in the mornings for their training rides. The Tom Simpson Grand Prix, run by Beurick, started and finished outside, and was won in its first year, 1964, by one Frans Brandts, with the world champion Benoni Beheyt in fifth place.

The 1965 BBC documentary 'The World of Tom Simpson' includes a long sequence shot in the café. A thinner and younger Albert pulls beers in a top with a British Cycling Federation badge. A sign over the door states that this is National Cycling Union-approved accommodation. Black and white photographs of the great Flemish cyclists line the walls as if to remind us that this is Belgium, not England. The cameraman didn't travel round the back, to Beurick's father's knackers yard, where cyclists would see an old horse arrive in the morning, and then see bits of it on their plates in the evening.

The cameraman pans from a billiard table in one corner to another with a long dinner table. A large group of thin, neatly dressed young cyclists in Buddy Holly glasses are eating bread and jam and drinking tea from a vast pot wielded by Beurick's mother. It is as if an English school canteen has materialized from nowhere in a bar in Belgium; Simpson is playing schoolmaster with a beer in his hand and a proprietorial air about him. Vin Denson sums up the way Simpson saw all this: 'He used to like people milling around, doing things for him.' The English king is in his court.

Beurick and Simpson were soon providing board and lodging for cyclists, on a grand scale, in the Velotel Tom Simpson, a large brick building five miles outside Ghent, with a massive banner outside made of a patchwork of at least 20 national flags. It offered bed, breakfast and two meals for 25 shillings a day, or 18s for those who stayed the whole year.

This was not the only business venture the pair started up to cater for the aspiring racing men from over the Channel. For a short while, from March 1962, they ran two-week 'cycling schools' for young amateurs from Britain. They used their contacts to provide a mix of training rides, racing and lectures on diet, preparation and race tactics. The instructors included the former world champion Georges Ronsse, Belgian team manager at the Tour de France; the racing included an outing in the amateur Tour of Flanders. The school did not make a great deal of money, but it was an enterprising piece of lateral thinking, and it was 30 years ahead of its time. Now, many former professionals in the English-speaking world trade on their names to run training camps and cycling holidays; it was almost unknown in the 1960s, and it remains rare for any cyclist to attempt diversification of this kind while still racing. In Simpson's case, it was probably more than mere money-making and self-promotion.

Simpson had travelled over to Europe alone, with £100 in his pocket and no support. He wanted others to follow the trail; the more English cyclists there were and the more successful they were, the greater the interest at home in cycling and in him. A major sponsor would also be more likely to come in and back the English team he wanted. It is not overplaying his stature to say that his interests and the interests of the sport were one and the same.

The derelict land between two Ghent canals had been empty since before Simpson died. The plot in Tweebruggen, part of the Visserij district, was bought by Simpson but never developed. It was the most striking image I was to find of what he was aiming for when he died. Overgrown with willow herb and long grass, a memorial to his financial ambitions, it was as poignant as the monument high on Mont Ventoux. Simpson speculatively acquired the land, roughly a quarter of an acre, together with a Mr De Roucke, mayor of a village outside Ghent through a specially formed company, Sidero.

Simpson had already invested in the Ghent property market, building two four-storey blocks of apartments on Maalderijstraat, a main road in St Amandsberg. The flats are still there, their slate-hung, near-vertical roofs all too clearly a product of the 1960s. They were reported to have sold for 750,000BF (£5,400) each. The Tweebruggen acquisition, however, turned out to be a misjudgement. Simpson spent a considerable sum on plans for the property, but could not get the owner of the house on the corner of the plot to sell, and his grand design was shelved for over 30 years, until Helen and Barry Hoban finally sold the land at a loss.

Most professional cyclists steer clear of business dealings during their careers other than those which relate to their racing: team contracts, endorsements, start money and so on. There simply isn't time to work out the best investments; it can detract from the training, resting and racing which earns the money in the first place. Simpson was clearly different, always looking out for a bit of extra cash. He kept his eye fixed on the medium and long term, as well as the short term.

'Tom was business,' says Beurick, pointing at his head to indicate that deals were always in Simpson's mind. Simpson was a wheeler-dealer, who would buy tracksuit tops in Ghent from a company called Riksport and sell them for a profit to English cycling club lads like Ray Pascoe, who were desperate for anything which looked 'Continental'. Beurick describes Simpson as a *deugniet* – the Flemish word for a lovable rascal with a finger in every pie. He still laughs about how, when he was moving from Paris to Ghent, Simpson tried to avoid paying import duty on a radio by smuggling it through customs – the radio had already been smuggled from Germany to France for him by a fellow cyclist – and, of course, he got caught. 'He was always trying to do things, sell and buy, take things to England, not pay tax. He was like a naughty boy.'

Land, though, was key to Simpson's plans. By the time of his death, he had bought a farmhouse near Harworth, split it into units and was renting it out. He and Helen were also renting out a semi in Doncaster, and they owned the property in Corsica. There were other projects, too, which never quite got completed.

When racing in Torremolinos with Jacques Anquetil, Raymond Poulidor and Jean Stablinski, he got into discussions with the race organizer about buying land for building in what was shortly to become one of Spain's biggest beach resorts. Stablinski now regrets that they did not take him more seriously in what would clearly have been a highly profitable venture: 'He pushed us to do it, and he was right.'

There was more behind Simpson's dealings than a simple love of money for its own sake. It was more of a need. His contemporaries all noted his financial hunger. It was something he spoke of in virtually every interview, and had begun early in his life. 'He was always on the lookout to make a dollar,' says his brother Harry. When he first arrived in Ghent, Simpson felt more than just the need to earn a living. He felt the fear that haunts immigrants: fear of having to return home empty-handed and the loss of face which that entails. 'In the beginning, when he arrived here [in Ghent], he was very, very careful,' notes Beurick. 'He was worried he would have to go back to England with no money.'

In the letters Simpson wrote to George Shaw, cash is a constant theme after Simpson leaves England for the Continent. No less than a third of his first letter to Shaw from Saint Brieuc deals with prize money and *primes*, the prizes awarded at intermediate points during a race. 'I arrived here on Thursday 3rd, raced on the 5th, but had two punctures and lost a crank. However I won about £2, 10s and some provisions in primes . . . I next raced on the 12th . . . I won two primes, 2,000 francs [£2], I got 35,000 for first, and a 5,000 franc bonus from my sponsor. So in two races I have made about £35.' Simpson was, of course, referring to 'old' francs, as this was before the currency was revalued. Simpson's tone is never boastful when talking about money: his manner simply suggests he was constantly aware of how much he was earning, and constantly wondering at how much money there was to be made compared with the smaller prizes on offer back in England.

The depth of his obsession glares through as the letter continues with the most intricate details of the prize money, lap prizes and win bonuses available: 'My sponsor is Santa Rosa, a wine manufacturer. He pays 40 francs a km [bonus] for a 1st, 30 francs for a 2nd ... this week I ride in St Brieuc 1st – 40,000 [£40] and about 80,000 in primes. The week after in a race 1st – 50,000 with a prime every lap of 1,000 (20) but two special primes of 10,000 on the 10th and 20,000 on the 15th.' The distance and course of the race are not even mentioned.

The precarious nature of the profession was clearly playing on Simpson's mind when he wrote to Shaw on May 12, 1959. The winter is still several months away, but he is already worrying about how he will get through. His winnings, he says, total £200 'so you will see I don't need any money, but I am saving very hard for I may have difficulty getting contracts in the winter on the tracks. So by the time I have lived Oct Nov Dec Jan Feb [sic] in Denmark and Germany, I expect my funds will be low.'

Simpson may have been keen to make money, but he clearly felt there were ways of getting it and behaving when you had it. A fellow English professional, Michael Wright, rode for Simpson at the world championship in 1965, but was not fit enough to help him much in the race. Wright refused to be paid, only for Simpson to insist he took the money as agreed. 'It was the correct way to behave,' says Wright.

Writing on July 9, 1959, Simpson inquired about Shaw's performance in the Tour of Britain, but not in terms which were familiar to the Corinthian British. 'The thing is not the position you finished,' he wrote, 'how much did you make [sic].' There is no question mark: this is a statement of fact. There could be no better summary of the philosophy of the professional cyclist.

Prize money was only part of what Simpson was seeking. In the 1960s, only a small proportion of a professional cyclist's income came from winnings and his retainer with his sponsored team. Contracts to ride 'criteriums' – short races held around villages and towns across France – and local track meetings were where the real money was earned. The purpose of the race was to show the stars to their public, who would pay to see them – as 25,000 did, for example, at the Château Chinon criterium after the 1967 Tour.

The rewards were high. In August 1963, it was estimated that Jacques Anquetil, cycling's top earner at the time, would earn £100,000 'in prizes, contract money and bonuses' for his fourth win in the Tour de France. But there was no security. There were too many cyclists chasing the same team places, creating a buyer's market for their services. In 1965, a third of the professionals in France were without a sponsor. And so a protectionist policy was introduced: the following year, French teams imposed a ceiling of four 'foreign' cyclists per squad. Sometimes it did not matter how good a cyclist was – in 1964, Simpson's fellow Ghent resident Alan Ramsbottom finished 16th in the Tour de France, but he was out of contract by the end of the following season and was not paid for four months.

Cyclists fell into three categories in the 1960s. At the top were the 15 or 20 *grands coureurs* – Simpson, Anquetil, Poulidor, Stablinski, Rudi Altig and their ilk. They took the bulk of the money available, receiving massive appearance money, and big fees to lead a team, or in some cases negotiating a looser retainer so that they could take start money for the major races as well as criteriums. The resources they commanded meant they could eat better food, pay for medical help, buy better equipment and get a better car to drive to the races. One, Louison Bobet, even had his own plane to travel from one criterium to the next.

In the middle were the *bons coureurs*, several hundred of them, classy cannon fodder, support riders to the stars. Usually they had contracts with a team, but sometimes their team place was purely on a verbal agreement or a handshake, and sometimes they were contracted for only nine months of the year. These were riders such as Hoban, Denson, and Ramsbottom, for whom much depended on their relations with the big stars as well as their ability to win. Their existence was precarious, because there was always another cyclist waiting to take their place, probably willing to accept less for a foothold on the ladder.

In the bottom layer were the *petits coureurs*. One was Simpson's teammate at Peugeot, Peter Hill. He describes a life close to the breadline in 1967: 'I got 650 [Belgian] francs – [£65] a month. You could just live off it. My mother-in-law took 12 francs a day for board and lodging, and then I had to pay petrol. Some guys were earning less. There were even Belgians who got a bike and a jersey. There was never any chance to make money.'

Even the most successful careers could end in financial and personal disaster. At the end of 1966, the pioneering Irish cyclist Shay Elliott, well known to Simpson and all the Ghent community, was bankrupted by a failed hotel venture and a divorce. Elliott had been a devoted teammate to Jacques Anquetil, and had worn the yellow jersey in the Tour de France, but returned to Ireland with next to nothing.

Simpson himself was made aware of the ruthless, ephemeral nature of the profession in 1961, when he injured his knee and missed much of the season. He wrote about that year in *Cycling*: 'I was almost dead and buried once I stopped winning. I thought I was finished. I only got seven [racing] contracts during the season. Fortunately for me, I had a contract with a cycling firm [his retainer with the St Raphael team], otherwise I would have been almost broke.' That was the year when Simpson won the Tour of Flanders, one of the biggest one-day races on the calendar, yet he says: 'My winnings totalled about £500 during the year. Barely enough to live on.' Appearance money would make up the rest.

Memories were short in cycling: before the world

championship win in 1965, Simpson's contract value had declined to £80 per race – after the victory, as world champion, his fee more than quadrupled. Small wonder that Simpson was earning as much as he could as quickly as possible, and investing heavily. Small wonder that he desperately wanted to keep his place at the top.

How much Simpson earned revolved around his agent, Daniel Dousset, who acted as a go-between for the riders and organizers, controlling the contracts for the races and the appearance money the riders received. Dousset operated in France where there was one other agent, Roger Piel. Belgium was the fiefdom of Jean Van Buggenhout. Italy was run by Mr Cinelli.

It was a cartel. If a cyclist was not on one of the agents' books he had no appearance money: nothing to live off other than prize money and whatever his team might pay him. As a result, the rider–agent relationship was one of dependence on the rider's side, exploitation on that of the manager. Dousset or Piel could always find new riders; the riders had nowhere else to turn. It was effectively a form of tied labour.

Half-Brazilian, half-Breton, the thickset Dousset had something of the mafia 'Don' about him, with his slicked hair and smart suits, his machine-gun style of speaking and dark glasses. And a little of the boxing promoter Don King, perhaps, in the way he operated. His nicknames among the riders summed up how they saw him: 'Monsieur 10 per cent'; 'Monsieur Rockefeller'.

'Dousset was a money merchant, quite ruthless,' says Ramsbottom. 'He made a fortune. He wasn't a likeable person. Some riders loved him, but I could see how much he was creaming off. He took his cut of what we got, you'd be going to events and there'd be 60 riders, doing it day after day, and you'd think, "He's sat back there, and we're doing this." But you had to go with them.'

The appearance races tended to have a script in which the local rider or the Tour star would win; this is well known. There were also said to be times when Dousset would effectively fix a major race, by ordering the riders contracted to him to produce a certain result, or by telling them to combine against a rider who was out of favour and prevent him from winning. All he needed to do was to offer contracts, or threaten to withhold them. Dousset was clearly fond of Simpson, most of the time. 'He liked flamboyant, extrovert guys because he could market them,' says Helen Hoban, adding, 'There were times though when Tom would rub him up the wrong way. Tom went skiing when he was world champion, broke his leg and Dousset went off his rocker.'

Dousset put it like this: 'A champion has to fight for his place constantly. The public continually demands new feats. This is a fast-moving time, and everything is quickly forgotten.' The agent was the first person to get to Simpson when he won Bordeaux–Paris, and he kissed the rider fondly. He knew what the victory was worth, to both of them. It put Simpson back among the elite after a spell with no big wins.

Cyclist and agent had to exploit successes quickly and fully. Simpson spent three weeks covering 12,000 road miles after winning the world title in 1965, racing 18 times at £300–£350 per race. This was not excessive for the time: Jean Stablinski, for example, recalls racing 48 times in 42 days after one Tour. Once the time spent travelling – in an age with few motorways, high-speed trains or extensive air networks – was added to the equation, the workloads now seem lunatic in their physical and mental demands. Simpson's schedule after his first Tour, the 1960 race, shows how relentless the business was. He finished in appalling physical condition, but in the next few days he was racing: in Normandy, Milan, Turin, Sallanches in the French Alps, Lyon, Belgium for a week, Nice – after a 24-hour drive –

and finally Central France. Not surprisingly, he ended up exhausted and ill – and checked himself into hospital for a week.

Interviewed in 'The World of Tom Simpson', the British No. 1 sums up the little world in which he was making his fortune: 'Professional cycling is a bit of a rat race, but if I'm one of the top rats I can bear it.' That was the situation which led to his death. Cycling was a better way of earning a living than working in a factory in England, but it was only worthwhile if he maintained his earning power.

The 1967 Tour came at a critical turning point for Simpson: he had been a professional for eight years, and 'had given himself another two in which he needed to put away a further £60,000', recalls Colin Lewis, Simpson's room-mate in the 1967 Tour. It amounted to the final push before retirement, or perhaps a brief, lucrative second career riding winter six-day races on the indoor velo-dromes. Simpson had more than his appearance money at stake in that Tour though. After five often frustrating years in the French Peugeot squad, he had reached a verbal agreement to ride alongside his close friend Felice Gimondi, the 1965 Tour winner, in the Italian Salvarani team in 1968. He would take Vin Denson with him. The size of his retainer with them would depend on his performance in the Tour.

The start of the year had gone well for Simpson, with the biggest stage race victory of his career, in the Paris–Nice 'Race to the Sun', and two other stage wins in the Tour of Spain. Fine victories as they were, however, these were not the kind of results which would draw the crowds to a village in central France or a track side in Brittany. They did nothing for his market value. 1966 had been a disaster, and he had not won a really big race since the Tour of Lombardy at the end of 1965. His public profile was slipping, and with it his market value. Hence Dousset's concern when Simpson rode the 1967 Tour de France in a restrained manner, merely holding on to the leaders rather that producing the popular do-or-die moves which were his hallmark. Overruling his instincts and riding a tactical race was, as he had told Harry Hall, the best way to ensure a high finish overall. Jean Stablinski, however, felt Simpson was making a mistake. He told him: 'You are the kind of rider who can wear the yellow jersey, win a stage, raise hell, but you can't last 22 days of racing.'

Dousset clearly put pressure on Simpson during that Tour. He told Simpson he needed to make a greater impact on the race, the very evening before the fateful Ventoux stage, when the pair had dinner in Marseille. 'They went out together and he [Simpson] came back at 9.30, which I remember vividly because it was late for him,' says Colin Lewis. 'He was concerned about something Dousset had said to him, and made a phone call to someone when he got back,' Lewis continues. 'He was a bit agitated. When he calmed down, he started talking about how important the stage was the next day, how it was a make-or-break day.'

Before his death, Dousset said that he had told the British leader that as far as he, Dousset, was concerned, the British leader was having a bad Tour. The scale of appearance money values which he would draw up for the criteriums would depend on the Tour result. If Simpson did not perform, Dousset told him, he would not receive his usual fee for the round of criteriums after the Tour. Simpson needed either to finish in the first five or win a stage. Even though Simpson was unwell, the manager had in effect held a gun to his head.

Tom Simpson was a victim of the system of exploitation and insecurity, but he had no illusions about what he was doing, and cannot be held up as an innocent. He was working the system as hard as he could, and it backfired.

Down the motorway from Ghent, on the other side of the

French border, lies the little town of Valenciennes, home of Jean Stablinski. Stablinski had much in common with Simpson: he was also an immigrant. Christened Jean Stablewski, he was the son of one of the Poles who moved to northern France in the 1920s to work in the mines and factories. Like Simpson, he was one of the *grands coureurs*; like Simpson, he was never really a man of the Tour de France, but a world champion and a consistent, popular winner of one-day Classics. They often travelled together to the criteriums. He speaks fondly of the Englishman; he liked talking to Simpson, who was one of the riders he sought out in the peloton for conversation when a race was quiet.

The small, dapper Stablinski is clearly enjoying a prosperous retirement. The car is big, but not ostentatious. The chintzy, lavishly decorated house is one of three on a plot of land he bought just before he gave up racing – the others have been sold. The coffee is served in thin, delicate china cups; the table on which the pot sits is ornate, in the 17th-century style. He is clearly a man of some stature in the local community: after talking to me, Stablinski's next meeting is with the mayor of a town nearby to discuss organizing a minor cycle race. After he hung up his wheels, he worked as a team manager, launched his own range of bikes, and did a bit of PR for a local firm. Now, he spends every July at the Tour de France glad-handing corporate guests and supervising the *anciens coureurs*. These are the old stars who work in the hospitality village and the guest cars, serving up pithy anecdotes and explaining racing tactics to deputy marketing managers from Coca Cola France, Nike and Crédit Lyonnais. Doping is not a topic he likes to discuss, but he will talk at length of his racing exploits and memories of Simpson.

Stablinski has not given up riding his bike, despite being slave to it for 15 years. He goes out for short rides, but makes a point of never carrying a bottle of water in the cage on the frame, so that he can stop in a café for a beer, which was something he never could do when the next race was always on his mind.

Financial security, status in the community, freedom to choose your own obligations: Simpson might have enjoyed these things in Corsica rather than northern France, but it is only necessary to visit Stablinski to see the future for which the Englishman was striving on that hot afternoon in July 1967.

More than anywhere else apart from Mont Ventoux, Simpson left his mark among Ghent's elegant cafés, big, curlicued churches like wedding cakes, trams and quiet net-curtained backstreets. As well as the remains, finished and unfinished, of his ventures into the property market, his bust still stands in the entrance hall to the indoor cycling track in the *sportpaleis*. It is nicknamed the *Kuipke*, the 'hip bath', because of its terrifyingly steep, Wall of Death-style bankings.

Beurick – who else? – was the driving force behind this permanent memorial in the days when Ghent was mourning its adopted son. A couple of months after Simpson's death, Beurick organized a race – starting, naturally, outside Den Engel – and managed to persuade Simpson's fellow professionals to turn up for nothing and without prize money. He raised 85,000 Belgian francs. 'In memory of a great gentleman', says the inscription on the pedestal, although on the day I visited, the great gentleman was adorned with plastic beer glasses and screwed-up programmes from a rock concert held there the previous night. Outside is a quiet park, which has hardly changed in the 40 years since it was used as the backdrop to a Belgian television film of Simpson, who appears in full 'Major Thompson' get-up of bowler hat, sharp suit and umbrella. Through the artificial grottoes and groves of trees he strolls, to a peaceful seat where he reads a *Daily Express*, which is leading with a story on the Cuban missile crisis. He plays the part to perfection.

The 'Sportpaleis' was where Simpson raced on his first visit here in 1958. Impetuous as usual, he did not ride to the preordained script and humiliated the locals. The outraged organizer threatened to shoot him if he did not get off the track, and added that he would never ride another amateur race in Ghent – but, as a professional, Simpson became a regular here.

British and Australian cyclists still come to Ghent to race – in 2001 it was home to the British national champion Jeremy Hunt – but they have never come again in such numbers or with such widespread local support. If there is a little reminder of the two-wheeled community which thrived here 35 years ago, it comes in November when British fans flock over in numbers to the Ghent six-day.

The Ghent outing is a tradition among British cyclists, particularly in the south of England, which dates back to trips organized by *Cycling* magazine in the 1960s to see Simpson ride the race – 120 of them, for example, in 1965. It is only appropriate that when the British fans enter the 'hip bath', they walk past the statue of the man whose feats prompted the magazine to bring over their predecessors.

Simpson's death had an even greater public impact here than in his home country. Belgian television devoted a whole evening's viewing to the man it described as 'English by birth, Belgian at heart'. They ran through his last interviews and the best racing moments of his career. The memorial service in St Amandsberg's Catholic cathedral was packed. 'In the streets, in the cafés, they talk of nothing else', wrote Marcel de Leener in *Cycling*.

Once Simpson had gone, the British cycling scene in Ghent slowly withered. Hoban and Helen stayed on in Mariakerke until Hoban retired from racing in 1981. When they returned to the UK, both Simpson's daughters stayed on in their adopted homeland; Joanne now lives in St

Amandsberg, close to Den Engel, while Jane's home is Laarne, on the outskirts of Ghent.

The Simpson Grand Prix ended in the early 1970s, when Beurick fell out with the president of the supporters' club, Mr Pauwels, who wanted to rename the race after himself. The Velotel Tom Simpson closed in 1976 and was turned into a disco. It burned to the ground a few years later. Beurick is still looking for the trophies, record books and photographs he left in Den Engel when it was sold.

Ramsbottom moved back to England; Denson and his wife Vi closed their bar and did the same. Beurick went through a period of disillusionment and depression after Simpson's death. He then offered his services to Graham Webb, tipped as Simpson's successor, bringing him to Ghent and looking after him when he turned professional. After winning the 1967 amateur world championship, though, Webb failed to produce the goods; both men brought Beurick only disillusionment. Meanwhile, as the willow herb grew on the corner of derelict land between the two canals in Ghent, Daniel 'Rockefeller' Dousset enjoyed a prosperous retirement in a villa in the south of France.

Sallanches, September 6, 1964
On the rain-soaked finish straight in the heart of the French
Alps, three men are sprinting for the world championship. The
Dutchman Jan Janssen is first, in his trademark dark sunglasses
in spite of the near dark. As he raises his arms to the sky in
celebration, the Italian Vittorio Adorni and Raymond Poulidor of
France are a few bike lengths behind.

Tom Simpson is sprinting too, head down, back bent, 20 metres
behind Poulidor. As so often, he is the moral winner. He has had
cuts down his side and a bent pedal since his crash on the fourth
lap, but was the only favourite who bestirred himself to chase
what would have otherwise been the winning escape.

For 42 of the 165 miles he rode alone in the soaking wet,
gradually closing the gap, but when he rode up to the last
survivor, the Frenchman Henri Anglade, the other favourites
were close behind. Janssen, Poulidor and Adorni had saved their
energy while Simpson had exhausted himself, and they rode past
him with ease.

The Englishman knew his only chance was to try again;
painfully he escaped the bunch, and in the final straight he closed
on the three leaders. If they had hesitated even for a moment, he
would have overtaken them; instead they sprinted for the line,
and he was left hanging. So near, but so far.

This frustration is painfully familiar: in 1959, with a mere
three months' professional racing under his belt, he managed
fourth. In 1961, he was ninth. Last year, in the little Belgian
town of Renaix, he could have won if the Irishman Seamus Elliott
had cooperated when they escaped the field. Simpson had offered
£1,000 to Elliott to help him but to no avail; today he would have
given £4,000 to anyone who would help him win. There were no
takers and, once again, no medal. Next year, he tells himself, it
will be different.

CHAPTER SEVEN

'If It Takes Ten to Kill You, I'll Take Nine'

'You big-headed bastard,' was Colin Lewis's first thought when he met Tom Simpson. Lewis was an amateur in the Milk Race round Britain event in 1964; Simpson was appearing in a circuit race at the Herne Hill stage finish. Simpson's verdict on the Milkmen was typically succinct: 'They look like a bunch of old men.' Lewis was not amused. Later that year, when the pair met again, Simpson struck the amateur as 'a miserable bastard, very egotistical'.

Yet if Lewis's large personal archive of magazine articles, photographs and cuttings about Simpson is anything to go by, he has since become fascinated by the man and the contradictions he presents. His memories of Simpson are stored on 12 hours of audio tapes, the fruit of a week-long trip to a Greek island to get away from distraction and to let his mind travel back.

Lewis ended up getting closer to Simpson than most. In the two weeks he spent sharing a room with the world champion before his death on the 1967 Tour, the insights Lewis gained into Simpson's personality made him realize he had got the champion all wrong. 'I warmed to him,' says Lewis. 'I started to respect him for his attention to detail. Everything was down to a T.'

It is said of professional cyclists that their quality comes out in the way they organize life on the road. Simpson was an object lesson to Lewis, who was in his first year as a professional. Everything he did before and after each day's stage was methodical, measured, to save energy and reduce stress. After the stage finish, for example, Simpson would empty his jersey pockets onto a table in the room, and would then divide the clothing into what could be worn again and what had to be washed. Jersey and shorts were folded up and put in the suitcase. This was in contrast with the more relaxed approach of Vin Denson, with whom Lewis was initially supposed to share. No sooner had Denson turned up at the start than he was involved in some larks with a group of Italian riders, who had drilled a hole in the hotel room wall and installed a fish-eye lens to watch the activities of a couple on honeymoon. The team manager, Alec Taylor, did not feel this was the right example to set a new professional, and made Lewis room with Simpson.

Lewis was struck by Simpson's ambition. He still says that he has never met a more competitive person than the British leader. As a boss, the ex-world champion was demanding – 'but he had every right to be,' says Lewis. 'He was going for the top three, with a makeshift team. He was a star, and he expected everything to be right.' He would spend at least an hour and a half being massaged each night by his *soigneur* Gus Naessens – a red-faced, sweaty Belgian of 18 stone or more, with a deep booming laugh and poor English – who did not seem interested in Lewis, but would occasionally grunt at him. Lewis's nightly session with the team's Dutch masseur Rudi Van der Weide would take a maximum of half an hour.

As the name *domestique* implies, the relationship between star and two-wheeled helper was feudal – and still is today. Lewis had a brand-new cotton racing hat with Great Britain on it, of which he was very proud. ('I'm a hat man,' he says now. 'I love those cotton racing hats.') Riding along one day, Simpson asked him for the hat, and Lewis asked why. Simpson replied, 'I want to have a shit in it.'

There are no toilet stops on the Tour de France, so answering nature's call is an improvised affair. Simpson stopped, went behind a lorry by the roadside, did what had to be done, and the hat played its part, as hats still do to this day. As Lewis remembers the episode, with a mixture of amusement and disgust, he recalls that, to add insult to injury, he was the one who had to tow Simpson back to the bunch afterwards.

Today, Lewis is a dapper 59-year-old, as slender about the midriff as when he raced as a professional. It seems a long way from the glamour of the Tour de France to repairing punctures and adjusting gears in his small, neatly kept cycle shop off a main road in the Devon resort of Paignton. There is the usual cluttered workshop out the back, a picture on the till desk of Colin, arms in the air, winning a big bike race back in the 1970s. Next to it is a child's first bike, waiting for repair.

When I began racing in the 1980s, I would often come up against Lewis, the terror of the south-west for all that he was then in his forties. He was a man with a certain aura: he had ridden the Tour de France and was one of the Holdsworth team who had dominated professional racing in Britain in the early 1970s. Lewis was also legendary for his ferocious competitiveness. There was a story that he once knocked another rider off for not pulling his weight on a club ride.

Lewis's urge to ride his bike is still there. A couple of months before we met, Lewis competed in a mass ride through the Pyrenees following the course of a Tour de France stage over three mountain passes, and was highly placed. When we met, he showed me the start sheet for the next weekend's event, which included most of the stiffest hills on Dartmoor. Even as we talked, he was worrying about fitting in his training ride that evening.

For all the fire in his belly, Lewis is not a man who is in cycling merely for what he can get out of it. As I sit in the back of the shop, a local schoolboy in full racing kit drops in. Lewis makes him welcome, chaffs him a little, drops a couple of hints about what he should be doing. The lad doesn't buy anything, merely shoots the breeze for half an hour or so, and then rides on. He has gained his little whiff of the Tour de France, however distant, and Lewis has given it to him without a hint of unwillingness.

I had known Lewis for some 15 years from races here and there, and the diatribe he directed at me when I first called about Simpson came as a shock. Lewis did not mind me telephoning. He was not angry with me in any way, but he could not prevent the fault lines of anger, running back 34 years, coming to the surface. His vexation with the whole business had been fed by the conflict which had sprung up with Simpson's widow Helen and her husband Barry Hoban three years previously when Lewis was interviewed by David Walsh for the *Sunday Times*. He still has the letter from Helen accusing him of betraying Simpson's memory. As a result, Lewis did not know what to do when I called him. The unspoken questions were not hard to imagine. Should he talk to me and risk further conflict? Did he want to be accused of blackening Simpson's name again? Was it worth raising the old ghosts?

Like many British cyclists, Lewis had begun racing abroad with a certain degree of naivety about performance-enhancing substances. At the world championships in Sallanches in the French Alps in 1964, he had finished 16th in the amateur race and was watching the pro race when, just as things hotted up, he heard a big-name French rider yell into the pits that he wanted *la moutarde* on the next lap. 'I thought the guy wanted a mustard sandwich and couldn't work out why.' *La moutarde* is cycling slang for a bottle containing a stimulant for the end of a race.

A season spent racing in France taught Lewis a little more about the ways of the continent – he would see riders injecting themselves at the start of races, and accepted that this was part of the European game. Nevertheless, he was taken aback at the 1967 Tour when one of the first things he was asked by his *soigneur*, Van der Weide, was whether he used drugs. 'No,' said Lewis. Did he want some? asked the soigneur. 'No,' was the answer.

Lewis saw enough on that Tour, from his privileged position as Simpson's room-mate, to convince him that the British team leader was a regular, indeed a heavy, user of amphetamines. Firstly, there was one evening he and Simpson came back to the hotel room after a stage. 'It had been hardish but not terribly hard. He went into the shower first, took his jersey off and put six tablets on the table. He used to keep them wrapped in foil.

'I'm in the bed, waiting to shower, he comes out and one [tablet] has fallen on the floor. He'd lost one tablet, and was accusing me of taking it. "Where's my stuff? If you want stuff, ask me, don't steal it." We scrabbled on the floor and it was under the table. It had dropped off and rolled underneath. He was contrite about it: "I'm glad, you don't need this stuff."'

Lewis does not like talking about Simpson's doping. He talks in rapidly delivered single sentences when the subject is raised and tends to eat his words. He seems slightly annoyed – not at me for asking the question, but at the subject itself. Perhaps Lewis is even posthumously angry at Simpson for having made him face Hobson's choice: say things about the champion which people will not want to hear, or cover up for him. The whole process feels as easy as pulling rusty nails out of a board.

Other former contemporaries of Simpson's are also prepared to discuss the subject. Alan Ramsbottom, who raced with him in Ghent, recalls that while he went on the Tour de France with one suitcase, for his kit, 'Tom went on the Tour with a suitcase for his clothes and another with his stuff, drugs and recovery things.' I cross-checked with Lewis, who remembers the same thing. Ramsbottom adds: 'Tom took a lot of chances . . . He took a lot of it [drugs]. I remember him taking a course of strychnine to build up to some big event. He showed me the box, and had to take one every few days.'

Another who believed that Simpson was a regular user was the doctor who attempted to revive him, Pierre Dumas. 'Did he really go for the drugs?' the doctor was asked of Simpson. Dumas's reply is unambiguous. 'He was well known for it, like [Roger] Rivière, all those guys.'

Like Simpson, Rivière came to a tragic end: he plunged into a ravine in the 1960 Tour de France, broke his back and never competed again. Three months after Simpson's death he admitted to massive use of amphetamines – a large injection and five pills for his hour record of 1959, for example. At one point, Rivière's soigneur, André Prévost, worked with the British champion.

Vin Denson also remembers Simpson and what the world champion called his 'Mickey Finns'. 'He used to feel that he'd be fine, as long as he listened to intelligent sports doctors – and there were one or two clever sports doctors in the Gentse Wielersport [Simpson's cycling club in Ghent]. He was told to keep within the bounds, take just eight milligrams of amphetamines.'

Eight milligrams of amphetamine, a former pro with an encyclopedic knowledge of drugs and drug-taking told me, is exactly what 'a rider who was being careful would take at the end of a long race', or in the second half of a circuit race. It's a small dose, in keeping with what a medical adviser would tell a rider to use if he wanted 'not to be dead by the age of 45' as my contact put it.

My former pro added that his research indicated that up to 50 milligrams per day was more like the norm at the time. Could Simpson have used a greater quantity than Denson's 'eight milligrams'? Quite possibly, because there are two factors which have to be taken into account. Firstly, the body acquires resistance to amphetamines, meaning that as a cyclist uses them over time, the more he has to use merely to gain the same effect. It would be easy to start with eight milligrams, but not so easy to continue. Additionally, the Festina inquiry suggests that there is a natural tendency among athletes to assume that the more they take of any substance, the better they will perform, and that there is a tendency to ignore the health risks. This applies to amateurs with multivitamins as it does to professionals with drugs. Hence, if eight milligrams worked, who knew what 16 or 25 milligrams might not do?

Simpson may have thought this way, if his remark about stimulants to another source is to be believed: 'If it takes ten to kill you, I'll take nine.' Consider the obsessive way Simpson treated other ways of improving performance, such as his diet: if he believed that more raw carrot meant you were more healthy, why should he not believe the same of a stimulant?

As for where the drugs came from, Lewis discovered the source later in the 1967 Tour, when two Italians came to the door of the hotel room he was sharing with Simpson. Italy was where the riders would go to buy amphetamines. They would ride over the border after training camps in the spring on the French Riviera and buy them. Simpson had a heated discussion with the two men in Italian, which Lewis did not understand, before eventually they shook hands and the two men left.

Simpson was given a box, 'exactly *that* size', says Lewis, and draws in the air with his hands a shape about six inches long, four inches wide and three inches deep. Lewis asked what was going on. 'That's my year's supply of Mickey Finns,' said Simpson. 'That lot cost me £800.' The amphetamine found on Simpson when he died, Tonedron, was one of the more expensive varieties – 'the Rolls-Royce of amphetamines', my ex-professional told me – compared to the basic and far cheaper Benzedrine.

Eight hundred pounds in 1967 was a huge amount of money. Lewis's wage from his professional team employer at the time was just £4 a week. Peter Hill was a new professional in Simpson's team, Peugeot, and he earned four times that, £16 a week. Even so, Simpson was spending almost as much per week on his supply of 'Mickey Finns'.

Lewis is still angered by the fact that Simpson could afford to spend four times his annual salary on drugs. The episode gives the lie to the notion that all the competitors in professional races at that time were on a level playing field because they had access to the same drugs. Instead, the opposite could be argued: the more money a rider had, the more – and better – drugs he could buy.

The same principle applied to the quality of medical support a rider could purchase. All the senior riders had their personal *soigneurs*. These men were more than mere masseurs: the word comes from the French verb *soigner*, which means to 'heal', or 'look after'. Before sports doctors arrived in cycling, soigneurs would offer a mix of sound advice and old wives' remedies on training, diet, lifestyle, give massage, medical support, a sympathetic ear, and in some cases, drugs.

The term 'soigneur' was removed from official used in cycling, however, after the Festina scandal of 1998, in which the soigneur Willy Voet was arrested while carrying his team's supply of drugs to the Tour de France. The word 'soigneur' has been replaced by 'team assistant' which does not have the same resonance. They must have qualifications, but are in many cases the same men doing the same job. Yet the soigneurs in the 1960s had no formal qualifications. Vin Denson was looked after by Bernard Stoops, who was a gravedigger by profession. Van der Weide, who massaged Lewis, was a fishmonger. Raymond Poulidor's soigneur was a wizened old Italian called Leoni, who slept on the floor in the corridor outside his rider's room.

These eminences grises traded on their mystique, their

secret remedies, their little tricks handed down from generation to generation, some of which still survive. It is impossible to define how much they actually delivered, how much was common sense and basic science, and how much was trickery designed to make the cyclists feel they were in possession of something – a drug, a dietary secret, a way of training – which their fellows did not have.

When asked by the press about Simpson's form in 1967, Naessens merely imitated an aeroplane taking off with his hand. Later, he was to be Willy Voet's mentor in his chosen profession. Voet learned much of what he knew from Naessens, who he described as 'one of the demi-gods of the profession . . . having your legs in his hands was simultaneously a measure of success and celebrity.' Naessens, says Voet, would split himself in two for his riders, who he regarded as his children. 'They were his life. He lost his marriage because of the time he used to spend away at races with them.' Naessens died in 2000, and Voet says he was shocked that not one of the many cycling champions he tended turned up at the funeral.

Before Simpson won the Bordeaux–Paris single-day Classic in 1964, Naessens lived with him and Helen for a month, giving Simpson massage, watching his diet, and advising him how to train. He did the same thing for a week before Simpson's unsuccessful bid to win the world championship in Renaix, Belgium, in 1963. Naessens certainly had his own trade secrets, like all his fellows. Harry Hall recalls: 'He used to buy cattle feed and boil it like a witch's brew in the hotel kitchen, then put it in the [riders'] bottles. It was so heavy, like thick rice pudding, that when they were handed up in the bags at the feed they would break the bags.' The theory was, apparently, that this would sit in the stomach as it was absorbed, and would prevent the stomach muscles from tensing and using up energy. Pure quackery.

It is not clear how much Simpson would have paid Naessens for tips like this but Voet suggests it might have been double the wage of a normal helper and certainly beyond the reach of mere mortals. As is clear from Simpson's business dealings, he believed in investment, and Naessens was just one more – and a costly one at that.

The comprehensive level of medical back-up which Simpson acquired is strikingly visible in the 1965 BBC film 'The World of Tom Simpson'. Lying in his hotel bed during the Tour de France, Simpson points to a powdered protein supplement on the bedside table, and brandishes in front of the camera a handwritten page of notes from his doctor, listing what he has to take every day in the Tour: 'What I need in tonics and medicine to see me through.'

The notes would presumably have come from one of Simpson's two doctors, Dr Castro and Dr Vandenweghe. Castro was the medical officer of Simpson's cycling club, the Gentse Wielersport, which, as we have seen, operated as an informal support network for the English professionals in Ghent. Dr Vandenweghe was president of his supporters' club.

Simpson opens up his box of small ampoules – about the same size as the one Lewis spotted – and describes the contents: 'Vitamin B complex, liver extract, muscle fortifier – I can't tell you what it does because it's too complicated for me. I believe what the doctor tells me because it's never done me any harm.'

'Muscle fortifier' could be innocuous, or it could be 'doctor-speak' for a steroid. There was one early hormone extract, Serodose A+B, widely available in cycling from about 1962, while Decca-dorabulin, the steroid most popular in the 1970s, was on the market from 1959 and available in Ghent in the mid-1960s. At the time Simpson was speaking, neither product was banned.

In his training, Simpson could be equally sophisticated. Lewis had spent a month with him as the British team prepared for the Tour de France, accompanying Simpson to Belgian kermesse races – circuit events based on a village fair. He had noticed that Simpson did not finish a single event. He used them as training, riding to the race, racing flat out for 60 miles to get an intense workout, then riding home to build his stamina for the Tour. Over 30 years on, a top cyclist today might well do exactly the same thing.

Although Simpson was ahead of his time in some ways, he was deeply flawed in one belief. He shared the popular misconception of the time that fluid replacement during a race was not important – and dehydration was to be part of the fatal cocktail when he died. And he did believe in some old wives' tales: in a training article for *Cycling* in 1964, he advises 'the cold water sit' – placing the buttocks and crutch in a bowl of ice-cold water – and the use of cocaine ointment to toughen up the crutch. These practices are bizarre, the kind of thing that would be passed on by an old soigneur to a new professional in order to impress the ingenuous newcomer.

Simpson's urge to go to any lengths to gain a competitive edge is explicit in an interview in 1966: 'I'm prepared to try anything, even hypnotism.' His way of thinking was not that there was a single magic remedy. Instead, his approach was holistic: if changing something would make you go half a per cent faster, that might not be a great amount, but if you could find 10 ways to gain that half a per cent on the opposition, suddenly you would be five per cent ahead. That is a considerable margin.

Every area merited investigation and experiment; diet, equipment, rest, training, the use of stimulants, hiring one of the best soigneurs. All are interdependent parts of a bigger picture. Stimulants might have helped Simpson to batter himself but their use would be pointless if he did not eat the right things and get the right massage to speed his recovery. Recourse to stimulants fits into a philosophy of total war: every means available has to be used.

At some point, Simpson must have made the decision to use his 'Mickey Finns': to lose his drug virginity. Was it a grudging realization that he had no choice but to do so if he did not want to go home with his tail between his legs, or a measured, systematic embrace of an extra weapon in the armoury? Or was it the first followed by the second? His enthusiastic, near-obsessive attitude to the other aspects of his profession – diet, equipment, medical and 'soigneur' back-up – and the eyewitness accounts would indicate this to be most likely.

Two of his contemporaries, both of whom lived close to him, would concur. 'He was not unwilling [to use drugs], no way,' says Lewis, his room-mate. 'There is an acceptance – you're a pro bike rider and you do it. You're either in it, or you're out of it.' 'He went looking for it, he went looking for a way to get right to the top', says Brian Robinson, his flat-mate.

Simpson was asked by the journalist Christopher Brasher in 1960 about taking drugs. Brasher used the answer he gave, about using caffeine, in an article in the *Observer* after Simpson's death headlined 'The cyclist who had to take drugs'. His words have the tone of a man trapped between a rock and a hard place, between his competitive instinct and need for money on the one hand, and on the other the demands of a system which has no mercy on the principled underdog. 'I am up there with the stars, but then suddenly they will go away from me,' Simpson told Brasher. 'I know from the way they ride the next day that they are taking dope. I don't want to have to take it – I have too much respect for my body – but if I don't win a big event soon, I shall have to start taking it.'

Such public statements about the use of drugs from any cyclist were rare before Simpson's death. Simpson, however, was one of the few to talk about the topic. He stirred up a hornet's nest among his fellow cyclists in 1965 with one of his ghosted articles in the *People* newspaper. 'I honestly don't think much doping, in the worst sense of that word, goes on in cycling,' Simpson wrote, referring to 'doping' as in handing up bottles spiked with drugs. 'Tell me where you draw the line between dope and tonics. Even the experts can't agree on that one ...' he continued. 'I admit that I also take vitamin injections and pills ... to me they are tonics – medical aids to help my body. You can't last the pace without tonics', was the conclusion he offered.

Simpson claimed that his words in the *People*, a mixture of bluster and evasion, were taken out of context, and that he was misquoted, but they echo what he told Ludovic Kennedy in 'The World of Tom Simpson'. 'I've never taken dope. I take medical aid to help my body. There is a big difference between tonics and dope.' The words have a tragic irony about them today: the 'tonic' he took on July 13 can hardly be said to have 'helped his body'.

Vin Denson remembers Simpson justifying the use of amphetamines on medical grounds: '"To ride 280 kilometres", he said, "it's unnatural, and amphetamines towards the end are actually helping the body". He'd been told it was more harmful to the body not to have them, which I thought was a load of junk.'

To anyone who has followed cycling's drug scandals of the last few years, Simpson's words have a hollow ring. To a man, the defence of the 'EPO generation' was that when they took drugs, they were doing so merely to look after themselves because the demands of their profession were such that it was impossible to compete 'clean' and remain healthy. 'EPO is medicine,' one top professional told me in the late 1990s.

Simpson also peddled the line – both to Kennedy and to the *People* – that drug use in cycling was an invention of the drug testers and the media. 'I don't worry about the suspicious officials with their obsessive inquiries and dope tests,' he told the *People*. To Kennedy, he said: 'There's not as much of it [drug-taking] goes on in cycling as the newspapers and TV try to make out.' Kennedy asks again: is doping going on? 'I doubt it,' replies Simpson.

He would not be the first, or the last, cyclist to be economical with the truth when it came to drugs, or to feign a lack of interest in the subject. It's the point where my liking of the man has to be tempered, where the 'buts' start creeping in. I can understand Simpson's drug-taking. I cannot honestly say I would have acted differently in his position. But the lies that surround drug-taking in cycling perpetuate the problem. In this aspect, Simpson seems no different from any other guilty cyclist.

Simpson's use of amphetamines on the Ventoux cannot be seen as an isolated incident. It was not a matter of the man reaching for a lifeline on one desperate day and finding some amphetamines. Virtually everyone who has come into contact with Simpson appears to remember him mentioning drugs in a way which implied that they were an everyday matter for him. There is Lewis's 'Mickey Finns', Denson's 'eight milligrams'. Harry Hall says that the line Simpson gave him was: 'If you keep taking the sweeties, you'll be all right.' Asked about the issue, Albert Beurick always mentions a day Simpson told him he was racing 'clean', and this merely makes one wonder if this was the exception which proves the rule. Finally, there is circumstantial evidence which backs up the eyewitness accounts. At one world championship, in 1966, Simpson was seen to get in a rage with his bike when he could not lift the machine over a barrier; he threw it on the ground with a vituperative yell. Mental instability is one sign of the amphetamine user.

Jean Stablinski speaks at length and in detail of Simpson's behaviour the night after winning the world championship when they shared a hotel room: not only was Simpson unable to sleep, he got out of bed every 10 minutes to put the jersey on and ask 'Stab' – Stablinski's nickname – 'am I really world champion?' His behaviour is either understandable joy, or the classic case of the man who has taken a large amount of 'speed' and cannot 'come down'. That a touching anecdote such as Stablinski's can be interpreted like this provides a depressing reminder of the way drugs in sport colour perceptions.

Colin Lewis is in a unique position. In his final act as Simpson's domestique, he supplied the leader he clearly so admired with another ingredient which contributed to his death: a dose of brandy stolen from a bar on the run-in to the Ventoux. Lewis had got used to the constant search for water each day on the Tour. It was his job, as a domestique, and the café raid on the road from Marseille to the Ventoux only seemed different in hindsight. 'I didn't really know what I was doing, there was this big bar, other riders were grabbing bottles, the proprietor was chasing one of them, although the customers were on our side.'

Lewis grabbed a bottle of Coca Cola and four other bottles, although he did not know what they were. 'I stuffed three of them into my back pocket, and the other down the back of my neck. Out of the bar, I worked my way through the convoy and back to the peloton. Tom was my major concern and I gave him the Coca Cola, which he was really pleased about. He took a long drink and handed it to the next guy. "What else have you got?" he said. I fished in my pocket and pulled out a half-bottle of brandy which was just a quarter full. "Bloody hell" he said, "my guts are queer today, I'll have a drop of that." He drank some and threw it over the heads of the other riders into a sunflower field.'

The French magistrate's report into Simpson's death lists alcohol as one of the contributory factors, and Lewis accepts that he is responsible for giving Simpson the cognac, although the British leader made a second café stop at the foot of the climb, where he drank more alcohol. He accepts the idea that what he gave Simpson may have helped to kill him, but points out that his leader knew what he was doing. His job was to grab what he could: Simpson did not have to take the bottle off him.

As a new professional, Lewis lost his innocence in the most devastating way, going from admiration to grief in the space of two weeks. Now, he cannot resolve the contradictions with which he was presented by living alongside Simpson and coping with his death. 'I've got a lot of respect for the guy. The guy was a champion. He was destined to be a champion. He had a spirit which was unquenchable, but that spirit was his own downfall.'

Another customer has driven down from Swansea with his six-year-old son. After getting dad his bike, Lewis brings him into the workshop to point out a second-hand, scaled-down racing machine. After a few adjustments, father and son take the bike for a small test ride, and the boy returns to be told that, if he behaves, perhaps Father Christmas will oblige in due course. 'I got a load of these a few years ago, they don't make them any more and they are hard to find,' explains Lewis. 'I sell them on condition that they come back when the child grows out of them. They're unbeatable – once you get a child on them, they're hooked.' The two extremes are rubbing shoulders again. Lewis won two national championships, was one of the best cyclists Britain produced, yet he is still worried about making children ride bikes.

Faced with the satisfaction Lewis takes in planting another little acorn at the bottom of the cycling tree and the lack of cynicism it reveals in him, I feel a little ashamed at the scepticism which the spate of drug scandals of the last few years has engendered in me. In spite of all he saw and felt in 1967, Lewis has clearly not lost his faith in the physical and spiritual value of riding a bike, and racing a bike. Whatever Simpson felt he had to do to get to the top, whatever illusions Lewis and the rest of us have lost, that at least endures.

Como, Italy, October 16, 1965
The world champion is alone as he circles the banked concrete velodrome in the town alongside the great lake north of Milan. Tom Simpson is alone, with the field far behind as he savours victory in the Giro di Lombardia, the final one-day Classic of the 1965 cycling season. Alone, as his childhood hero Fausto Coppi was on each of the five times he won this 165-mile race through the mountains that surround the lake. Like the 'champion of champions', Simpson is 'un uomo solo al comando': on his own and in control. The best cyclists in the world have been powerless to follow him.

In his white jersey with the rainbow stripes around his chest, he is easy to recognize when he rides in the bunch; when the world champion makes his move, the whole peloton knows, as they knew when Simpson attacked in the previous weekend's Classic, Paris–Tours. He was easily spotted, and they all followed. The terrain is tougher today, and Simpson made his move early, with 125 miles and four mountain passes to go before the finish. His attack drew a dozen of the strongest in the field. One by one, they weakened and dropped off the pace until only the Italian Gianni Motta was left. On the little climb of San Fermo della Battaglia, nine miles from the finish, he too gave his best. It will be three minutes until the little group which is chasing Simpson comes onto the track.

The 'tifosi' packed around the track know they are witnessing history. Only one world champion has won Lombardy before, one of their own greats, Alfredo Binda, 38 years ago. Few have won it in such style. Among the crowd is Simpson's wife Helen. Five weeks ago she broke the sofa in their house in Ghent as she jumped for joy when he became world champion. She rarely sees her husband race, but today she can share in the most crushing win in his career.

CHAPTER EIGHT

The Past is a Foreign Country

A tape-recording of a dead man's voice, crackling into my ear for three hours as the French and English countryside sped past the high-speed train. A man with his own little ways of talking, a man laughing the occasional guttural chuckle, asking his companion if he had enough to drink, the clink of water jug or wine bottle on the glasses. Dr Pierre Dumas's voice was there in my ear, still living in the cassette recorder. That, however, was as close as I would ever get to knowing the Tour de France's former doctor, who fought to save Tom Simpson's life, who took a large amount of the blame for his death. But I could feel the man's humour, his relative detachment after 20 years away from cycling, even if I could barely put a face to the deep voice.

In reading an interview or watching it on television, the editing process invariably gets in the way: the writer edits the quotes, the sub-editor cleans them up again. This was different: it was eavesdropping on an uncut conversation, and, like any eavesdropper, I felt I was intruding. And it was frustrating to hear a colleague, Philippe Brunel of *L'Equipe*, doing something I wished I could do myself. Sometimes I wished Philippe had asked a different question. I would wonder why he had not pressed a point home here, not sought a specific answer there.

In every photograph of Simpson dying on the Ventoux roadside, Dumas is a central figure: stubbled face, mousy hair, his gut bulging under a black string vest, his climbing boots and running shorts spread in a variety of bizarre angles across the rocks as he crouches to blow air into the lungs of the inert cyclist.

As I trawled through back copies of cycling magazines of the time, something else struck me. There were other pictures of the doctor doing the same thing to other cyclists in 1955 and 1965. Both his posture as well as the props – oxygen mask, oxygen cylinder – he used were identical. The cyclists, Jean Malléjac and Lucien Aimar, looked the same as Simpson did – inert, comatose – and had come close to the same fate as Simpson. Dumas looked younger and thinner when tending to Malléjac, but that was the only difference. Obviously, when the doctor ran up to Simpson's body, took the pulse, and applied the oxygen mask, he had been there before. It was not a new experience for him, until he realized – within a couple of minutes – that Simpson was not going to get up.

Simpson's death could not be seen as an isolated incident: it was one of a series of collapses on mountains on the Tour during the 1960s. This one happened to end in a fatality. As the doctor responsible for the physical well-being of cyclists at the race from 1952 to 1969, Dumas was the man best placed to put the tragedy in its context. Largely forgotten by the world of cycling, Dumas gave one major interview before he died in February 2000; to Brunel, the chief cycling writer at *L'Equipe*, a cycling historian who was fascinated by the Simpson tragedy. Brunel had crossed the Atlantic from Mexico in January 1999 solely to meet the doctor, then a semi-invalid living in retirement in the outskirts of Paris.

On my behalf, Philippe had hunted high and low among the piles of cycling magazines and books in his central Paris apartment. What he had found for me were three small tapes of one conversation which connected three different aspects of the Simpson story. There was the visual evidence of men lying prone by the mountain roads, the unseen world of syringes and pills, and the official attempts to stop the cyclists from using drugs. Dumas was the missing link.

The young doctor should have been on a climbing holiday in the Alps in July 1952. He was a black belt in judo, an instructor at the ENSEP teacher training college who knew nothing of the Tour de France, and the offer of the doctor's job on the race came at short notice. He cancelled the trip and was immediately thrust into a small, enclosed world, far removed from the sprawling enterprise of today. The Tour was a rudimentary affair, a hamlet compared to today's small town: 'rustic' is the word the doctor uses continuously to describe it.

The race's intimacy meant that Dumas could quickly get to know his charges: the riders, the men who looked after them, the tiny press corps, the organizers. Medical back-up was minimal, so he was welcomed by the cyclists. Using performance-enhancing substances was not banned, so the men he looked after had no inhibitions about letting him into their secrets. 'They told me everything, because they did not have the impression that they were doing anything wrong.'

Dumas arrived in cycling close to the end of 'the witch doctor time', as he called it. This had been a period of almost complete ignorance in matters medical and physiological, in essence little changed from the years between the wars. The bike racers came from what he calls delicately 'a certain *milieu*: they were country boys, blacksmiths'. His implication is that they were poorly educated.

The men who looked after them were the soigneurs, whose 'value was in their valise', as Dumas's pun has it. Their status and income depended on the magical remedies they carried in their suitcases. These might be medicines bought for one old franc and sold on for 100 with the label scratched off. 'It was all part of the mystery,' says Dumas. Among other things, they would provide *la topette* – a small bottle containing a stimulant. The French word is still used today to mean doping. In one soigneur's case, the mix was coca, cola and quina – the active agent in quinine.

Attention to hygiene was minimal: Dumas saw riders 'injecting each other with syringes which had just been used by a friend, with dirty hands'. Saddle sores on the crutch were common owing to dirt from the roads and the lack of basic hygiene; they led to a condition which Dumas called 'the third testicle', a large swelling caused by infection of the perineum. Training was rudimentary: if one cyclist had ridden 5,000 kilometres before a race, he was felt to be better prepared than a colleague who had covered a thousand fewer. Diet came down to volume as well and, as a result, the cyclists ate like weightlifters. Dumas would watch the Tour men consuming 20 hard-boiled eggs at a sitting. The more fuel in the machine, the better. There was no understanding of how the body consumed energy. To combat hypoglycaemia, in French cycling slang *la fringale*, a kilo of sugar or honey might be consumed at a time.

As for stimulants, 'the cyclists took everything they were offered,' says Dumas. 'It didn't matter what they took, as long as they believed in it.' In the suitcases and on hotel room tables were numerous arrays of flasks, boxes of pills, suppositories, ampoules and syringes. Dumas's charges took extract of bee's or toad's venom, which were popular cures for rheumatism; pure cola, which was a remedy dating back to the 1900s; and ether, which could be smelt from 60 feet away. Each had his own remedies: Jean Stablinski, for example, would take two egg yolks in a glass of port.

Shortly after Dumas's arrival at the Tour de France, the philosophy, and, as a consequence, the drugs, gradually began to change, as the cyclists and their advisers became better educated. As the doctor puts it: 'Then we came to a more civilised period, when they began to read the *Vidal* [a popular medical directory]. They began to think about the problem, as well as using the information which was handed down.'

Then followed what Dumas calls 'the semi-scientific period, roughly speaking Jacques Anquetil's time'. Anquetil raced from 1955 to 1969: Simpson's career fell within those years. This was a period of transition, when basic medical information was becoming widely available, but its application to cycling was still empirical, and the old philosophy of 'the more the better' was still followed. Simpson, with his thirst for knowledge and his drive for the latest remedies, fits into this picture. In place of the witch doctors' brews came what Dumas terms 'the Anquetil cocktail': painkiller, stimulant, sleeping pill. Morphine or palfium, which was given to terminal cancer patients to ease their agony, was injected into the riders' legs to deaden the muscle pain.

'During the race?' asks an incredulous Brunel. 'Oh! *Enormément*,' comes the deadpan answer. Brunel cannot believe what he is hearing: 'You saw them inject themselves in front of you?' Dumas doesn't see the question as shocking, doesn't take Brunel's surprise on board. 'They weren't embarrassed,' maintains the doctor, who would have witnessed it from his car or the motorbike he sometimes used, immediately behind the bunch. And there were no rules to prevent it.

The opiates deadened leg pains, but they slowed the rest of the system down: a stimulant was needed in order to counteract this. It was usually amphetamine, produced in vast quantities during the Second World War to keep the Armed Forces awake during operations – 72 million for the RAF, for example – and used in slimming pills by the 1950s and 1960s. Caffeine, in tablets and suppositories, was also used.

The stimulant's effects might last long after the stage finish, which meant that sleep was often impossible; hence the sleeping pill, usually Gardenal. And there were the 'lung-openers', such as Solucamphre, injected to improve the breathing. There were no rules against this, and no stigma about the issue, so drugs could be used in quantity.

During one Tour, Dumas intercepted a package addressed to one well-known soigneur, Julien Schramm, who worked with Anquetil. It contained 50 ampoules of 20cc of the popular amphetamine Tonedron, known universally as 'Tonton'. (Its twin sister, Pervitin, is 'Tintin'.)

Schramm told Dumas the capsules were for his personal consumption – ironically, the same defence Willy Voet would use 30 years later when he was stopped by customs at the start of the Festina affair. 'I offered to inject him myself,' says Dumas. 'He refused, and I said, "You're a little shit you are: it's OK for the other guys, but not for you." '

Among the cyclists, there was, Dumas maintains, little awareness of the potential risks of doping. 'If someone won a stage using a certain product, they all wanted it. They had no idea what they were doing. It was like when someone has a toothache and their neighbour says "Ah, I've got this medicine in my cupboard, some of that will make you better." ' Ignorance, the desire to finish the race, and the need for cash overrode any appeals for caution or inner doubts.

The young doctor's medical skills were put to the test in ways which now seem completely sickening. If one of Dumas's charges had a serious crash and had to be taken to hospital, he would have to find the soigneur before the cyclist could be treated. It was necessary to find out what drugs the patient already had in his system, to avoid overdoses and bad reactions. 'It was OK as long as the cyclist was conscious and could tell me; if he was in a coma we would have to work out the dosages ourselves.'

As a smattering of badly applied science entered the minds and methods of the Tourmen, Dumas soon developed the feeling that he had no control over what they did. In 1960, he found the race winner Gastone Nencini lying in his bed with a drip infusing primitive hormones into both arms – and smoking a cigarette. He had a similar shock in 1962 on the day after Simpson lost the yellow jersey at

Superbagnères in the Pyrenees, when 20 riders fell ill in an epidemic known as 'the rotten fish affair'. The mass infection was blamed on eating bad fish; Dumas realized that this was not a credible explanation, and put it down to a single soigneur giving all the riders a drug which had affected their health. On the tape, Dumas's reaction to the practices he saw leaves nothing to the imagination: 'I was horrified. All this stuff scared me shitless.'

This is the world in which Simpson arrived as a new professional in 1959. In English racing, by and large, drug-taking did not happen. The financial rewards to make it worthwhile were not there; there was no culture of soigneurs with magic remedies; there was a history of Corinthian amateurism in the sport. All Simpson's English contemporaries speak of seeing drug-taking going on when they arrived in Europe, and being shocked by it. 'It was a big jolt, seeing it right in front of you,' says Arthur Metcalfe. 'Living in England you didn't hear much about it. You would hear rumours of lads who were taking stuff, but you never saw anything, you didn't actually discuss it.' He adds: 'I remember a criterium in Belgium, when we were all lined up at the start and the police drove up. I can remember the sound now: *click, click, click, click*, all the pills dropping onto the ground.

Jean Malléjac was the doctor's first big scare. The Breton collapsed by the roadside on the lower slopes of Mont Ventoux on an afternoon of searing heat in 1955. 'It chilled my blood,' says Dumas. The cyclist remained unconscious for a quarter of an hour, laid out on a blanket on the rocks. Dumas had to prise his jaws apart to save him. He gave him oxygen and injected the stimulant solucamphre to restart his heart. At last he came to in what Dumas described as 'a state of delirium tremens'.

Placed in the race ambulance to be taken to hospital,

Malléjac 'talked, waved his arms, yelled, asked the way to the finish, and wanted to be let out', reported the newspaper *L'Equipe* the next day, adding blandly that he had had to be tied down for his own safety. According to one account, Dumas had to use his skills as a judo black belt to pacify the cyclist.

The Tour organizers empowered Dumas to open an inquiry and issued a statement calling upon teams, their managers and their soigneurs to avoid 'the use of certain products issued without prescriptions'. The only outcome was that a soigneur who worked for Malléjac's trade team, Terrot, was requested to leave the race, although the organizers were unwilling to link this to the incident. All Dumas could do was express his concerns and hope that persuasion might work. The men who ran the race preferred to push the issue under the carpet.

Just two years before Simpson's death came the clearest warning signal of all – events on a baking hot afternoon during July 1965 on the Aubisque pass, in the Pyrénées. André Bayssière and Charles Grosskost, two of the riders in the Tour de l'Avenir, the amateur race run alongside the Tour de France on a shorter course, fell by the wayside. In the Tour itself, the rider who was to win in 1966, Lucien Aimar, and his Dutch teammate, Arie Den Hartog, did precisely the same thing.

In each case, the sequence of events was the same as it had been with Malléjac and would be with Simpson: the riders were climbing strongly when they lost control, zigzagged across the road, and then collapsed unconscious in the gutter. With Aimar, there was a surreal note: he had begun walking up the mountain pushing his bike once he was unable to ride – and he dropped his bike shortly before he fell. The key development was that both Grosskost and Bayssière admitted using amphetamines – Aimar did not and none were found on him. Dumas, reportedly outraged by the whole episode, had examined Grosskost and Bays-sière's baggage, and said, 'As far as I'm concerned, this isn't funny any more.' The use of drugs had become illegal on June 1 that year, so there were consequences: the two cyclists were given bans.

It is still part of the game for professional cyclists to reach their physical limit in the mountains: drugs do not have to play a part. But physical collapse is rare. The image of Stephen Roche being given oxygen after a stage finish in the 1987 Tour is familiar to most cycling fans; I remember the Italian domestique Giovanni Fidanza being put under the mask after a desperate battle to make the day's cut in 1994. Eddy Merckx and fellow Belgian Martin van den Bossche had the same treatment on the Ventoux in 1970. But these were precautionary measures: Roche and Fidanza never lost consciousness.

Given what he had seen, and his feelings on doping, it was no surprise that on the morning before Simpson died, Dumas should have a premonition of what might occur. This is according to the veteran journalist Pierre Chany, who met the doctor at about seven in the morning near Marseille's main street, the Cannebière. 'The air was warm already. We exchanged a few words and he [Dumas] said something to me which I'll never forget: "The heat will be terrible today. If the guys start to play about with dope we're liable to have a death on our hands."'

There was a context in which recourse to stimulants, for all that it was reprehensible and dangerous, was entirely understandable. Merely consider the demands placed on the cyclists by race organizers in the 1960s. Here too, cycling was on the cusp between antiquity and modernity: the sport still harked back to the pre-war years, when superhuman feats over superhuman distances were the norm. The longest stage in the 1967 Tour de France covered 225 miles, from Clermont Ferrand to Fontaine-bleu, lasting 11 hours and starting at 7.40 a.m. – at the end of three weeks in the saddle. The following day there were two stages totalling 95 miles. When Simpson's teammate Arthur Metcalfe finished that year's race, he was 'like a skeleton', he says, with his blood pressure so low that he would black out whenever he stood up.

It was not just the Tour de France which placed extreme demands on the riders: the Bordeaux–Paris one-day Classic, which Simpson won in 1963, was 348 miles, mostly paced behind small motorbikes at high speed, starting at around two in the morning and finishing some 14 hours later. The Corona London to Holyhead one-day race was 270 miles, covered when Simpson won in 1965 at an average of 26 mph and after 11 hours in the saddle. Today, the maximum permitted distance for professionals has been cut to a more reasonable, but still daunting, 175 miles.

The 1967 Tour de France in which Simpson died was 3,000 miles long, one of the longest in the post-war years, and the Tour organizer Jacques Goddet later said that Simpson's death came as a message to him to make the race shorter. The following year it was reduced by 200 miles, and the Tour would never again reach such distances. In fact, it would rarely break the 2,500-mile mark for the next 20 years. The total distance of the 2002 Tour is exactly 1,000 miles less than in 1967.

The spectacle of cyclists driving themselves to their physical limits and beyond, for entertainment and profit, creates a moral dilemma both for the race organizers, who devise the route, and for the journalists. They can simulta-neously admire the men's courage and yet wonder if the human cost can be justified. Goddet was both organizer and reporter: in his editorial in *L'Equipe*, he describes the Aubisque stage as 'a fabulous day', and waxes lyrical about the 'pitiless cruelty of cycling, a sport of total effort'. A dozen years earlier, he had described the near-tragedy involving Malléjac, which ended the careers of at least two other riders, in a similar eulogy.

It would be too strong simply to say that the Tour organizers at the newspapers *L'Equipe* and *Le Parisien* were blind to the risks simply because of the copy that such spectacles made; Goddet had become aware of the doping problem as early as 1931, when he wrote in the newspaper *L'Auto*, 'the riders are addicted to poison'. He told the journalist Pierre Chany of his worries about the issue as early as 1951. The organizers were, however, prepared to take the chance and Goddet admitted later that Simpson's death 'posed a grave ethical problem and he felt guilty'.

The Tour had been founded in 1903 in order to make headlines and sell newspapers by turning the participants into supermen who managed feats beyond mere mortals. That was no longer the overt message, as it had been in 1903, but Goddet and Levitan were still at the same time creating the Tour route and profiting from the headlines and sales the superhuman feats in the race brought to their papers. Nowadays, that would be seen as a conflict of interest.

However, the problem was not simply the matter of races over inhumanly long distances. The duration of an event does not cause doping. Athletes still feel the need to take drugs to win a 100-metre sprint lasting 10 seconds. Even when the Tour was a relatively benign 2,000 miles in 1988 and 1989, there were still positive drug tests.

The volume of racing was equally important. The nature of professional cycling at the time, dominated as it was by agents such as Daniel Dousset and Roger Piel, meant that the more often a cyclist raced, the more he earned, as long as he performed. There was little incentive to save energy and prepare carefully for a single objective. Doping was an inevitable consequence of the combination of miles spent in the saddle racing and miles spent at the car wheel between races. This was acknowledged by a group of cyclists approached by Dumas for a random test at a track meeting in 1969. They refused on the grounds that they had used amphetamines to keep them awake while driving, and would test positive – unfairly, they claimed, as there was no law against 'speeding' in a car.

One of the greatest Belgian cyclists ever, Rik Van Steenbergen, wrote in a newspaper article in 1967: 'I've had to drive to Paris, then immediately after the race get back in my car for a 10-hour trip to Stuttgart where I had to get on my bike at once. There was nothing to do. An organizer would want this star or that one on the bill. He would pay for it. Another would want the same ones the next day, and the public wanted something for its money. As a result, the stars had to look fresh in every race, and they couldn't do that without stimulants. There are no supermen. Doping is necessary in cycling.'

Jacques Anquetil summed up the situation perfectly when he said: 'You would have to be an imbecile or a crook to imagine that a professional cyclist who races for 235 days a year can hold the pace without stimulants.' Rudi Altig made the point more simply: 'We are not sportsmen, we are professionals.'

Dumas was the man who found the little tubes in which Simpson had kept the amphetamines he took during the stage. That is common knowledge. What the tapes reveal for the first time is when he found them: at the start of the desperate attempt to revive Simpson. 'I began coming across them as we undressed him to give him cardiac massage, and said to myself, "There you are."'

A photograph taken on the day shows the unconscious cyclist lying there with his white Union Jack jersey pulled up above his waist, revealing the braces he wore to keep his shorts up. The picture Dumas's sentence evokes is devastating in its clarity: the doctor rolls the jersey up the inert torso, feels the pillboxes through the woollen material of the pockets in the back and thinks, 'Oh right, I know what these mean.'

Dumas does not sound surprised that he found the drugs. He had seen Simpson drive himself into the ground before. He had watched from his car Simpson's vain fight to continue in the Tour the previous year in spite of an appalling open wound in his arm. He knew that the rider used stimulants. He was clearly fond of the British leader but that did not mean he was blind. 'We were very good friends. He told me everything. He'd told me himself that he was taken to hospital during the Tour of Spain [three months earlier]. I'd been obliged to hospitalise him after the finish of a stage of the Tour, a time trial two or three years earlier. He generally recovered very quickly.' The word 'generally' is the giveaway here: this was a regular occurrence as far as Dumas was concerned.

At the hospital in Avignon that evening, the doctor took the three tubes out of Simpson's jersey and passed them to the head of the Tour's detachment of *gendarmes*. One tube was labelled Tonedron, the others unlabelled. One was half-full, the others empty. He showed them to the race organizer, Jacques Goddet, who spoke of seeing 'little tubes of explosive products, and all empty'. This lends a new weight to Goddet's editorial in *L'Equipe* the next day about the tragedy. 'We had already wondered if this athlete, who when under pressure had a painful look, did not make mistakes in looking after himself . . . Doping? We can fear the public revelation of a tragedy caused by this scourge.' Goddet knew for certain when he wrote this that Simpson had indeed used drugs. He was effectively preparing public minds for the scandal that would follow.

The gendarmes placed the little tubes under lock and key, and Dumas set off the process of interrogations, medical expert's autopsy and judicial inquiry which was to result in the 'Simpson affair'. 'I said to myself that it wasn't natural that an athlete in his prime should die in this way, so I refused permission for burial.'

Dumas could have ignored the tubes. He could have failed to put two and two together. He could have thrown them away. He might have done, had he felt that Simpson had a right to privacy in death, or had he considered that the rider's drug-taking was not an issue; or, perhaps, if he had not had several hours since he came across the drugs in which to reflect, at least briefly, on what steps to take. Had he acted differently, Simpson's death might have been quietly forgotten like the near-tragedies that had preceded it.

The moment Dumas refused interment was the moment when the Simpson tragedy took on a different dimension. Once Dumas decided to set the investigation in motion, the tragedy merged into the wider history of drug-taking in cycling and in sport in general. In this context, it came at a key moment: the mid to late 1960s were a time of increasing awareness and debate about the issue, with a new willingness among the press to recognize the problem, and a new readiness among the authorities to fight against it.

Dumas played a key role here as well. In 1960, after coming across Nencini and his drips, he had gathered team doctors on the Tour de France to discuss the topic. The Tour doctor spoke at another conference, a Europe-wide one, in the Alpine resort of Uriage-les-Bains, in 1963, held by the French sports ministry to define the problem and ways of combating it.

A year earlier, cycling's international governing body, the Union Cycliste Internationale, had thrown out a motion from the Polish Federation to make the UCI responsible for combating doping. Measures against the use of drugs in cycling, when they came, were led by police in Italy, Belgium, Switzerland and France. They treated action against sportsmen as an extension of their operations against drug traffickers and behaved accordingly. The sports federations followed, empowered by new laws, such as the one passed by 356 votes to 0 in the French national assembly at the end of 1964, and ratified on June 1, 1965. It prohibited 'the deliberate use of any substance designed to enhance artificially the physical capability of a sportsman where the substance is known to be harmful to health'. There would be fines from £35 to £350, and prison sentences of one month to one year. Amphetamines, such as Simpson and the other cyclists used, were banned by this law.

Early anti-drug operations at cycle races were crude, did nothing to make cyclists feel well-disposed towards their imposition, and lacked any credibility. In April 1965, for example, 'medical examinations' were carried out at the Het Volk one-day race in Simpson's home town of Ghent. All roads into the city were sealed by police, all cars involved with the race were searched. The first five finishers were tested, apart from two who 'did not understand the situation'. It was a farce: a vast show of strength which had been easily subverted.

The mix of attempted coercion and official laxity continued through 1966. At Royan in the Tour de France, Dumas accompanied gendarmes as they carried out the first drug tests on the race. They checked pulse rates, looked for needle marks on riders' arms, and took urine samples. The riders went on strike, marching down the road for 200 metres the next day shouting, among other things, 'Piss yourself, Dumas!' But six men, among them the cyclist who finished sixth overall, Herman Van Springel, tested positive for amphetamine and its derivatives. It took over a year for the legal process to result in Van Springel being fined.

Jacques Anquetil, by then a five-times winner of the Tour, and the biggest star that cycling had ever seen, summed up the feelings of the Tour men: 'We find these tests degrading. Why do cyclists have to be suspected and controlled while any other free man can do what he likes and take what he likes?' The sentiment that cyclists are unfairly penalised by those who would prevent them 'looking after themselves' is one that persists to this day.

Anquetil's denunciation was countered by Levitan in his editorial in *Le Parisien*: 'Was this a revolt? No, it was an admission. An admission of concern about the test and its consequences. An admission of inability to move away from suspicious practices. An admission that minds are troubled by the determination of the authorities.'

There are claims that Simpson, the world champion at the time, did not participate in the strike. In his biography *Mr Tom*, his nephew Chris Sidwells writes: 'Tom made a point of not getting off his bike. He was one of the few who rode the infamous 200 metres.' Simpson's behaviour during the episode is a central part of Sidwells' argument that he did not willingly use drugs and supported the authorities, but it is by no means clear what Simpson's feelings were.

In his book *Doping: Cycling Supermen*, the journalist Roger Bastide suggests the opposite. Simpson was merely the first to break ranks: 'After three minutes Tom Simpson got back on his bike and provoked a furious breakaway.' Pierre Chany wrote that Simpson criticised the strike only because it raised the profile of the issue.

The conflict between testers and tested came to a head at the 1966 world championship in the Nurburgring in Germany, where the first six finishers refused to give urine samples. This was not uncommon: both Jacques Anquetil and Rudi Altig had refused tests in Belgium in the spring, and had forfeited wins in the Liège–Bastogne–Liège and Flèche Wallonne classics as a result. Anquetil and Altig, that year's world champion, and the runner-up to Simpson the previous year, were among the Nurburgring six, along with four of the biggest names in cycling: Gianni Motta,

oureur

SPORTING
CYCLIST

APRIL 1960

TOM SIMPSON

and

Jean-Claude

TWO SHILLINGS AND SIXPENCE

At home in Saint Brieuc, in spring 1960 with Jean-Claude Murphy, whose parents were Simpson's hosts on his arrival from England. The photograph was taken by his close friend, *Sporting Cyclist*'s editor, the late Jock Wadley.

Tour de France 1961, and the British team rides to the start in Rouen: Simpson and his boyhood rival Pete Ryalls have a good look at the photographer.

A rare moment at home with Jane, Joanne and Helen, with a world title to savour in November 1965.

Champions on the grass: Simpson, Jacques Anquetil, Rudi Altig and Eddy Merckx in the track centre at the Piste Municipale, Vincennes, France.

A little light music with the locals early in the 1966 Tour. There were no smiles by the end of the race, following a lisastrous crash in the Alps.

High on Mont Ventoux, the Simpson memorial is always covered with souvenirs – on the right of the statue is a plaque left by his daughters when they rode up the mountain on the 30th anniversary of his death.

Raymond Poulidor, Italo Zilioli and Jean Stablinski, who was world champion in 1961. Stablinski says the strike was over the procedure of the test: there was apparently no doctor present. Poulidor, hilariously, had apparently got lost trying to find where he was to be tested.

What followed was farcical. Stablinski was banned for two months, Poulidor for one month, but the suspensions lasted all of 10 days before the UCI Congress cleared the cyclists. There were no penalties, and the top three finishers retained their medals. It can only have left the cyclists with the impression that the cycling authorities were not consistently prepared to take serious measures against the biggest stars if they refused tests; and that race organizers who wanted the stars at their races would come down on their side.

It was total incoherence, a fist of cotton wool in an iron glove with no coordination of measures or penalties between countries. Anquetil's fate after the Grand Prix des Nations time trial that October can only have confirmed the impression. 'Master Jacques' was the most outspoken of all the top cyclists in his opposition to the tests and told the press: 'We have to take stimulants for such a race. Yes, I have taken stimulants today.' He was fined 2,000 francs, but did not receive a ban as 'a gesture of mercy to the cyclist and his comrades'. This was due to 'the great honour bestowed on international cycle sport, to wit his [Anquetil's] Légion d'honneur'. He was saved by the gong.

It is only fair to Simpson to speculate on the effect this climate would have had on him at the time he died. By July 13, 1967, the use of drugs had been banned for two years. Amphetamine use was illegal. Drug tests were being carried out, but not in a way which lent the process the slightest credibility. The sport was in a state of flux. The most senior cyclists of the day, Simpson's peers and friends, were actively contesting the imposition of drug testing. The arguments for the use of drugs were being at least as strongly put as the arguments against. It was not clear by any means whether the economic weight of the senior riders and promoters would be overruled by the punitive powers of the authorities.

It was not set in stone that if a cyclist like Simpson won a race while using drugs he would be tested, or that he would be punished if he refused a test. Dumas had warned riders and managers before the start of the 1966 Tour that measures would be taken, but the world championship strike had left the issue hanging. If Simpson had become a regular user of amphetamines before the day he died, as seems highly likely, what incentives were there for him to give up the practice?

'Dear Tom Simpson,' wrote Jacques Goddet in his editorial the evening before the start of the 1968 Tour de France, 'You will not have fallen in vain on the stony desert of the Ventoux. Doping is no longer a mysterious sickness, hidden, uncontrollable, uncontrolled. For it really seems that there is a common determination among the riders to be rid of this scourge.' Sadly, Goddet was wrong: drug-taking in cycling did not cease from the moment Simpson died. There would be a major drug scandal on the Tour roughly every 10 years after, and a constant low-level flow of positive drug tests. What changed was the official attitude to combating the practice.

A month to the day after the Simpson tragedy, Désiré Letort was found positive after winning the French national championships, having taken an amphetamine-based product. A campaign was mounted to have the decision overturned. Delegations from his home region of Brittany lobbied the French Cycling Federation but the gold medal was simply not awarded.

Anquetil remained the most virulent critic of the movement, calling the anti-doping law 'an idiocy' in a Sunday newspaper shortly after Simpson's death. He again tried official will power in September that year, in refusing a test immediately after setting a new hour record in Milan and delivering a sample 48 hours later, by which time it was a meaningless exercise. He and his manager Raphael Geminiani – the same Geminiani who was to be one of Dr Dumas's fiercest critics – had a furious argument with the doctor conducting the test, and came close to throwing the medic out of the track. But the cycling authorities stood firm: Geminiani was fined, the record was never ratified. The same policy was followed when the track rider Pierre Trentin 'broke' the 500m world record, without a test.

As well as the new official line, Simpson's death came in a period when dirty two-wheeled linen was washed in public with a readiness which would only be matched 30 years later after the Festina scandal of 1998. There were Anquetil's revelations, followed by the confession of Roger Rivière – 'I took drugs' – across seven columns of a daily newspaper. There were the six positive tests out of 30 samples from the Tour de l'Avenir – a 'contagion', wrote *L'Equipe*. There was the string of positive tests at the world championships, and there was the death of an obscure Belgian, Roger de Wilde, in a kermesse. In normal circumstances this would have attracted little comment, but de Wilde died of a heart attack brought on by the use of amphetamines. To lose one cyclist in this way looked like bad luck; to lose two smacked of carelessness.

In late November, the UCI Congress passed new international penalties for doping – a one-month suspension for a first offence, life for a fourth. This may sound lenient in contrast with today's sanctions, but the Simpson affair had provided the impetus for a key development: consistent rules across the world.

The cycling world which gathered in the sedate little spa of Vittel for the Tour of 1968 was changed for ever, according to Dumas, who notes that the tragedy had, in the most brutal manner possible, made the organizers and the cyclists themselves aware of the potential for disaster. 'Firstly, they knew what they did wasn't good; secondly, they had never weighed up the risks before.' The 1968 Tour was billed as the 'Tour *de Santé*' (the Health Tour) – something which would also find echoes 30 years later when the first post-Festina Tour was sold as the 'Tour of Renewal'. The 'Tour *de Santé*' was more than a mere label. 'The Tour of 1968 established certain principles,' wrote Geoffrey Nicholson eight years later in *The Great Bike Race*. 'If a rider took dope he might be caught. If he was caught he would be punished. And if he was punished he could expect no intervention from his fellow professionals.' One Simpson legacy, then, is the little caravan at bike race finishes bearing the words '*contrôle anti-dopage*'.

When I met Jean Stablinski to discuss Simpson, we talked about the effect his friend's death had on the discussions of the time about doping. Stablinski felt slightly aggrieved that Simpson's death had been exploited by the proponents of dope testing, who included Dumas, *Monsieur Anti-doping*, to the peloton. They had, felt 'Stab', used Tom's tragedy as a vehicle to promote their case. It should, perhaps, be seen the other way round. It is hard to conceive how else the man to whom I listened on the scratchy tape on the Eurostar would have felt. Dumas had saved two of Simpson's fellows *in extremis*, and he then put his fingers on the pillboxes even as he tried to bring Simpson back to life. The doctor already felt that doping was a phenomenon he could not control, which endangered the lives of the men he had to look after: here was living, or rather dying, proof of what he had feared for 12 years.

More than three decades after Simpson died, the notion that performance-enhancing drugs can be a health aid is still doing the rounds in cycling. Since Simpson's death, however, it has been impossible to put the theory forward with any credibility. Any moral argument for the use of banned drugs died on the Ventoux on July 13, 1967.

The Past is a Foreign Country

Col de Montgenèvre, July 8, 1966
The pain is too much for the world champion. The bunch is not climbing fast, but the riders have left him behind early on the steady Alpine ascent which divides France from Italy. Simpson's right elbow is heavily bandaged, thick padding and gauze over the deep gash with its five stitches.

Last night, after his crash as he chased the leaders at 50 miles per hour down the hairpins of the Col du Galibier, he was close to collapse with the effort and loss of blood. Yesterday, he was trying to win the Tour de France; today he has to survive. Turin lies on the other side of the mountain. There the Tour will rest for a day. He can recover. Perhaps win a stage later in the race.

But he did not sleep last night. His legs cannot turn the pedals quickly enough. He cannot use his arm to pull on the bars to help the legs. He is lopsided on the bike, no strength in his right hand. The mechanic has put padding on the handlebars, but each bump in the tarmac jars the wound. Behind him the photographers gather on their motorbikes: the world champion quitting will be a good picture. The doctor, Pierre Dumas, watches impassively through his Ray Bans, sitting on the car door with one leg dangling in the road as they grind upwards. 'Tom,' he says gently as they approach the summit, 'will you be able to pull on the brakes on the descent?'

Simpson nods slowly, but three miles down towards Italy he pulls to a halt by the roadside and waits for the ambulance. He cannot hold the brake lever. He cannot descend in safety or at speed. He cannot go on. He weeps. This is not a fitting way for a world champion to leave the Tour de France. A journalist asks: 'What will you do now?' The answer comes in halting phrases, his voice dull. 'I don't know. I'm heartbroken. My season is ruined.' There is a pause, then he adds: 'I know I will start again though. You always start again. That's your job.'

CHAPTER NINE

'It is Not Natural'

When it came to working out why Tom Simpson died, I faced a dilemma. 'My' Tom had begun life as a set of racing results, some black and white images, and a strip of cine film showing a man wobbling up a hill and dying. Over time, with each fresh or rediscovered clue, he became far more tangible and three-dimensional. Every so often I would feel a connection with the man, his life and his mind: the smutty postcard he sent to George Shaw from training camp, the little diet book in the Hobans' kitchen, the race number in Harry Hall's study, the waste ground on the canal corner in Ghent which he never managed to build on, the pranks he played as a schoolboy.

I began to understand his sense of humour, some of his likes and dislikes, and could imagine the kind of person he must have been. He became stressed when the pressure was on between races. He loved to drive too fast. He had wild dreams, firm ambitions and dirty thoughts. He liked to talk. Life at his home revolved around catering for his thirst for success.

There seemed to be a bit of every cyclist I have known in the man. The wheeler-dealer with an eye for a bit of extra cash here and there. The cyclist who would custom-build bits for his bike. The expat professional at the top of his game who would go out on club runs with the lads when he visited home. The Jack the Lad with an eye for a pretty girl and a way with a joke. The top dog with the vicious sense of humour. The cyclist who took drugs because that was the way of cycling. The driven competitor who would never admit defeat. The teenager who was the apple of his mother's eye. The planner who was constantly pondering his next move and the four or five after that.

I could also find little bits of myself in Simpson's story. None of the distinguished parts struck a chord but the homesickness in France and the teenage ambition certainly did, as did the Geordie accent of his parents, who sounded like my grandparents. He had been dead for almost 35 years, but I ended up liking him and laughing with him. This did not make it particularly easy or palatable to turn myself into an amateur pathologist. Tom would be reduced to an imaginary corpse on the slab, with a set of symptoms which needed to be explained. But it had to be done, because of the ambiguities and unanswered questions which stem from his death.

The first issue was Albert Beurick's assertion at the film show that Simpson received the wrong treatment from Dr Pierre Dumas and his colleagues, an accusation which I'd seen repeated elsewhere. There had also been the allegation that Harry Hall and Alec Taylor effectively killed Simpson by putting him back on his bike. And there were, and still are, the claims from members of the cycling community that Simpson's death had nothing to do with amphetamines.

The starting point had to be the brief report into Simpson's death released by the autopsy team on August 4, 1967. 'Death was due to a cardiac collapse which may be put down to exhaustion, in which unfavourable weather conditions, an excessive workload, and the use of medicines of the type discovered on the victim may have played a part.' The report continues: 'The dose of amphetamine ingested by Simpson could not have led to his death on its own; but on the other hand it could have led him to go beyond the limit of his strength and thus bring on the appearance of certain troubles linked to his exhaustion.'

Behind the French legal jargon is a simple enough statement: Simpson died on July 13, 1967, because he rode up a mountain on one of the hottest days of the summer under the influence of amphetamines. That would seem self-evident, but it is all that most people have had to go on for more than three decades. The inquest was closed on September 3, 1968, with a *non-lieu*: there was no case to be answered by any of the people involved. The full report seems to be lost in a miasma of French bureaucracy.

Simpson's dying actually began during the first Alpine stage three days before his collapse. Here he showed the first signs of gastric trouble, when Harry Hall had to clean his diarrhoea-spattered bike and when Colin Lewis and Vin Denson had to try to make him eat. Vomiting and diarrhoea involve considerable fluid loss from the body, causing the depletion of vital electrolytes – potassium and sodium for example – which assist the body in functioning normally. Potassium deficiency, in particular, has been linked to heart dysfunction – something which I will discuss later. The only cure is rest, accompanied by regular intake of fluids and minerals to restore the balance.

Rest has never been available in any great quantity on the Tour and, in the 1960s, liquid replacement was at a primitive stage. In Simpson's day, dehydration was common among the cyclists, who were not even permitted to take on bottles of water from the support cars driving behind the race, because the organizers were worried that they might take illicit tows. The cyclists would start the stage with two small bottles – *bidons* – carried on their bikes, and they would get another two with the feed bag, the *musette*, which was handed up midway through. Otherwise they had to rely on kindly fans at the roadside bearing hoses, quick visits to roadside fountains, and bar raids of the kind in which Colin Lewis and Simpson himself stole brandy on that fateful day. Barry Hoban, for example, would finish stages of the Tour feeling 'as if he'd just ridden across the desert' and would see his fellows pouring down bottle after bottle of the free Perrier at stage finishes.

As we have seen, Simpson had a habit of running out of steam close to the end of races. He himself put this down to what the French call *la fringale* and English cyclists call 'the bonk': hypoglycaemia due to failure to eat sufficient food during the race. It is just as likely to have been dehydration or heat exhaustion: the symptoms he describes – dizziness, physical weakness, nausea, mental confusion – can be caused by either.

Among professional cyclists in the 1960s, there was a widely held belief that drinking too much water was damaging. For example, it was recommended that cyclists train in hot weather without drinking water, and that they should take salt fish with them to condition their bodies to working without water in the heat. At the training camp Simpson held for British amateurs in Belgium in April 1962, the top Belgian trainer George Ronsse offered the following advice: 'Avoid drinking when racing, especially in hot weather. Drink as little as possible, and with the liquid not too cold. It is only a question of will power. When you drink too much you will perspire, and you will lose your strength.' Simpson had received similar advice from George Berger back in 1958.

Brian Robinson recalls his team manager limiting him to 'four small bottles for a long stage [of the Tour], it was frowned upon to drink more'. Nowadays, it is recognized that staving off dehydration is vital if heat exhaustion is to be avoided: eight or ten small bottles during a stage would be the norm for a Tour cyclist, together with 'pre-loading' – an increased intake of fluid before the start.

Simpson's stomach trouble continued as far as the Ventoux stage – he had bouts of diarrhoea the night before – and he must already have been dehydrated when he arrived at the mountain after five and a half hours on his bike in the heat of Provence. If, as Jean Stablinski maintains, he had been advised by his soigneur to put pure carrot juice in his bottles, that would not have helped matters: carrot juice is high in vitamins, but is too concentrated to offer much in the way of fluid replacement. During the stage, he would have become even more dehydrated by drinking Coca Cola and brandy *en route*, from the bottles stolen in the café raids. He was looking to caffeine as a stimulant and alcohol as a painkiller, but both are also diuretics, stimulating the body to lose water. To sum up, Simpson's dehydration would have been a key factor: his body would have been unable to produce the sweat he needed to cool down as he rode up the mountain.

Cyclists of the time seem to have been half-aware of the dangers of extreme heat: there was an unwritten convention that they did not use amphetamines or other stimulants in such conditions. The professional cyclists of the 1960s cannot have known it, but this corresponds with what science says about 'speed'. Amphetamines have a double whammy effect on body heat: their use leads to a temporary increase in the body's core temperature and at the same time it also impairs the body's capacity to regulate this internal heat. The body gets hotter, but it becomes unable to deal with this efficiently. This would be unsafe under any conditions, but it is a highly dangerous state in extremely hot weather.

There is a third reason why amphetamines are unsafe. They are not physical stimulants but a mental pick-me-up which distorts the central nervous system to produce a feeling of euphoria, self-confidence, alertness and invincibility. Amphetamines do not give the body more energy, or increase physical capacity in any way, but merely make the mind push the body harder. They distort the user's perception of reality, overriding physical and mental warning signals from the body. A threat of external danger or physical damage is observed, but ignored. This is perhaps why so many of them were produced for British airmen during the Second World War, and why in some quarters they were credited with having won the Battle of Britain. It is also, of course, precisely why a tired cyclist would take them.

As heat exhaustion sets in, you experience symptoms such as nausea, muscle weakness, lightheadedness and headaches. They are warning signals that the body's heat regulation mechanisms are being dangerously overloaded. An undrugged person will usually have no choice but to slow down; the amphetamine-taker is more likely to attempt to continue in spite of these symptoms, or will simply not notice them.

Alcohol, too, affects a person's judgement. If Simpson had taken the 'half of a half bottle' described by Colin Lewis, he would probably have come up positive in a police breathalyser test. If, as seems likely, he topped up at the bottom of the mountain, he would have been climbing under the influence of two mood-altering drugs. This would have been on top of the ability to ride himself into a state of collapse which he had shown from an early age.

The first of Simpson's 'troubles' would have been an increase in his internal body temperature as he rode up the mountain. Core body temperature rises during sustained intense effort. When a cyclist rides up a mountain in hot weather, the effect of the heat is made worse by the slow pace, which means there is less air flowing over the body and sweating is less effective as a means of controlling temperature. No official records are available for the heat on the mountain that day, but there is a much-quoted apochryphal report of a thermometer reaching 54 degrees centigrade and bursting at Chalet Reynard, the large café-restaurant two-thirds of the way up the mountain. The heat would have been intense, and on a hot day in Provence that means at least 40 degrees.

The body of a trained athlete is usually able to deal with

conditions such as this. On his first ascent of the Ventoux during the 1965 Tour, on a slightly cooler day than he would encounter two years later, Simpson himself noticed how much he perspired. 'It was the only time I have got off my bike and my pants have fallen down. They were soaked and heavy with sweat and I had to wring out my socks because the sweat was running into my shoes.' This perfectly illustrates the copious sweat which the body produces to counter its temperature rise caused by cycling up a mountain in the afternoon heat. July 13, 1967, was a far hotter day but, in contrast, when Harry Hall laid Simpson by the roadside, he noticed that his skin was dry. Sweating is the most important way in which the body loses heat: by the time he keeled over, Simpson was no longer able to produce any sweat at all.

The human body needs a stable environment to function properly and remain alive. This is maintained by a process of delicate reactions known as homeostasis, which keeps the internal workings of the body within certain limits, enabling it to counter external factors such as heat, cold, dehydration and altitude. But what the body cannot cope with are extremes – very low or very high external temperatures, or the rarefied air of high altitude, for example – or a combination of factors all at once. As he climbed up the wooded lower slopes of the mountain, desperately trying to stay with the early leaders, Julio Jimenez and Raymond Poulidor, Simpson's body overheated like a car engine with a malfunctioning radiator. The effect would have been devastating.

The rise in Simpson's body temperature would have led to heat exhaustion. It is actually possible that he was already suffering from this when he arrived at the mountain. He could have been showing the symptoms when he asked Vin Denson for water and told Colin Lewis that his 'guts were feeling queer'.

If heat exhaustion is not treated, heatstroke sets in: an uncontrollable rise in body temperature which causes damage to the body's organs as the cells die off owing to the heat. The medical term for the condition is hyperthermia: when the body cooks slowly from within. Usually, heatstroke patients have to be treated in an intensive care unit.

Heatstroke can result in irrational behaviour: the bizarre conduct which Lucien Aimar observed when he overtook Simpson and his refusal to ride up the mountain at a sensible pace would be typical, as was Simpson's obsessive desire to continue. The lack of sweat on Simpson's skin ties in as well: it is common in the acute stages of the condition.

Simpson's heart would have felt the strain first. The heart of a top cyclist going up a mountain beats between 160 and 200 times per minute, but Simpson's pulse rate would have increased drastically above this. It would have entered a state known as 'tachycardia', where the heart beats very rapidly and less efficiently: the contractions are so brief that less blood than is needed is pumped around the system. From the British team car, Harry Hall filmed Simpson zigzagging up the mountain. It ties in with tachycardia: the reduction in the supply of oxygen to the brain would result in confusion and a lack of coordination, similar to that seen in climbers at extremely high altitudes.

It is possible for the heart to revert naturally to a normal rhythm following a brief spell of tachycardia, but Simpson's heart had no chance to do so. He had been climbing the mountain for almost an hour, and his internal temperature would have been too high, even though he had slowed down and by now he was in the cooler part of the climb. He would then enter a state known as 'ventricular fibrillation', where the heartbeat becomes completely uncoordinated and there is no blood flow through the body. This is not a heart attack, which is when the heart actually stops beating owing to a blocked cardiac artery. Heart attacks are virtually unknown in athletes with no history of heart disease in their family. In a state of fibrillation, on the other hand, the heart is still moving but the muscles are merely twitching and pumping no blood. Once this has begun, death usually follows between two and three minutes afterwards. The brain is starved of oxygen, and is irreversibly damaged.

The waxy nature of Simpson's skin, and his yellowish colour, both described by Harry Hall, would suggest that there was no oxygen in Simpson's blood when he fell for the second time. The way in which Simpson's fingers gripped on his handlebars is typical of the muscular spasm which happens as a result of the sudden severe chest pain caused by heart failure. I asked a retired Home Office pathologist about Simpson's fingers, and he gave me a chilling answer: 'He would have had a violent cardiac cramp and would have hung on like grim death.'

Nowadays, these are well-known syndromes; many large public buildings in the United States have defibrillators, which apply an electric shock to an abnormally beating heart to jolt it back into a normal rhythm. The machines are carried in the ambulances at most major cycle races. If a modern-day Simpson were to collapse on the Ventoux in a similar state in the 2002 Tour de France, he might be kept alive, if a doctor were on the spot immediately, which is of course by no means likely. It would, however, take the best of modern resuscitation aids: the defibrillator, plus an electrocardiograph (ECG). Pure oxygen might be administered via a tube down the throat, with a bag used to pump air into the lungs. At the same time, he would have to be treated for the heatstroke.

In 1967, however, Dr Dumas did not arrive on the scene immediately. The Tour caravan would have been spread over at least six miles of mountain road, so it would have taken a fluke for him to be in the right place at the right time. The doctor had a primitive oxygen mask and cylinders; but Simpson's heart needed to be functioning for the equipment to have any effect. There is virtually no chance that he could have been saved, unless he had happened to fall off in front of a hospital with an intensive care unit. This is worth bearing in mind, given the claims directed at Harry Hall and the late Alec Taylor, who obeyed Simpson's final order to put him back on his bike. Hall has been accused to his face of failing to prevent Simpson's death, and there have been comments such as this from Simpson's teammate Roger Pingeon: 'Tom was unlucky that the Tour was being contested by national teams. His [trade team] manager would never have put him back on his bike.'

Another point should be made regarding Hall's and Taylor's action. Simpson was the boss, in charge of the team. Hall makes it clear that Simpson had the final say on virtually everything that went on, down to which of the two mechanics would travel alongside Taylor in the team car on which day. All of Taylor's orders were prefaced with 'Tom wants this'. Simpson's status and experience were vastly superior to that of either the mechanic or the manager. It was not their job to deny him.

Dr Dumas has also been blamed for Simpson's death. Albert Beurick's theory is that, when Dumas put Simpson in the helicopter to transport him to hospital, the doctor killed his patient by taking him to a higher altitude and depriving him of oxygen. This view does not stand up: Simpson was already being given oxygen, to no effect, and was put in the helicopter at least 40 minutes after his collapse. Dr Dumas maintained that he was dead 'a long time' before then – 'you could see it: his blood pressure was not rising'.

Both Jacques Anquetil and his manager, the former cyclist Raphael Geminiani, claimed for many years after Simpson's death that Dumas was to blame. In an interview with the magazine *Velo* in 1984, Geminiani claimed: 'Pierre

Dumas made Simpson die. Simpson died of a cardiac arrest which can happen to anyone. You have to immobilize the sick man, keep his head lower than his feet [to ensure some oxygen reaches the brain] and inject adrenaline or Maxiton to reanimate the heart.' The same claim is still there on Geminiani's website today, quoting its source, a newspaper article written shortly after Simpson's death by one Dr Philippe Decourt.

But Simpson was immobilized. Keeping his head lower than his feet would have been pointless if his heart was not beating, and could not deliver the oxygen. Today, an adrenaline injection might indeed be given, but it would be just one of a wider panoply of measures. Whether on its own it would have had an effect on an athlete suffering advanced heatstroke is debatable.

There are other, less pernicious, Simpson myths which are worth dealing with briefly. His death has been blamed on the fact that he came from a mining family and had inherited undersized lungs from his father. No medical doctor I have spoken to feels this is worthy of consideration. Had Simpson had damaged lungs, he would have been unable to win the toughest cycle races in the world, with or without drugs. Then there is the claim from Jacques Anquetil at the time that Simpson's death was due to the newly instituted drug controls, because he would not have used his usual drugs and might have tried something more dangerous. This has to be put in the context of Anquetil's war on drug testing. Great cyclist he may have been, but he was hardly objective when that topic came up.

Decourt could not claim to be writing from an objective standpoint either, although his allegations, now also on Geminiani's website, were widely quoted in the press after Simpson's death. A former employee of the Rhône-Poulenc drug company, Decourt claimed to have been responsible for inventing the amphetamine marketed as Ortedrine. It could be argued that he had a personal agenda: blaming

Dumas meant that the drugs were cleared of any responsibility. He makes the link explicitly in his article: 'Amphetamine did not cause Simpson's death. He did not receive appropriate care.'

Geminiani and Anquetil belong to the same school of thought. On his website, over 30 years since the publication of the autopsy report, Geminiani maintains that Simpson died 'of cardiac collapse due to hypoglycaemia'. Anquetil, for his part, told *Velo* magazine in 1979: 'As far as I know, Simpson died due to a cardiac collapse which was not caused by the use of amphetamines.' The five-times Tour winner and icon of cycling, and the popular 'Big Gun', as Geminiani is known, are in prestigious company. The late Robert Chapatte, former Tour cyclist and head of sport at French national television Antenne 2, wrote this in his autobiography *When the Doors Slam*: 'The tragedy of the Tour de France 1967 calls for a definitive answer about the use of stimulants by certain sportsmen. In Simpson's case, the answer was no he did not.'

Even Simpson's great friend the journalist David Saunders, who ghosted his autobiography *Cycling is My Life* falls into the same trap. In his book *Cycling in the Sixties*, Saunders wrote: 'I think the drug played a very small part in his [Simpson's] death ... It relieved him of much of the pain and suffering.'

As revisionism goes, it is hardly Stalinist, but, like Beurick's 'helicopter' theory, it all serves to muddy the waters and steer attention away from the amphetamines. In Saunders' and Beurick's case, it can be explained as blind loyalty: they do not want to admit that what their friend ingested may have helped kill him. Anquetil and Decourt also have their own agendas.

Part of the confusion arises because it is perfectly possible to die of exertional heatstroke without taking 'speed'. Heatstroke kills a small number of participants in long-distance runs every year, and it also claims a few US army recruits. In these cases, it is excessive motivation, extreme weather conditions and possibly a lack of fitness which are to blame. There is no drug link.

In Simpson's case, the drug was present. Amphetamines did not directly cause his death, in the same way that alcohol does not directly lead to the death of a driver who has a few beers, then goes off the road and crashes into a tree. But they would have caused his body temperature to rise, they would have hindered his body from dealing with that situation, and they would have prevented his mind from being aware of what was going on. The background to his death and his symptoms point to exertional heatstroke as the cause: amphetamines would have played their part along with the other factors.

The question which follows immediately is this: if amphetamines did play a part in Simpson's death, and given that they were being widely used by cyclists at the time, why was Simpson the only cyclist to drop dead on the Ventoux on that day? My search for the answer took me a long way from Mont Ventoux. Surfing the Internet using the search terms 'hyperthermia' and 'amphetamines', I came across the best modern parallel: the deaths of nightclubbers who have used Ecstasy, which is itself a form of amphetamine. Deaths are extremely rare in relation to the volume of drugs being taken.

In Britain, 500,000 Ecstasy tablets are estimated to be downed in one weekend. Exactly as in Simpson's case, there is no apparent explanation why one particular person takes the same pill as another under the same conditions and survives while the other dies. The available evidence from the 1960s is that a lot of amphetamines were being used in cycling. And, as is the case for Ecstasy-popping clubbers of today, the mortality figures imply that the game was probably worth the candle.

So was it plain bad luck that Simpson died when others

did not? Not for nothing do the French refer to the force which drives cyclists on as *rage à vaincre*, or 'rage to win'. But '*rage*' also refers to the madness of rabies. Simpson's friends, contemporaries and family all comment on his ability to drive himself further than most people could manage, from an early age. Simpson said himself that he could ride 'into such a state of fatigue that you don't know what you're doing'. 'He would fire off and explode and we would all pass him lying in the gutter,' says his professional mentor, Brian Robinson, who gives the impression that the sight of Simpson lying by the roadside surprised no one. Indeed, at the top of the Ventoux, when Vin Denson, Colin Lewis and Barry Hoban saw him being treated by Dr Dumas, they assumed he had just tried too hard – as usual.

Indeed, Simpson made a habit of continuing to race far beyond the point where common sense would dictate withdrawal in the interests of damage limitation. Simpson summed up his philosophy thus: 'I find it hard to think a rider is ever justified in retiring from a major race.' The 1965 Tour de France was a good example: the poorly treated hand injury left Simpson with severe blood poisoning, bronchitis, a kidney infection and one abscess after another, but he did not quit until he was made to by the race's doctor. In his first Tour, 1960, he lost two stones in weight, finished in a state of exhaustion, and then raced himself to a standstill afterwards in appearance events.

Given cyclists' minimal understanding of physiology at the time, it was normal for them to go over the limit in races: they did not know whether or not they were harming themselves. Barry Hoban says now: 'We had no idea how often we were pushing ourselves into the red.' In his autobiography, *Watching the Wheels Go Round*, Hoban describes an incident in 1963, in the Paris–Luxembourg race. 'Edouard Delberghe and I were so smashed that we were zigzagging along the road. Delberghe went off the road completely. He was suffering from heatstroke and was taken to hospital, delirious. I managed to struggle on . . . I crumpled like a piece of jelly . . . There was no strength left in my legs. They carried me to the team car. I was so smashed I couldn't go downstairs for dinner [in the hotel].'

Simpson, however, is the only cyclist I have come across to drive himself so hard that he managed a near-death or out-of-body experience. It happened in a two-man team time trial in Italy in 1964, the Baracchi trophy, when he was partnered with Rudi Altig. He would beat the German a year later to win his world championship, but on that day Altig was far stronger and pushed Simpson to a point where he could barely keep up. The day after, Simpson went out training with Vin Denson, and told him about it. It clearly made a huge impression on Denson.

'He said "Christ, I died." He said everything seemed to be coming and going. It was a sensational feeling, you could see things totally clearly, then it all closed up and you could see nothing. Then it came back again, it went and came back like being in a tunnel. He said he felt peace of mind and wasn't afraid to die. He said, "I'm sure I died and came back again." He said he would have been happy dying.'

This sounds like the sense of detachment from the body and from physical discomfort which athletes describe when they enter 'the zone'. In Simpson's case it may have been caused by a shortage of oxygen in the brain due to the effort of trying to stay with Altig, or by endorphins, the body's natural painkillers. It could have been both of these, with or without the effects of 'speed'. Nonetheless, it is an eerie premonition.

Acceptance of mortal danger is integral to cycle racing. Just as a top Formula One driver can find an extra 10 mph over the rest on a given bend, on the road the best cyclists will perfectly calculate their descending speed and the expert sprinter will spot a minute gap between the wheels of a group sprinting for the finish at 40 mph. Even in a sport where every participant has a mass of scars from 'road rash' on elbow and thigh, Simpson fell more often than most other riders. His wife Helen wrote to George Shaw on July 18, 1963: 'Tom fell off yesterday and cut his head rather badly, not bad enough though to prevent him from riding today. That's the second fall in two days.'

Injuries were not something he took seriously. On September 1, 1960, he wrote to George and Marlene Shaw from a Paris hospital: 'Raced almost every day since the Tour (the money's OK). I'm in hospital – it's nothing serious, just a leg I can't walk on. I don't like me bike, it's to'ard [*sic*].'

Many of Simpson's contemporaries felt that he did not merely flirt with disaster, but warmly embraced it. When racing on a banked indoor velodrome, Simpson would sometimes ride up the vertical advertising boards at the top of the bankings, Wall of Death-style, to please the crowds. 'We admired it, but we said "the guy's a bloody idiot. He will kill himself one day",' says Norman Sheil. Racing with Simpson in France, Sheil saw him crash twice, once sliding down the road on his back for 100 yards, another time piling into a heap of gravel at full speed. 'I told him to his face: "one of these days you will kill yourself".'

To the outsider, cycle racing can look suicidal – descending mountains at 60 mph, sprinting into the finish elbow-to-elbow in a group of a hundred riders travelling at 40 mph. But, to the cyclist on the inside, the risks are part of the business, in the same way that a jockey accepts sitting on a horse galloping at 30 mph or so, or one rugby player flings himself at another. I have enjoyed the constant flirtation with danger myself. It's a game of courage, instinct and adrenaline, where the man who gets closest to the line that says 'disaster' without stepping over it is most likely to win. Understand this, and you understand something of why

Simpson died, why it is possible for a man to leave part of himself behind when he gets on a bike.

There is an element in the best bike racers, amateur and professional, which is beyond the bounds of rational behaviour. They have times when the inner need to win overrides any sense of danger, and the physical effort becomes almost irrelevant. There is a kind of split in the personality involved. On two wheels, I have seen the friendliest, most level-headed people become possessed with a will power which turns them into a human machine with tunnel vision.

Simpson should be remembered as an impulsive, intelligent, articulate and supremely charismatic man who had a single blind spot: his need to win at any cost. He was not a bad man, nor a foolish one, nor was he unprofessional in his approach to his sport, but he chose to join others in cheating and got caught out in the most dramatic manner imaginable. He transgressed no more than many others did, and still do. Unlike Richard Virenque, who lied for two and a half years, and then confessed, served his drug ban and returned to stir the hearts of cycling fans once again, there is no way back for Simpson. That is his enduring tragedy.

Mont Faron, March 13, 1967

Below the steep mountainside, strewn with limestone rocks, the port of Toulon stretches into the distance in the late afternoon sun. On the hairpins close to the top of the great hill, two men are fighting the gradient: Eddy Merckx, broad-shouldered, round-faced, bending over his handlebars, and the willowy Tom Simpson. They wear the same colours, the black-and-white chequerboard of Peugeot-BP, but they have a common objective: victory in this year's Paris–Nice 'Race to the Sun'. They are friends and teammates, but they have not spoken for 48 hours, since Simpson slipped into a breakaway group in central France, finishing over 15 minutes ahead of Merckx.

The Belgian's supporters have accused Simpson of doublecrossing his teammate; Simpson's fans say that Merckx was not strong enough to get in on the move. It is a classic conflict: the established team leader against the young upstart. But now they are united and in the lead, with a single purpose: gaining time on the rest of the field, who are over two minutes behind. They will not see them again.

At the finish that evening in Hyères, Simpson will let Merckx cross the line a few yards ahead for the stage victory, knowing that he, not the Belgian, will pull on the white jersey of race leader. He will wear it in triumph at the finish on the Promenade des Anglais in Nice in two days' time. It is his biggest stage race win, and it puts him on the shortlist of favourites for the Tour de France.

Payback time is five days away: Simpson will support Merckx as he wins the Milan–San Remo single-day Classic. Out of conflict, a close bond is born: on a rainy day in five months' time, the Belgian will be the only European professional at Simpson's funeral.

CHAPTER TEN

'Your Neighbours Are the Unknown Stars'
Jacques Goddet, 1955

As you fly towards Marseille down the Rhône Valley, the great mountain emerges gradually to the left through the afternoon heat haze, beyond the sprawl of buildings that is the town of Avignon. This is Mont Ventoux: a glowering east–west ridge with a wisp of cloud on the top which is soon lost again, like the back of a shark rolling out of a wave and returning to the sea.

The first time Tom Simpson rode up the Ventoux he saw it as 'another world up there among the bare rocks and the glaring sun'. And on a summer afternoon almost 35 years on, with its lower slopes lost in the haze, its summit merging into the thunderclouds, the 'Giant of Provence' has an aura which is not quite of this world. This is frequently the case. With nothing so high anywhere near, the Ventoux continually draws the eye, but from a distance it never looks quite real. 'You wonder what it's doing there, between the Alps and Provence,' wrote cycling historian Philippe Brunel. As with all mountains, its appearance is constantly, subtly, changing, depending on the angle from which it is seen.

From Nîmes, 40 miles away, Mont Ventoux appears as a near-perfect dome, akin to Mount Fuji. From the autoroute south of Avignon it is like a beached, white-backed whale towering over eastern Provence, a steep head to the west, a gradually sloping tail to the east above the Côtes du Ventoux vineyards. The first time I saw it was in spring and the white rocks on the summit deceived me, as it has many others before and since, into thinking that there was still snow on top.

Simpson's life ended here on July 13, 1967, but the mountain spawned something equally potent: the Simpson myth. The 'Giant of Provence' is a defining factor in his story. The peak where Simpson died stands alone, visible for 65 miles on a clear day, dominating an area of some 2,000 square miles, give or take a few. Had Britain's greatest ever cyclist happened to collapse in a coma by some anonymous roadside in, say, the Berry or Calvados, his death would not have had the same lasting impact.

Of all the mountains climbed by the Tour de France, the Ventoux is the one which most readily takes on a personality, believed the philosopher Roland Barthes. 'The great cols, be they Alpine or Pyrenean, and tough as they are, are ways of getting through the mountains: the col is merely a passage which struggles to take on a personality; the Ventoux, thrusting abundantly skywards, is a god of Evil to whom sacrifice must be paid. A true Moloch, a despot of cyclists, it never pardons the weak and exacts an unjust tribute of suffering.'

When Barthes wrote that, 10 years before the mountain took a terrible tribute from Simpson, the Tour had climbed the Ventoux only three times. It had not taken long for the mountain to gain a fearful reputation for the toll it demanded of 'the giants of the road'. 'We have seen riders descend into madness due to heat and stimulants,' wrote the journalist Antoine Blondin, 'some going down the hairpins when they think they are going up, others brandishing their pumps above their heads and calling us murderers. There are few happy memories attached to this witches' cauldron, which is always climbed with a heavy heart.'

Memories of Simpson linger not only at his memorial near the summit, but also in the little towns at the mountain's feet. In Carpentras, where he picked up his last bag of food and where the news of his death was revealed to the world. In Bedoin, where he dashed into a bar to get a final drink before he climbed the mountain. In Malaucène, where his dazed teammates attempted to come to terms with the loss of their leader and the police arrived to question his team manager and masseurs.

It is now something of a cliché to say that Simpson's dramatic death created the headlines in British newspapers that he craved throughout his career, and that he would have found this amusing. That may be true, but there is another twist which would have amused his sardonic mind every bit as much. In dying on the Giant of Provence, one of sport's larger-than-life characters inadvertently annexed a whole mountain, the greatest memorial that nature itself could have put in his way. Had he wanted to be remembered, he could have chosen no better place.

I pedalled out of the sleepy little village of Bedoin one August morning in search of Simpson. Somewhere in this huddle of stone houses on the south slope of the Ventoux, he went into a bar in search of water to cool him as he climbed, and alcohol to ease his stomach pains. As you roll past the last house and into the lavender fields, the mountain soars up to the left, the white tower of the observatory on the summit pointing to the sky like a lone finger. Close to, the mountain creates a feeling of insignificance like Ben Nevis seen from sea level in Fort William. Relatively speaking, it is only a little higher: 5,000 feet above Bedoin to Ben Nevis's 4,400 feet from the loch-side town. The top of the Ventoux is 13 miles away as you engage bottom gear. For the moderately fit cyclist, that means at least two hours of hard toil. The record, in Simpson's day, was just over an hour, set by the 'angel of the mountains', Charly Gaul of Luxembourg.

The road does not look steep – yet – but it is gaining height deceptively through the vineyards, which will soon give way to oak woods. After four miles along the flank of the mountain, the gradient eases and the road swings to the left in a vast hairpin, the Virage Saint Estève. In the 1960s, the sweeping corner still had a massive, shallow banking of concrete setts on its inside, for the motor races which were first held up here in 1902. It has since been filled in, but the Ferraris and BMWs still race up, in the French hill climb championship, for example, between Bedoin and the summit.

Thus far, the road has been heading east, away from the summit, which is directly above Bedoin, but the hairpin swings the road completely back on itself. For a brief second, the observatory comes into view high up above the straight ahead, framed by the trees on either side of the tarmac. It is an unpleasant reminder of how much height has to be won.

Climbing away from Saint Estève, you soon notice something which sets the Ventoux apart. There are no hairpins to break the rhythm here as there are on other mountains. The road through the Bedoin forest snakes a little in its rock cutting, but is essentially heading straight up the flank of the mountain at somewhere between one in 10 and one in eight.

There is no respite, no slackening of the gradient. If you were not riding through it on a bike, the forest would be a pleasant enough place. It was planted in the late 19th century after woodcutters and farmers had turned the slopes bare, and begins with stunted oak trees lower down, which gradually give way to delicately scented cedars, fir trees and pines. Wild boars roam here and the oak woods provide some of the finest truffle-hunting in France for the locals and their dogs.

On two wheels, this road plays with a cyclist's mind. There are no landmarks in the forest. The road is featureless, enclosed by the trees and sometimes by shallow rock cuttings. You simply pedal, never knowing quite when the pain will end. Other cyclists may be just a few metres ahead, but you cannot increase speed to join them – an extra half a mile per hour can ask too much of your legs and lungs. The sweat pours down your face, making the eyes sting – and this is on a cool morning. Simpson came up for the last time in the heat of the afternoon, his constitution sapped by 12 days in the saddle, with lighter men forcing the pace. It is said that the air actually contains less oxygen here than higher up; because of this, in the early days of motoring, it was here that cars would break down.

Jean Malléjac got no further than the top of the forest when the Tour came up in 1955. Foreshadowing the Simpson tragedy, the talented Breton cyclist, who had finished second in the 1953 race and was lying ninth overall, keeled over onto a pile of gravel by the road, still turning one foot which had remained strapped to its pedal. 'Pouring with sweat, haggard and semi-comatose, he zigzagged on a road which was no longer wide enough for him,' the journalist Jacques Augendre wrote that evening. 'He was no longer in the material world, still less that of cycling and the Tour de France.' He was saved, but never raced again.

That day also ended the career of Ferdi Kubler, who had won the Tour five years earlier. The effervescent Swiss had sprinted up the foot of the mountain in his usual cavalier style, ignoring the heat, which was bad enough to melt the tarmac. He was warned by Raphael Geminiani: 'Watch out, Ferdi, the Ventoux is not like any other col.' Kubler replied: 'Ferdi's not like the other riders,' and sprinted on. Soon, however, the gradient and the heat got the better of him. He wobbled to a halt, cursing in German and imploring the spectators to 'push Ferdi, push Ferdi'. He did eventually get over the mountain, about 20 minutes behind the leaders, only to fall at least three times on the descent. Later in the stage he was seen entering a bar close to the stage finish in Avignon, where he downed one beer after another, then set off for the finish – the wrong way. That evening, covered in bandages, he called a press conference and announced his retirement with the words: 'Ferdi is too old . . . Ferdi hurts too much . . . Ferdi has killed himself on the Ventoux.'

In the horrendous heat – 'a furnace' says the report – half a dozen other cyclists collapsed in varying states of distress. 'They shivered and shook and yelled inarticulately like madmen,' reported *L'Equipe*. Some ran desperately for shade. The next day, worried by the near-death of one of their colleagues, many of the riders in the field threw away their '*explosifs*', as *L'Equipe* called them. The day's events, the mix of heroism and near tragedy, also inspired some of the most purple prose the Tour organizer Jacques Goddet, a director of *L'Equipe*, ever produced about the 'Giant of Provence'. His daily editorial hailed 'all the men who passed the Ventoux, without exception. Yes, all, lost in the rocky immensity of the Ventoux, baked white hot by the fiery sun, have the right to the admiration of the public, and to its esteem.'

Malléjac's near death, Kubler's breakdown and the collapse of at least six others merely added to the spectacle, as Goddet saw it. 'On this accursed ground, the battle raged, while all along the fiery mountain men fell by the wayside, beaten down by sunstroke, empty, drunk with the effort and the struggle, heaps of brave men who were once so solid and so resolute . . . Nothing stops the rhythm of the 1955 Tour de France.'

After the forest, and the single hairpin among the trees – towards the top and known, baldly, as Le Virage du Bois, or 'the hairpin in the wood' – the forest thins out, and the top of the mountain shoulder can be made out: 'the sloping desert' as Goddet called it. At Chalet Reynard, huddled in the scree slopes, the road from Sault – the newest way up, opened in the 1950s – comes in from the right. 'Up there, you leave planet Earth,' wrote Goddet in 1955, and in the final metres before the café, Provence opens up behind your back wheel like a map spread out on the floor: green vineyards, honey-coloured villages, brown forests. Past the café, the road swings to the left, between poles which mark it out in the snow, and the bare scree slopes begin, with a few last vestiges of vegetation among the 'Sahara of stones'. 'You turn left and it's parched white, in that heat it was like going into an oven,' recalls Vin Denson of the day his leader died.

The top of the Ventoux is a hostile place, formed between 100 and 130 million years ago when vast plates of limestone were pushed up beneath a vast sea. The great scree slopes are produced by constant erosion in the extreme climate: the rocks split as water on and inside them is frozen in temperatures which can plummet to minus 27 degrees centigrade, and the bits are then bounced about by the wind.

No precise figures exist for the speeds of the Ventoux's winds. The weather station on the summit was closed in 1960, and France's meteorologists do not accept the accuracy of readings prior to 1980. It is said that the gusts regularly exceed 150 mph and that they once hit a world record 200 mph but the local weathermen do not take the latter figure seriously. Meteorologists stationed on the summit years ago recall that the gusts used to break their anemometer. The wind would bend iron poles, move parked cars, and blow stones as big as a man's fist up the slope. The gap between the two hummocks that form the summit was not lightly named the Col des Tempêtes.

For obvious reasons, there is speculation that the name Ventoux comes from the Latin for 'windy': *ventosus*. 'Windy mountain' seems the tidiest theory, but there are others. One is that the name comes from the word *vinturi*, which is Ligurian – the language once spoken up the coast to the east – for 'mountain'. Mont Ventoux could actually mean 'mount mountain' or perhaps 'mountain of mountains'. Others hold that the root is *vintur*, Gaulish for 'victory'.

The summit has its own microclimate, averaging about three or four degrees centigrade. In climatic terms, from bottom to top you travel from Provence to Lapland in just over 10 miles: from lavender fields in Bedoin to ski lifts at Chalet Reynard. The temperature can be up to 20 degrees colder between summit and foothills and this was exploited to the full in the 19th century when 30 people earned a living on the mountain producing ice, which was laid down in the winter in specially dug pits and then exported in summer as far away as Arles and Marseille.

It is a complex, exotic ecology. Among the 60 rare plant species are the subalpines found on the summit: saxifrage from Spitzbergen and a poppy found in Greenland and the North Cape. One resident, the rare Tengmalm's owl, is a native of Finland and northern Russia; the wild boar, salamanders and vipers complete the mix. Since 1990, much of the mountain has been a UNESCO biosphere nature reserve, with 'its feet in the Vaucluse, its head wanderiing between the Arctic and the Antarctic', in the words of the writer Louis Nucera.

All the way up, I had Tour heroes for company, or at least their names written on the road in fading paint when the race finished at the summit in 2000: Jan Ullrich, Erik Zabel, Udo Bolts 'and company' with the vast 'T' logo of their Deutsche Telekom team; Richard Virenque and his fellow in drug-taking disgrace Pascal Hervé; Jaja, for Laurent Jalabert. Danes, listed one by one – Bo, Nikolai, Jesper. Every Belgian in the race, in a neat line: Mattan, Baguet, De Wouwer.

After Chalet Reynard they were joined by the man who was to win that stage, Marco Pantani, in a perfect yellow stencil repeated every 10 yards for a mile, and, poignantly, the name Ochoa. It could have referred either to Ricardo, mown down and killed by a car while out training in March 2001, or his twin Javier, disabled in the same moment. Pantani, whose name now spells ambiguity over drugs; Ochoa, a name linked forever to two-wheeled tragedy.

Men have been riding bikes up here for over a century.

The road from Bedoin was opened in 1882, to great fanfare, to enable the construction of the weather station, which took another seven years. Soon after its opening, Adolphe Benoit, director of *La Provence Sportive* newspaper, became the first to make it up the mountain on two wheels. In his editorials, Benoit encouraged his readers to emulate him, and by 1905 they were racing up, in 'Le Marathon du Mont Ventoux'. The marathon was won by a local woodcutter, Jacques Gabriel, a broad-shouldered young man who hauled his single-geared, fat-tyred clunker over the 19 miles from Carpentras to the summit in two hours, 29 minutes. It is a time which would shame many today, and, indeed, made the two hours I took over the shorter distance from Bedoin look pedestrian.

The road down the other side of the mountain, the steeper northern face above Malaucène, was opened in 1932, and major cycle races such as the Tour du Vaucluse and Dauphiné Libéré began to make occasional visits from 1935. It was not, however, until well after the war, in 1951, that the Tour visited for the first time, scaling the north side, and not until the following year that the Tour men struggled up from Bedoin, led by Jean Robic, a gritty little Breton known as 'Biquet', the little goat.

As well as sorting out the mountain goats from the flatland lambs, the Ventoux provided 'monumental decor', in Goddet's words. It fitted well alongside such spectacular Tour staples as the rock columns of the Casse Déserte, on the Col d'Izoard in the Alps, the spiral road around and up the dead volcano of the Puy-de-Dôme in the Massif Central, and the precarious track which clung to the mountainside nearly 9,000 feet above sea level on the Col du Galibier. Conquering such places turned the Tour riders into giants. That was how the Tour's first organizer Henri Desgrange intended it, and that is precisely what Goddet called his riders – 'these miniscule beings climbing a fiery

VENTOUX... TOUT ET TOUT !

De gauche à droite et de haut en bas : Geminiani, Favero, Bobet, Nencini, Mahé, Schmitz, Stablinski, Anquetil, Dorto, Anglade, Robinson, Bauvin, Picot, Privat, Elliott, Bergaud, Busto, Polo, Pipelin, Groussard, Brankart, Colette, Graeser, Christian, Rohrbach, Walkowiak, Darrigade, Van Est, Graczyk.

Calvary with a backdrop of desolation' – when the Tour came up in 1955.

There was nothing else to approach the near-fatal episode of that year before the Simpson tragedy but there were more warning signs of the potential for disaster when the Tour finished on the top in 1958. The winner, Charly Gaul, was 'on the edge of asphyxiation' as he headed straight through the crowds at the finish and into the race ambulance to recover.

The qualities which set the Ventoux apart are shown in a newspaper cartoon of 1958 by the artist Pellos who depicted it as a vast, squat monster, troll-like and sadistic. It has an ironic smile on its face as it pulls the tongue out of the mouth of an anguished-looking cyclist, while his fellows look up in awe from below. The Alps, on the other hand, are shown as two smiling giants on the sidelines.

For at least 2,000 years the Ventoux has drawn men to it, inspiring this mix of fascination and dread. Pottery trumpets found on the summit are believed to be ex-voto offerings brought up during the Iron Age. According to the writer Seneca, Julius Caesar had a temple built on the summit and dedicated it to Cicius, the god of the Mistral. The first to record climbing the mountain was the Italian poet Francisco Petrarch, who ascended with his brother during a moonlit night on April 25, 1336, to watch the sunrise. He clearly appreciated the view, writing to his father: 'Owing to the unaccustomed quality of the air and the effect of the great sweep of view spread out before me, I stood like one dazed.

'I beheld the clouds under our feet, and what I had read of Athos and Olympus seemed less incredible as I myself witnessed the same things from a mountain of less fame. I turned my eyes toward Italy, whither my heart most inclined. The Alps, rugged and snow-capped, seemed to rise close by, although they were really at a great distance.'

For the intrepid and sure of foot who want to follow in the poet's footsteps nearly seven centuries on, companies in Malaucène and Carpentras organize walking trips to the top to watch the sunrise.

Petrarch was right about the view from the top: to call it spectacular is an understatement. On a clear day, Marseille can be seen 100 kilometres to the south, while in the east the panorama begins with the Pelvoux massif and it runs west to the hills of the Cévennes via the Lubéron massif and the Rhône Valley. To the north, the hills of the Drôme rise and fall like vast waves on a sea of land, rolling to the feet of the snow-capped Alps.

Shortly after Petrarch's visit, a chapel was constructed just below the summit, dedicated to the Holy Cross, and endowed with a box containing one of the many bits of the 'true' cross which were touted around Europe in the Middle Ages. The winter climate at the summit was too harsh for the resident hermit, however, and he lived in a house further down the mountain rather than in the chapel.

As late as the 18th century, the annual pilgrimage to the chapel on September 14 would still attract 500 people and in the 19th century up to two thousand were believed to climb the mountain annually. It was clearly a perilous business. The 16th-century writer Thomas Platter writes of 'numerous crosses' on the path to the top where pilgrims climbing to the chapel 'had found death by fatigue or accident'.

As with all mountains, part of the fascination of the Ventoux must derive from the hostile forces the mountain can unleash. Hurricanes could wipe out up to 90 sheep and 30 goats in one fell swoop, and flash floods would wreak havoc in neighbouring towns. The mountain was known for its wolves until the late 19th century and, to complete the picture, its caves were reputed by local legend to lead down into hell itself. Even the very stones are to be feared when the wind gets up. In one midwinter storm in the 1970s, the body of a woman tourist was found just below the summit. The car she and her husband were driving had been blown off the road, its windscreen smashed by a stone driven by the wind and she had then attempted to walk the few hundred metres to the observatory for help. Her body was virtually unrecognizable due to bruises from the windblown rocks. 'She had been stoned. Killed by the rocks. It seemed incredible,' said a soldier stationed at the summit at the time. Her husband, who had also gone for help, was blown over a wall at the observatory but survived.

In winter, the upper part of the mountain is frequently cut off by snow. Soldiers at the observatory recall blizzards that lasted nine days, and the little garrison on the summit being cut off for weeks at a time and running out of food. One man talks of wandering for five or six hours in one of the white-outs, until his dog found the way. Others were not so lucky: in 1936 two soldiers got lost in a white-out close to the summit. One was found shortly afterwards, frozen to death. It took 40 hours to locate the other, blown 500 yards down the slope; in a tragic twist, he was discovered to have died only a short while before the rescue team came across his body.

The motor races claimed the life of at least one driver, in 1960, and just above Simpson's memorial is another stone dedicated to a cycle-tourist who died up there. Even watching the Tour is not without risk: in 1994, on the day the Tour came up the mountain, a young German fan was killed by lightning close to the summit.

Mont Ventoux remains a hostile place even in summer. The heat is perhaps most feared, but the massive variations in temperature are the greatest danger. In July 2000, high winds, hail and snow on the summit forced the curtailment of the annual mass participation event, the Etape du Tour, that year run up the Ventoux. Half the 7,000 participants were turned back at Chalet Reynard because of the risk that someone would die of exposure. Two days later, when

Pantani and Armstrong led the Tour to the summit, the wind was blowing so strongly that it was hard to stand, and much of the race's infrastructure had to be left in Carpentras as it would have been blown off the top. There was no elaborate finish flag for Marco Pantani to ride under when he won – the bald cyclist on the 'bald mountain' – and no massive inflatable podium for him to stand on and celebrate his victory. Yet again, Roland Barthes's 'god of Evil' had shown its power over the devices of mere mortals.

As you approach the memorial, retracing Simpson's final miles, the road snakes across the bare scree slopes. The thinness of the air begins to make itself felt in your lungs. There is a slight sensation of breathlessness to add to the sheer effort of getting the pedals round after almost two hours climbing without a let-up. To the right, the great mass of sunbaked limestone soars into the sky. Far below, to the left, what looks like the whole of Provence is on display, with row after row of rolling blue hills to the south. As the road crosses the mountainside, still climbing steeply, a series of vast U-shaped bends go into the heart of the rocks and out again onto the shoulders of the summit. These great bowls are natural suntraps, where the sun's heat bounces off the bleached rocks. They feel like a succession of vast natural kilns, as if designed to draw in the maximum amount of heat. The last of these, which is also the largest, is one and a quarter miles from the observatory, just below the point where Simpson took his last breath, with his objective for the day within reach, just a few minutes away.

The memorial stands to the left, a kilometre before the summit. Here, the road on which Simpson wobbled to a halt for the last time is so steep that merely walking up it is an effort. The granite profile of a cyclist with the words 'Olympic medallist, world champion, British sporting ambassador' was paid for by a subscription fund, launched by *Cycling* magazine the week after Simpson died. The idea of putting a monument here was inspired by the Guthrie memorial on the Isle of Man, which records the death of a motorcyclist in the TT. There are still bike races through Guthrie's corner, as there were in Simpson's day: the landmark was well known to cyclists of the time. One of the men who launched the fund, the journalist Peter Bryan, recalls the response as 'overwhelming, a national thing'. Cycling clubs held whip-rounds and raffles, raising around £1,500.

While looking for Simpson's autopsy in the local archive in Avignon's Palais des Papes, I came across Bryan's letters to the local *préfet* requesting permission to use the land where the memorial stands. They are in the same red-bound, string-tied folder as the local police report recording the cyclist's death. So too is a copy of the black-bound Simpson memorial issue of *Cycling Weekly* sent to oil the wheels of local bureaucracy. The memorial was unveiled in 1968 by Helen, Hoban, and Taylor, and when, in 1970, the Tour passed for the first time since the tragedy, Eddy Merckx, no less, tipped his cap and crossed himself as he led the race past. This was only natural: Merckx was a former teammate and the only fellow professional to attend Simpson's funeral.

The feet of the faithful have worn the stone leading up to the monument into rough steps, giving it a much-visited feel, rather like the amply marked grave of Jim Morrison in the Père Lachaise cemetery in Paris, and with a similar pile of offerings. To the writer Julian Barnes, it is 'the tumultuous altar of some popular if dubious Catholic saint'. Over the years, a heap of ex-votos from the two-wheeled Simpson faithful has accumulated and rotted in the wind and sun. When I visited in July 2000, the collection included tubular tyres, half a dozen cotton racing hats – with stones on top to stop them blowing away – a broken wheel, energy bars, a French racing licence in the name of

Sylvie Reverand, sunglasses, a tyre lever, a bottle cage, a saddle, two lollipops and a dinosaur from McDonald's.

A clean-up in the summer of 2001, when Helen and Barry Hoban had removed three bin liners full of artefacts, had left the memorial looking neater this time: a cotton hat from Holland (Van Vliet containers, with the date, 15/8/2001, in felt tip), another from Belgium, a couple of feeding bottles, a single bunch of flowers. The new vogue, it seems, is to leave stickers on the plinth – from Germany, Ireland, Holland – or to pick up stones from the mountainside and inscribe them in felt pen. 'A symbol of the struggle for perfection, you will always be remembered,' says one, left there by an English family. On the left of the stone there is a small plaque, placed there by his daughters Jane and Joanne, who retraced their father's last road in 1987. It reads: 'There is no mountain too high.'

In an echo of the thousands who used to struggle up the Ventoux to pay their respects in the Chapel of the Holy Cross, people on bikes now come from all over the world, drawn by the memorial and the mountain – it is hard to tell which is uppermost in their minds. When the Tour visits, they flock in their hundreds of thousands, much to the consternation of the local ecologists. Some go to extremes in their devotion to the mountain, like the newly wed couple who rode up in specially made white cycling shorts and tops, the bride's outfit topped with a veil, perfect lipstick and a big, if wobbly, smile. It earned them the front cover slot in the local magazine, *Les Carnets du Ventoux*.

On a midweek day in mid-August, the 21st-century pilgrims are there in all shapes, sizes and ages: slender adolescent youths on second-hand Gitanes handed down from the 1980s, Marco Pantani wannabes in full team replica kit, fat old cycle-tourists on tired-looking bikes with bellies bulging in their jerseys, young men on mountain bikes spinning tiny gears, club cyclists from every corner of France and Britain. They race, huff and puff, and wobble.

In some cases, they walk up, painfully pushing their bikes. The cycle-tourist from Kent who follows me up to the memorial is climbing for the second day in a row, once on each of his two bikes.

Often, husbands are followed by their wives. Patiently, the women overtake their other halves every few minutes in their Renault Clios, shout encouragement from the lay-bys and take photos as if hubby is riding his own private, miniature Tour de France. The ritual ends with a brief halt at the memorial; a slippery walk up the rocks in stiff-soled cycling shoes to leave the obligatory souvenir; a coffee in the bar by the observatory; and a long look at the view before they put the bike on the car roof rack.

At the turn of the last century, the public appeal of the Tour de France lay in the fact that the competitors were pioneers, setting off to do things no right-thinking mortal would attempt: circumnavigate France in 250-mile chunks on dirt roads, risk being eaten by bears while ascending the Pyrenean passes. That was the great attraction for its first organizer, Desgrange; that was why his paper's circulation went up during the Tour. Now, however, much of the Tour's popularity comes down to the fact that its great set piece venues, the mountain passes of the Alps, Pyrenees and Massif Central, are all open to the public, the weather and the legs permitting.

To be convinced of the strength of the fans' desire to emulate and empathise with the supermen, you have only to drive the route of a mountain stage of the Tour de France in the hours before the race passes. Hundreds of thousands of cyclists – the same mix as were there on my mid-August ride up the Ventoux – throng the roads, defying the gravity and the heat and risking life and limb among the advance Tour vehicles.

'*Faites-nous rêver*', say the placards on the Tour route, and it is written in faded paint on the Ventoux's tarmac: Make us dream. And that is why people will always climb the 'bald mountain' and its brethren. Unless you are friendly with the ground staff, you cannot go to Headingley and fantasise that you are Ian Botham destroying Australia in 1981, but you can get on your bike and pretend you are part of the great moments of the Tour: Eddy Merckx's epic escape of 1969 through the Pyrenees, or Marco Pantani's destruction of Jan Ullrich on the Galibier in 1998.

So it is with Simpson. Motor-racing fans can leave bouquets, but they cannot gain any empathy with what Ayrton Senna might have felt as he sped around the Imola track before careering off the Tamburello curve and into the great Formula One paddock in the sky. But for the price of a low-cost air ticket to Marseille and a night in a Ventoux hotel, however, you can retrace the final kilometres of Tom Simpson's gilded but tortured career, if a little more slowly.

The act of riding up the mountain is a shared experience. All Simpson's teammates who were with him on the Tour when he died have made the pilgrimage, as has Harry Hall, who picked him up off the road and obeyed his order to put him back on his bike. When his daughter Joanne rode the mountain in 1997, she was specific about the reason: it was 'to finish what Daddy didn't do'.

You can share some of the dull ache he must have felt in his calves and buttocks as he shoved on the pedals and the lactic acid built up. You can sense the hot sun on the back of your neck as he did under his pushed-back white Great Britain cap, and feel the dryness in your throat as the rocks suck the moisture from the air. Your eyes will probably sting as the sweat pours into them but you can cast them up to the observatory. Its constant presence exudes the immense power which the 'Giant of Provence' exerted as Simpson fought his way towards its summit. Perhaps, if the pain permits, you can reflect on the contradictions in the man and his sport.

There is more to Simpson than a tragic end, more than a

world champion's jersey, more than an enduring controversy stemming from three tubes of pills. He has also kept his place in cyclists' hearts and minds for 35 years because we can go and get some idea of what he was trying to do when he died and what it must have felt like. On that August morning, that is why we were there.

Afterword

July 2007 marks the 40th anniversary of the death of Tom Simpson on Mont Ventoux, that watershed in English cycling history and the first and greatest of what is now a long litany of drugs scandals in the sport. Simpson's collapse remains one of the most memorable sporting moments of all time, according to one magazine; more so, unfortunately, than his victory in the world professional road race championship or his brief spell in the yellow jersey, five years before his death.

July 2007 will also mark the fifth anniversary of the publication of this book. It is a respectable spell for any work to remain in print, and a reasonable milestone at which to pause briefly to assess how the Simpson story has moved on.

Although I had no particular intention of adding to the undertow of controversy surrounding Simpson's death when I embarked on writing this book, with hindsight I should not have been surprised by the reaction *Put Me Back on My Bike* prompted. My postbag was surprisingly large; and though the responses were overwhelmingly favourable, emotions remained raw. As to why Simpson's drug-taking matters now, the answer is in some of those letters. Many of those who wrote to me following publication attacked the culture of silence within cycling. The view of Glenn Meredith of London was typical: 'The world of cycle sport has, for many years, suffered from a massive collective denial on the doping issue.'

In chapter one I described my feelings at witnessing the Festina scandal of 1998 and how they were linked to

Simpson's death thirty years ago. Events since the publication of this book have further underlined the intractable nature of cycling's drug culture and the need for openness.

One drug scandal has followed another, culminating in a positive drug test for the winner of the 2006 race, Floyd Landis. Those revealed to be drug takers include Simpson's heir apparent, David Millar, who ironically had a particular fascination with Major Tom's story. It was Millar who sat with me the day after climbing the Ventoux in 2000, fingering a pebble from the mountain that had been given to him by one of Simpson's daughters. Millar is, like Simpson, a hugely talented, charismatic and intelligent cyclist, but those qualities did not enable him to resist the lure of performance-enhancing drugs.

There has also been a spate of premature deaths among professional cyclists, including two examples of self-destruction that match even Simpson's premature, wasteful demise: the deaths of the climbers José Maria Jiménez and Marco Pantani through cocaine abuse.

This is why Simpson's death and the reasons for it remain important. If we cannot examine dispassionately the death of a cyclist 40 years ago, where drugs were involved, what chance do we have of getting to grips now with the biggest threat to the future of the sport?

Amid the climate of uncertainty, I uncovered new evidence of Simpson's dependence on amphetamines and the warnings that were given to him to stop riding in the Tour. The initial clue came from Jean Bobet, brother of the triple Tour de France winner Louison, who raced as a professional and later worked on the Tour as a journalist. He recalled, almost in passing, that Simpson's long-time *directeur sportif* at Peugeot, Gaston Plaud, had told his English leader to quit the race the night before the Ventoux.

In his flat high above Tours' Avenue de Grammont, in

the summer of 2006, Plaud explained that on the 1967 Tour he had come across Simpson at the start in Marseilles. He had supervised Simpson at his trade team since the start of 1963, but the 1967 Tour was, of course, contested by national teams, so he was not in charge of the Briton in that race. They had not always seen eye-to-eye during Simpson's four years at Peugeot. They fell out over races that Simpson allegedly sold, and over his interviews with the *People* in September 1965; for his part Simpson was sometimes frustrated with the back-up he received from the team. However, Plaud could claim to know Simpson as well as anyone on the professional circuit.

'The face I saw was that of a very tired man. His features were drawn and he was very white. I knew he was not good in the heat, and I said he should not go up the Ventoux, because he was not healthy enough.' As Plaud put it, Simpson was '*au bout du rouleau*' – at the end of his tether. One of the photos taken that morning shows him at the start with the sunken cheeks of a corpse. Simpson, naturally, ignored the warnings. He had never spared himself throughout his career, why should he do so now?

The Peugeot team manager had good reason to be fearful for Simpson's health. He had previous chilling experience of what Simpson was capable of doing to himself. In the Tour of Spain earlier that year, Plaud told me, Simpson collapsed on the Puerto d'Envalira, one of the toughest mountain passes in the Pyrenees, an episode which foreshadowed almost identically his fatal zig-zag up the Ventoux.

Simpson had escaped the field and was riding ahead alone to the finish in Andorra, seemingly destined to win the stage – he had won one stage already and would win a second – when he began to wobble across the road, clearly out of control. Plaud stopped him, even though with 30 kilometres to the finish, he was assured of the stage victory.

'I stayed with him for a long time, until he was really

back on the rails. It was a long time because the field had time to catch him and come past. He was extremely tired that evening, but was OK the next morning.' Plaud's account ties in with a throwaway sentence from an interview with the late Doctor Pierre Dumas, which I quote on page 167. Here the doctor states that Simpson told him he was 'taken to hospital during the Tour of Spain'. This had intrigued me at the time but I was unable to follow it up.

The Peugeot manager makes the point that on the Envalira he had to overrule Simpson in the most emphatic manner to prevent him from harming himself, because his leader was utterly, irrationally, determined to go on. 'He did not want to stop. He wanted to remain on the bike. I had to stop him physically. I caught him when he was still on his bike.'

Simpson's collapse in the 1967 Vuelta is significant in another way. It was the latest in a series of life-threatening incidents – and perhaps cycling's last warning of a preventable and needless tragedy. Since Jean Mallejac's *défaillance* in the 1955 Tour, there had been several other incidences of riders zig-zagging up mountains out of control and keeling over. Simpson wasn't the first British rider to succumb; that honour must go to Victor Sutton in the 1960 Tour. The featherweight climber collapsed on the final Alpine stage, and was hospitalised with an apparent heart attack, a forewarning of the heart trouble that would end his life in 1999. Like Simpson he was over-raced, having just finished fifth in the Tour of Switzerland; like Simpson there was an amphetamine connection. In his account of racing in France with Sutton, *In Pursuit of Stardom: Les Nomades du Velo Anglais*, Tony Hewson states categorically that Sutton was using the drug.

Simpson's collapse in Spain adds weight to Doctor Pierre Dumas' view that the Briton's drug-taking had reached excessive proportions by the time he died (see page 142). Both Plaud and Simpson's team-mate Roger Pingeon reiterated this during *L'Equipe*'s 2002 investigation into Simpson's death.

Interviewed for the television documentary *Death on the Mountain*, the French sportswriter Philippe Brunel concluded: 'In the month before the stage up the Ventoux, certain riders were surprised by a change in Simpson's behaviour. According to Michel Nedelec, another Peugeot rider, who was with Simpson at criteriums "he lacked lucidity and was abusing drugs".' This backs up one eyewitness who told me of Simpson's apparent 'amphetamine rage' at the 1966 world championships.

Death on the Mountain, produced by Alastair Laurence at BBC Bristol, came out in 2005 and finally gave Simpson the in-depth small-screen treatment his story deserved. In essence, it achieved what Ray Pascoe had set out to with *Something to Aim At*, but in a different register. It was rightly crowned best documentary in the Royal Television Society awards at the end of the year. It is an intriguing mix of archive footage and interview, interspersed with reconstruction: a young cyclist on a fixed wheel bike training in the Yorkshire Dales; a more mature rider on a 1960s Peugeot taking on Mont Ventoux. Laurence interviewed the main players, with the exception of Harry Hall and Albert Beurick: he spoke to Vin Denson, Colin Lewis, Jean Stablinski, Helen and Barry Hoban and George Shaw. There were also interviews with Lucien Aimar – who was riding in the same group as Simpson on the fatal day – and, most significantly, Jean Bobet.

The documentary added further flesh to the story I told in *Put Me Back on My Bike*, with two small but significant revelations. Together, these indicated that Simpson's drive to keep racing in the 1967 Tour against common sense and sound advice was even stronger than I had imagined.

Denson told Laurence that he had advised Simpson to

give up his attempt to win the 1967 Tour after seeing him close to collapse in the Alps. After the stage to Briancon, when Simpson had stomach trouble, and Harry Hall had to clean the diarrhoea off his bike, Denson had said to him, 'Don't push it further, settle for what you have got and then go for the world championship.' But, according to Denson, Simpson wouldn't hear of it.

Those who retain the belief that Simpson did not abuse drugs should listen to another of Laurence's finds, Jean Bobet's account of his final encounter with the Briton. Bobet has no agenda, no need to be mealy-mouthed about drug-taking; like Colin Lewis, he is uneasy talking about Simpson. He was, he says, utterly fond of the British star.

One of the great 'Major Simpson' images is the photograph published in *L'Equipe* the day after Simpson took the yellow jersey in the 1962 Tour de France. Bobet was the man behind the picture. As he told me when I was researching *Roule Britannia*, my account of British racers in the Tour de France, it remains his fondest Simpson memory.

'We got him sitting on an old staircase in the hotel, wearing his bowler hat, and with his umbrella. He was like a small boy who had just been given the most beautiful Christmas present. I remember his smile for us. It was totally genuine. It made a huge impression: this young cyclist who had come from nowhere and was so happy to be there.'

In his interview with Laurence, Bobet uses the present – '*j'aime Tom*' [I'm fond of him] – but his final image of the British star today is of his 'terrible grimace', as he 'poked his tongue out and there were five tablets, almost certainly Tonedron because that was one of his favourite "medicines"'. Simpson excused himself for speaking in slightly muffled tones – the tablets presumably were getting in the way – and he joked that they were what he had needed to wake himself up that morning.

This sounds like a man for whom amphetamine use was casual, everyday, a joke in spite of its life-threatening implications. Plaud told me of Simpson slipping some of his 'medicine' to a dog at a party following the 1966 Paris-Tours race. Fortunately there was a vet not far away.

In hindsight, perhaps I let 'the Major' get off too lightly. This was not, however, because I had any fear of criticism that I was exploding cherished myths. It was because, although I never met Simpson, I came to like him. Reading his letters word for word, spending months attempting to get inside his head, how could one not? He was a charismatic man with a personality that drew people to him. The fondness I felt for him caused me to pick my way more gingerly through the drug-taking minefield than I should have done.

Put Me Back on My Bike and *Death on the Mountain* may have settled the arguments about whether Simpson used drugs to excess and whether the amphetamines contributed to his death, but, clearly, they will never resolve the argument about whether Simpson is unfairly targeted over his drug-taking. Should the story of what happened on 13 July 1967 be examined again? Or is it time to let Simpson and his drug-taking rest in peace?

For Barry Hoban, the answer to the latter question is 'yes'. In an interview with the magazine *Cycling Weekly* following publication of *Put Me Back*, he told Keith Bingham: 'The only thing Tom did wrong was to die . . . [He] was doing nothing more than certain other riders were doing. Everyone knew that Tom took drugs but the use of the word "cheat" [in *Put Me Back on My Bike*] is wrong.'

Perhaps Hoban and I are singing from the same hymn sheet in one sense: I felt, and still feel, that Simpson's drug-taking has to be seen in context. However, the question of whether Simpson was a cheat can be answered in this way. He broke the rules, as they were at the time. That many others were doing likewise, that the rules were new and poorly enforced, and that we can understand the reasons why he broke them does not change that fact. The amphetamines were still taken deliberately in order to gain an advantage. Tonedron was no mere placebo.

Simpson's drug-taking should not be glossed over. It was as much part of his life as his wheeler-dealing, his dreaming and his will to win; indeed, these four sides of his personality were all tangled together. And his use of amphetamine clearly played a key part in his premature, tragic death. What he did 'wrong', was to take drugs, apparently to excess (according to at least six different witnesses), and to ignore the advice of those around him whom he should have trusted. His death followed from that.

The last five years have produced other new snippets in the Simpson story, even if none of them is on quite the same dramatic scale as Plaud's revelations. Among the pile of letters that arrived following publication was one from Robin Gambrill, whose brother Mick was on the British team with Simpson at the Melbourne Olympics in 1956.

It is to Robin that I am indebted for a cutting from the *Daily Mail* of 31 July, 1967, which builds on the account of Simpson's death provided by Harry Hall. Hall estimated the distance Simpson covered between his first fall and his final collapse as some 500 yards; J.L. Manning, the *Mail*'s reporter, climbed the Ventoux shortly after Simpson's death and found two piles of stones 420 yards apart.

'At the first was scrawled on a piece of paper "here Tom Simpson fell". On the second was written on cardboard: "Here Tom Simpson died tragically on the 13th stage of the Tour de France."' Manning wrote. The picture his article conjures up is a poignant one: cycling fans marking the spot in an impromptu manner before the memorial was erected, in the same way that they would mark the point where the Italian Fabio Casartelli died in the 1995 Tour.

Manning is also probably the source of the reported temperatures on the Ventoux of 54 degrees centigrade; he interviewed the proprietors of the Chalet Reynard, who told him their thermometer had reached 55 degrees on the afternoon of 13 July.

The *Daily Mail* man's conclusion over Simpson's death, from his interviews with the police inquiry team, is similar to the one I reached in chapter nine.

'Simpson, knowing the Ventoux was a formidable challenge, took stimulants as he was in the habit of doing. Why else was a supply carried on him and in the baggage car?

'As he struggled in the last half-hour of his life, these drugs screened the approach of desperate fatigue. In the intense heat his breathing gradually failed and his judgement was too impaired to realise that the limit of endurance had been reached.'

On a lighter note, research into *Roule Britannia* brought further insights into Simpson's alter ego Major Thompson, the fictional Englishman created by Pierre Daninos. Clearly, Simpson both appropriated and subverted Thompson. He wore the dapper outfit (bowler, brolly, sharp suit, *The Times*), as sported by the Major, and was regularly referred to in the press as 'Major Simpson' but of course he ended up totally integrated into Europe – at home in Belgium and France, speaking Flemish, French and Italian – whereas Thompson was written as an affectionate mockery of the way the English remained a race apart.

Simpson subverted Daninos's comic hero in another way, of course. Thompson is the quintessential upper-class Englishman (educated at Rugby, Trinity and All-Souls); quite a contrast with a miner's son whose academic career was mainly notable for the way he mimicked the teachers at Worksop Technical College.

Interviews for *Roule Britannia* also offered more detail on Barry Hoban's stage win at Sete the day after Simpson's death; as I pointed out in *Put Me Back*, the victory remains controversial to this day. Jean Stablinski, the senior pro on the Tour and the *patron* in the absence of his leader Jacques Anquetil, had already told me that '*en principe* the stage was for [Vin] Denson. He was older than Hoban. We thought Denson was supposed to win.'

For the sake of completeness it is worth adding Denson and Hoban's respective versions of events to this. Not surprisingly, they differ. In his autobiography *Watching the Wheels Go Round*, Hoban wrote: 'I suggested that one of the British-based riders be allowed to win, but the general feeling was it should be Vin Denson or myself. We just rode along ... Suddenly I looked round and there was nobody there. I hadn't jumped away ... the others must have slowed down together. They had made their decision.'

As Denson tells it, however, Hoban did 'jump away' and the decision was not comfortably made. '[During the stage] suddenly Barry went from behind, Stablinski came crashing up and said "Get him back, this is not what we want". I said [chasing him down] would be like fighting for someone's gold ring after they had died and we would be the laughing stock of the press. "Let him get on with it".' It is hardly a dignified image, but then Simpson's death was not exactly dignified, for all its drama.

The Simpson story has a dynamic of its own, and fans of the great man are unlikely to be short of material in the near future. To start with there remain witnesses out there who have not yet told their side of the story, primarily the British team mechanic Ken Bird.

Ray Pascoe has continued down the Simpson trail, and has produced another video, largely featuring the 1965 BBC documentary *The World of Tom Simpson*. George Shaw is likely to publish the letters he received from the young Tom, as quoted extensively in these pages, with his own commentary.

The project to build a cycle racing circuit in Simpson's

home village of Harworth appears stillborn, but Simpson is likely to be celebrated in other ways: there is a project for a feature film of his story, not to mention the fruition of a dream so unlikely that not even the ultimate two-wheeled dreamer Major Tom could conjure it up: starting the Tour de France in London. That is part of Simpson's legacy, shared with Robert Millar, Barry Hoban, Chris Boardman, Sean Yates and David Millar.

The Tour is, however, in a dubious condition 40 years after its first great drug scandal. Cycling's flagship event epitomises the wider state of professional road racing, which is still at the sharp edge where modern morality rubs up against an ingrained culture of cheating that goes back to well before Simpson's day. Every passage past the monument on Mont Ventoux reminds us of that.

The future of the sport remains unclear. Whether it will have the ability to cure itself of the drug habit is as yet uncertain. But if the sponsors, public authorities and the fans eventually lose all patience and professional cycling withers away, it may be that in years to come Simpson's death will acquire new significance. The afternoon of 13 July 1967 will be pinpointed as the turning point, when cycling began a painful, and terminal, downward spiral from one doping scandal to another.

Major Simpson shows no signs of resting in peace. But that most dynamic and mercurial of sporting heroes probably would not have wanted it any other way.

Epilogue

A pile of letters sits on the table in Helen and Barry Hoban's farmhouse high on a mid-Wales hillside: three big bundles, perhaps 150 or 200 of them. Every kind of envelope, postmarks from around the world – Arizona, France, Tahiti, Germany, New Zealand, Britain. They arrived at Helen and Tom Simpson's house in Vijverstraat, Mariakerke, in the weeks after his death, as cycling fans around the world shared in Helen Simpson's grief. The message is overwhelmingly universal: the writer does not know what to do, and finds an outlet in writing to Helen.

Some letters are addressed simply 'Mrs Tom Simpson, Mariakerke, Belgium'. One has been sent to the Saint Martha Hospital in Avignon. Another is directed 'care of the French Cycling Federation'. They are from fellow cyclists, old ladies in rural France, the British consul in Brussels. Collectively, they are a more eloquent expression than I could ever provide of why Tom Simpson mattered and still matters.

The first one Helen and I opened was written on July 13, 1967, within hours of Simpson's death being announced, from Tony Dickson of the Catford Cycling Club in south London: 'Cycling is going to stand still for us all. Although fully grown I keep getting watery-eyed and would not try to conceal it. It's partly sadness, disbelief and partly pride at having been here when Tom took the world and put Britain on it too. I respect and almost love him without ever having met him.'

Tom Simpson: Race Record

Born: November 30, 1937, Haswell, Co. Durham.
Height: 1.81m.
Weight: 69kg.

1956   Amateur: silver medal, national individual pursuit championship; bronze medal, Olympic Games team pursuit (Melbourne).

1957   Amateur: gold medal, British League of Racing Cyclists national hill climb championship.

1958   Amateur: gold medal, national individual pursuit championship; silver medal, Empire Games individual pursuit (Cardiff); silver medal, British League of Racing Cyclists national hill climb championship.

1959   Independent (until August): major wins: stages in Essor Breton and Route de France stage races.

Professional from August with Rapha-Geminiani team: wins: two stages Tour de l'Ouest. Selected place: fourth in world professional road race championship (Zandvoort, Holland).

1960   Rapha-Gitane: wins: Tour du Sud Est, Mont Faron hill climb, two criteriums.

Selected places: 3rd, Genoa–Rome; 7th, Flèche Wallonne; 11th, Liège–Bastogne–Liège; 9th, Paris–Roubaix; 3rd, stage three Tour de France (29th overall).

1961   Rapha-Gitane: wins: Tour of Flanders, stage 1B Tour of Eibar, two criteriums; joint winner team time trial Four Days of Dunkirk and Paris–Nice, Challenge de

France team event.

Selected places: 2nd, Menton–Rome; 5th, Paris-Nice; 9th, World Championship. Abandoned Tour de France stage three.

1962 Gitane-Leroux: wins: Tour de France yellow jersey, stage 12; Challenge de France team event; joint winner team time trial in Paris–Nice.

Selected places: 5th, Tour of Flanders; 6th, Ghent–Wevelgem; 6th overall Tour de France.

1963 Peugeot-BP: wins: Bordeaux–Paris, stage one Tour du Var; Manx Trophy; three criteriums; joint winner: GP Parisien team time trial, World Cup (team trophy).

Selected places: 2nd, Paris–Brussels; 2nd, Ghent–Wevelgem; 2nd, Paris–Tours; 3rd, Tour of Flanders; 8th, Paris-Roubaix; 10th, Flèche Wallonne; 10th, Tour of Lombardy. Did not start Tour de France.

1964 Peugeot-BP: wins: Milan–San Remo, stage Circuit du Provençal, five criteriums.

Selected places: 2nd, Kuurne–Brussels–Kuurne; 4th, world road race championship (Sallanches, France); 10th, Paris-–Roubaix; 14th overall, Tour de France (2nd, stage nine).

1965 Peugeot-BP: wins: world road race championship (San Sebastian, Basque Country); Tour of Lombardy; London–Holyhead; Brussels six-day (track); three criteriums.

Selected places: 3rd, Flèche–Wallonne; 3rd, Bordeaux–Paris; 3rd overall, GP Midi Libre; 3rd overall, Circuit de Provençal; 7th, Paris–Roubaix; 10th, Liège–Bastogne-–Liège. Abandoned Tour de France, stage 20.

1966 Peugeot-BP: wins: nine criteriums; joint winner, team time trial, Four Days of Dunkirk.

Selected places: 2nd, stages 12 and 13, Tour de France. Abandoned stage 17.

1967 Peugeot-BP: wins: Paris–Nice (3rd, stage four; 2nd, stages six and seven); stage and overall, Tour of Sardinia (2nd, stage two); Manx Trophy; two stages Tour of Spain.

Selected places: 33rd overall, Tour of Spain; 4th, stage nine, Tour de France. Died stage 13.

Bibliography

Continental Cycle Racing, Noel Henderson, Pelham, 1970
Cycling is My Life, Tom Simpson, Pelham, 1965
Cycling in the Sixties, David Saunders, Pelham, 1968
Dopage, l'Imposture des Performances, Dr Jean-Pierre de Mondenard, Chiron, 2000
Doping, les surhommes du velo, Roger Bastide, Solar, 1970
La Fabuleuse Histoire du Tour de France, Pierre Chany, Editions de la Martinière, 1997
Le Tour de France, Pierre Chany, Plon, 1972
Le Tour, Geoffrey Nicholson, Hodder & Stoughton, 1990
Le Tour de France, Lieux et Etapes de Légende, Jean-Paul Ollivier, Arthaud, 2000
Les Grandes Heures du Tour de France au Ventoux, Bernard Mondon, Equinoxe, 2000
Mr Tom, The True Story of Tom Simpson, Chris Sidwells, Moushold Press, 2000
Mythologies, Roland Barthes, Seuil, 1957
The Great Bike Race, Geoffrey Nicholson, Hodder & Stoughton, 1977
Watching the Wheels Go Round, Barry Hoban with John Wilcockson, Stanley Paul, 1981

Cycling and *Cycling and Mopeds* were invaluable sources of reference, as were *L'Equipe* and *Miroir-Sprint*.

Ray Pascoe's film *Something to Aim At* was an important resource, as were Les Woodland's 1987 articles on Simpson in *Cycling Weekly*, Philippe Brunel's features on Simpson and Dr Pierre Dumas in *L'Equipe* from 1997 and 1999, David Walsh's 1999 article on Simpson and Colin Lewis in the *Sunday Times*, and Julian Barnes's essay on the 2000 Tour de France in the *Guardian*.

Index

235

Slaying the Badger

Richard Moore

LeMond, Hinault and the Greatest Ever Tour de France

Heroes and villains, spectacle and controversy, mind-games and endurance – this is the 1986 Tour de France.

Greg LeMond, 'L'Américain': fresh-faced, prodigious, newcomer. This is supposed to be his year.

Bernard Hinault, 'The Badger': aggressive, headstrong, five-time winner of the Tour. He has pledged his unwavering support to his team mate, LeMond.

The team is everything in the Tour, so the world watches, stunned, as LeMond and Hinault's explosive rivalry plays out over three high-octane weeks. *Slaying the Badger* relives the adrenaline and agony as LeMond battles to become the first American to win the Tour, with the Badger relentlessly on the attack.

'So engrossing, you don't want it to end'
Scotland on Sunday

'Captivating'
Times Literary Supplement

'Entertaining'
Richard Williams, *Guardian*

'From the opening pages this is a book that grips. Combining great insight, interviews and anecdotes with wonderfully vivid writing, it is thoroughly researched and well written'
Scotland on Sunday

'The race and the book build towards a gripping page-turning climax which you don't want to end'
Daily Telegraph

My Time

Bradley Wiggins

On 22 July 2012 Bradley Wiggins made history as the first British cyclist to win the Tour de France. Ten days later at the London Olympic Games he won gold in the time trial to become his country's most decorated Olympian. In an instant 'Wiggo', the kid from Kilburn, was a national hero.

Outspoken, honest, intelligent and fearless, Wiggins has been hailed as the people's champion. From his lowest ebb following a catastrophic attempt to conquer the 2010 Tour and the loss of his granddad who had raised him as a boy, *My Time* tells the story of his remarkable journey to win the world's toughest race.

'Fascinating'
The Times

'Listening to Bradley Wiggins is a pleasure unmatched in British sport'
Sunday Telegraph

'Like the man himself, captivating'
Daily Express

'Revealing'
Observer

'Raw, thrilling Wiggins'
Sunday Times

How I Won the Yellow Jumper

Ned Boulting

Dispatches from the Tour de France

'Paris, 4 July 2003: My first Tour de France. I had never seen a bike race. I had only vaguely heard of Lance Armstrong. I had no idea what I was doing there. Yet, that day I was broadcasting live on television. I fumbled my way through a few platitudes, before summing up with the words, "...Dave Millar just missing out on the Yellow Jumper." Yes, the Yellow Jumper.'

Follow Ned Boulting's (occasionally excruciating) experiences covering the world's most famous two-wheeled race. His story offers an insider's view of what really goes on behind the scenes of the Tour. From up-close-and-personal encounters with Lance Armstrong to bewildered mishaps with the local cuisine, Ned's been there, done that and got the crumpled t-shirt.

Eight Tours on from Ned's humbling debut, he has grown to respect, mock, adore and crave the race in equal measure. What's more, he has even started to understand it.

'I thought Ned was an old hand at the Tour. Evidently he was clueless... Told with panache'
David Millar

'Candid, insightful and often hilarious'
Alastair Campbell

'Quirky, warped, enthusiastic and funny'
Chris Boardman

'Genuinely funny'
Richard Williams

French Revolutions

Tim Moore

Cycling the Tour de France

Self-confessed loafer Tim Moore, seduced by the speed and glamour of the biggest annual sporting event in the world, sets out to cycle the course of the Tour de France. All 3,630km of it. Racing old men on butchers' bikes and being chased by cows, Moore soon resorts to standard race tactics – cheating and drugs – in a hilarious and moving tale of true adventure.

'Bill Bryson on two wheels... A one-liner every other line... Not so much witty travelogue as self-examination in a joke-heavy trial by fire'
Independent

'Moore is a talented and funny writer, who, through a combination of slapstick, absurd simile and a healthy suspicion of French civilisation, gives us something to laugh at on almost every page'
Daily Telegraph

'Moore's floundering attempts to emulate the Herculean feats of his cycling heroes unfold with eyewetting hilarity'
The Times

'Moore unleashes a high-energy torrent of astute observation and hilarious self-deprecation. Hailed as the new Bill Bryson, he is in fact a writer of considerably more substance... The jokes come thick and fast'
Irish Times

'Hilarious and inspiring... It is embarrassingly laugh-out-loud'
Daily Express

'One of the funniest books about sport ever written'
Sunday Times

ABOUT THE YELLOW JERSEY PRESS

In cycling, the yellow jersey is worn by the leader of the Tour de France. It symbolises achievement, effort, bravery and quality. When Yellow Jersey Press was created in 1998, it was to publish sports writing with these same values. Since then it has established itself as the premier list of high-quality sports writing, publishing five winners of the prestigious William Hill Sports Book of the Year award.

Yellow Jersey Press's range of cycling books is second to none. It is the home to some of the peloton's greatest heroes like Bradley Wiggins, Tom Simpson, Stephen Roche and Laurent Fignon, as well as some of the sport's best writers like William Fotheringham, Paul Kimmage and Richard Moore.